BRINGING
UP MORAL
CHILDREN

BRINGING UP MORAL CHILDREN

IN AN IMMORAL WORLD

A. LYNN SCORESBY

SHADOW MOUNTAIN®

Library of Congress Cataloging-in-Publication Data

Scoresby, A. Lynn.
  [Bringing up moral children]
  Bringing up moral children in an immoral world / A. Lynn Scoresby.
    p.   cm.
  Originally published: Bringing up moral children. Salt Lake City, Utah : Deseret Book Co., c1989. With new preface.
  Includes bibliographical references and index.
  ISBN 1-57345-366-8 (pbk.)
  1. Child rearing—Moral and ethical aspects. 2. Moral education. 3. Child rearing—United States. I. Title.
  [HQ769.S343   1998]
  649'.7—dc21   97-45977
                                           CIP

Printed in the United States of America   72082

10 9 8 7 6 5 4 3 2 1

CONTENTS

PREFACE

We live in a world of changing values and complex challenges. Never have more forces combined to threaten the strength and integrity of the family. Never has there been a greater need to teach values and morality to children. Teaching children how to think and act morally is a positive approach to parenting. It provides them a foundation for making judgments, acting responsibly, and developing a set of standards to live by.

This book will help you teach morality to your children—not just sexual morality, but moral behavior that affects all aspects of a person's life. Unlike many parenting books, *Bringing Up Moral Children in an Immoral World* teaches that our children's behavior and choices must be based on a firm moral foundation. Where many scoff at morality as old-fashioned, this book advocates that we must teach our children to be responsible for their choices and actions, that they must learn to respect and value others, and that morality is never out of style. The book teaches moral reasoning, moral judgment, and moral conduct, and gives strategies on how to effectively teach these to our children.

The first five chapters of this book, therefore, do not contain the usual simplified techniques commonly found in books about parenting. Rather, they contain accurate information and effective approaches—based on experience and research—for teaching morality to children.

These chapters on morality lay the groundwork for the rest of the book.

Chapters six and seven discuss sexual morality and chemical abuse. Our children will encounter situations where they will have to make choices about these issues and where their morality will likely be challenged. Rather than wait for morality to mature "naturally" as these situations arise, we can prepare our children now so that they will know how to act in a high-risk situation before it occurs.

Friendship, money and property, authority, work, and school are all important issues in teaching children morality. They can present children with moral challenges in terms of fairness and equality. Chapters eight through eleven discuss these issues in detail. They explain, for example, how children build friendships, how some negative behavior in children can be a response to certain types of authority, why some children don't complete tasks they start, and how to teach children cooperation.

Children have to learn the sometimes difficult task of being morally responsible for their own well-being. Chapter twelve discusses this problem by considering the different manifestations of self-destructiveness, including eating disorders and, most tragically, suicide. It discusses issues that may underlie self-destructiveness, including lack of self-respect, stress, depression, and abuse.

Sometimes certain children present special difficulties to parents and others who try to teach them. Chapter thirteen talks about how to deal with "difficult" children whose unique needs require us to make mental and emotional adjustments in our teaching in order for them to learn moral behavior. This chapter includes strategies and techniques for effectively dealing with difficult or at-risk children.

Hypocrisy, which can be such a hindrance to teaching morality, is discussed at length in chapter fourteen. This chapter teaches what to do when children are deceitful and how to turn children's misbehavior into a positive teaching tool.

The book concludes with a chapter on love and morality. Love remains the basis for all good teaching, and it is ultimately through patience, hard work, and the teaching power of love that we are able to bring our children to an understanding of morality, even in an immoral world. By committing our families to moral standards, we can find greater happiness for ourselves and our children, and enjoy more healthy and loving relationships.

CHAPTER 1

PARENTS AND MORAL CHILDREN

As a child psychologist, I work with children in trouble. Many of these children are like the fifteen-year-old boy who sat across the room from me one day—defiant but also ashamed and discouraged. This boy was trying to change his life, but to this point he had failed. He had dropped out of school, unwilling or unable to maintain a responsible schedule of study. His life revolved around weekend parties. On Friday and Saturday nights, he got drunk. He had sex. Sometimes he knew the names of the girls he was with, and sometimes he couldn't remember. He was not on good terms with his parents. Like all children, this boy deserved love and help, but, like many I have seen, he had placed himself beyond the reach of those who cared about him most.

Sexual promiscuity, alcohol, and drugs are now almost a routine part of adolescent life. These things are harmful, even deadly. But something about the boy in my office was more distressing to me than his drinking or promiscuity. He had an intense disregard for himself, shown partly by his complete apathy about the consequences of his actions for himself or anyone else. The problem was not that he knew something better and chose not to do it. Rather, it was that he knew nothing else, at least not well enough to do anything about it. The most important thing to him, and to many other children like him, is the sensory thrill that drinking, drugs, and sex provide. If such children are asked about other values, such as school achievement

or family relationships, they will respond with indifference.

These children scare me—not because they threaten
me with physical harm, but because they are evidence of
a terrible failure. For although someone, perhaps many
people, may have tried, no one has succeeded in teaching
these children something else; no one has been able to help
them find something of substance, significance, and true
worth—something enduring. The selfish pursuit of material things, the constant need to look good in order to
impress others, and the persistent seeking for sensory pleasure are not the goals of people who have a mature understanding of life, of themselves, and of their relationship
to others. Children who seek only these things are empty,
and in their hollowness they find little to contribute. Unless
they change dramatically, they are lost to us, and we to
them. Their actions so occupy their attention that they do
not see any danger. We may call out to them or get angry
at them. We may plead with them or cry over them. They
are our children. We have loved them from birth. They
have such great promise. Why, we wonder, do they make
such choices?

Some of us start out as parents with enthusiasm, believing in the enjoyment we will find. We soon learn that
rearing children is sometimes a tiring and thankless task.
Parenthood has its rewards, but we begin to understand
why so many of us need help. We begin to rely on
churches, schools, other institutions, and even television
to assume major roles in rearing our children. Financial
necessities and other pressures exhaust us. Teaching children some important lesson often requires so much effort,
so much energy, that we are secretly thankful when a
church program involves our children, or when a good
television program occupies their attention. We tell ourselves that only this once we will not follow through; we
will do our parental duty next time, when we are not so
tired.

Few of us are wholly consistent and responsible as parents. We fail to do our best at one time or another. If the world around us is safe, we will have other chances to make up what we miss. But if people and conditions around us are dangerous, then we may not have enough "other chances." So we hope that our children will learn from other caring people. Unfortunately, however, the people in church, school, or other institutions, though they may be helpful, are limited in their ability to influence a child's development. Specifically, in the absence of strong parental guidance, organizations are notably ineffective in one important area: developing morality. Any thoughtful observer can see that during the past several years, while parents have increasingly turned to other people and organizations for moral training of their children, increased numbers of children are less moral. A United States government commission reported in 1985 that at least 15 percent of American youth under age nineteen are so impaired by drug abuse, or by criminal, illegal, or other debilitating acts, that they will never be competent members of society.

And if we consider that the trend is clearly toward a worsening condition and that many of these young people will one day be parents themselves, then we foresee a truly alarming number of children who will not receive adequate moral training in the future.

Parents are, or at least ought to be, the guardians of their children's moral development. If we accept that role, we can help our children develop the sensitivity, the compassion, and the standards of moral people. If we do not teach them, or if we teach them poorly, our children may never know how to live as moral beings.

Some of us don't want to believe that. We would rather believe that teaching morality is the exclusive domain of our churches, and we have even managed to feel somewhat secure in letting church programs play the primary role in this aspect of our children's lives. Also, some of us hesitate to get very much involved with teaching morality because morality itself has an unfavorable image these days. Perhaps the very word smacks of narrowness or misguided ideals or even of bigotry. Perhaps *morality* puts us in mind of Puritans or Inquisitors or holy wars, or perhaps we think of grim parents and religious fundamentalists who over-regulate and emotionally abuse children in an attempt to preserve them from the devil and his influence in this fearsome world. For these and other reasons, some of us find it easier to forget about morality. We may even think that we are doing our children a favor by our indifference.

That attitude is unfortunate. For even though history and our own observations can reveal to us many people, nations, and cultures who have used private standards they called "moral" to excuse what we can see only as bad behavior, real morality is something else. Morality actually means honesty, concern for others, responsible work, and mature judgment. A truly moral life is a rich life. If we understand it that way, we are less likely to find the notion of morality unpleasant.

Teaching Morality in the Family

The idea that parents are in the best position to teach morality is satisfying because of the values we traditionally hold about close families and good parents. Many religions, school systems, and communities openly emphasize the importance of "good" families. This emphasis alone, however, does not seem to provide sufficient motivation for many parents to do what may be necessary to adjust work or play schedules and learn new teaching skills. Many children are in trouble because their parents have been indifferent to their real needs or ignorant of them. In my view, it is imperative that parents learn what to teach their children and also how to teach it. Teaching morality must be an act of love, the result of wholesome and warm concern. Attempts to teach it any other way, by force or with angry threats, will so frighten or distract children that they will not be able to learn what is professed. If we start out knowing the importance of love and compassion in teaching morality, we can use the ordinary events of family life to ensure that our children grow and learn in a positive way.

Family members are usually bound by intense emotional bonds. These are established through the shared experiences family members have from childhood to old age. This makes anything learned in the family more memorable than what might be heard or seen elsewhere, such as in church or school. Combinations of people of either sex and of different ages give opportunity for variety, organization, adjustment, and regulation of family relationships. Families make rules, build traditions, and develop styles of communication and ways of expressing and receiving affection. These patterns are often carried by children outside the family as moral standards.

Family members must also perform work of some kind. The tasks vary from family to family, but all families divide their work to some degree. As with other family practices, how the work gets done creates attitudes children have about themselves that may last throughout their lives. As children work, play, love, and communicate, parents evaluate their actions and words. What is good and bad or right and wrong is first understood by children from these parental judgments. Parental approval and disapproval provide a child's first and most profound lessons about the moral standards of community and society. If we know how to teach these lessons, we can give our children a moral standard within the family that will serve them well in many situations outside the family.

Let me emphasize that living a moral life will not make children less happy. A moral life is not excessively structured by rules and obligations. Moral children are more successful than others during adolescence, and they grow up to have happier marriages. Having developed character based on faith in standards of honor and commitment, these people seem, at every stage of life, to live fully. They are respectful and law-abiding members of their communities. And they are likely to honor their parents. Few of us would complain of that.

If we are afraid that teaching morality will prevent us from sharing the joys of childhood with our children, we need to recognize that in teaching morality we will find the real joy and fulfillment of parenthood. Teaching morality lets us enter our children's lives and have something to do with the formation of the kind of people they will become. Fulfillment and satisfaction come from contributing to and watching such development, as our children come to love knowledge, respect truth, and live in ways that will help those around them. That is possible for us if we teach the principles of morality.

Public Consequences of Private Acts

In recent years, our society has focused on the rights of individuals, hoping to allow each person as much freedom as possible. We have courted the idea that any private act is acceptable as long as it does not infringe upon the rights of others. This line of thinking seems to imply that we do not have to maintain shared standards except as they are codified in our legal system. Some parents even excuse their failure to teach moral values by appealing to such reasoning. These parents assert that if they do not bother anyone outside the family, they have the right to neglect or abuse their children or teach them unusual behavior. One man explained to me why he physically abused his son. "My father hit me," he said, "and I turned out okay. Besides, what I do in my family is my own business." I explained to him that his reasoning failed to consider what his son, angry and hurt, might do to other people. Parents who rationalize in this way are protected from seeing their own immorality. And because the effects of private acts are often not immediately seen in public, the parents are protected from public censure and from a chance to understand the long-range effects of their behavior.

I have heard many people defend promiscuous sexual behavior, abusive parenting, and chemical abuse with the inadequate and shallow rationale that what they do does not hurt anyone else. During our rush in the past twenty years to accommodate new sexual freedoms, few could have anticipated that the private sexual acts of some would have such a terrifying public consequence as Acquired Immune Deficiency Syndrome (AIDS). Now that we are more aware, we can more accurately recognize the public consequences of those private acts in human suffering, in enormous financial burdens, and in human life itself. This one disaster provides a lesson that no one can easily forget: private acts have public consequences.

What we teach or fail to teach our children in the privacy of our homes will someday have public consequences. Our children will go from us and either contribute to the general well-being of others while they pursue individual goals, or else they will be a drain on society because the hurt they bring to others diminishes life for all involved with them. Justice may require us to put such people where they will not be able to continue to do harm, at great cost in dollars as well as in human pain.

I once heard a man say as he contributed to a Boy Scout fund-raising project, "I would rather pay a few dollars to help boys succeed than pay triple the amount for the cost of a new prison if they don't." Such a sentiment can lead us to consider the role parents have in maintaining a stable and productive society. Every organized group of people establishes standards to govern individual members. Some of these standards may be formal laws; others may be behavioral prescriptions that enable people to get along with each other socially. Although many of us do not teach our children much about the legal system of our society, we do teach them how to act in public so they will not be

offensive to others. For example, when I was a boy my
mother always made sure that I carried a clean handker-
chief, and I still follow her teaching in this matter to this
day. Almost all parents have standards of this sort. Some,
for example, insist that their children have clean teeth and
fingernails before they leave for school or church or the
neighbor's birthday party. Some want hair done neatly or
clothes carefully matched. Some parents like their children
to speak quietly and play cautiously. Other parents think
it more important for children to dress as they please, to
deal with danger in their play, to shout if they want to.
For almost all parents, some standards will vary according
to the public context for the behavior—"best behavior"
might be required for church but not for a picnic.

Our attempts to teach children about appropriate public actions indicate the existence of community standards.
Community standards are acceptable ways of acting that
all members of a community (religious, language, or ethnic
group) share and understand. These standards exist in our
minds, and we hold them in common, though some var-
iations might exist from family to family, religion to religion, region to region, and so forth. Some easily recognized
examples of such standards are standing and placing our
hand over our heart while our flag passes by, not taking
all the credit for a team victory even though our own performance may have been the very best that day, or being
quiet in a museum.

When we try to teach these standards to our children,
we discover that they usually behave better when we are
around to supervise. We conclude that we must do something to help our children behave according to these standards even when we are not around. When a child acts
appropriately without supervision, a community standard
has become the child's personal standard.

Knowing about community and personal standards
helps us understand the important role parents have in
helping children become contributing members of society.

We are the first to teach them about how to act in public. We maintain this unique teaching relationship with our children throughout our lives. We also have a major role in helping them form "character" and the personal standards that will last them a lifetime.

A Definition of Morality

Of course, morality is much harder to teach than it is to define, but even defining it can be difficult. A really useful definition requires the resolution of a long-standing argument. Some have said that moral standards cannot be universal because what is moral in one situation may be immoral in another. Further, what may be moral for one person may not be moral for another person in the same situation. Those who think in this way see morality as relative and situational. From their point of view, no general standards exist for everyone, and morality is merely a matter of personal choice.

Others have argued, in contrast, that some moral standards should be recognized by all, regardless of the differences between people or the situations they are in. People who accept this idea have a more absolute interpretation of morality and make a fairly clear distinction between what is right and what is wrong. According to this view, what is right is nearly always right and what is wrong is nearly always wrong.

In the definition I offer here, I attempt to resolve these two points of view. I give morality an absolute definition: morality helps. Morality contributes to mental, emotional (spiritual), and physical well-being; it promotes general welfare. Behavior that hurts people, behavior that contributes to mental, emotional (spiritual), or physical distress, behavior that disrupts the general welfare, is not moral: it is immoral. To be moral, people must know how to promote their own welfare and both how to help and how to avoid hurting others. Using this definition, we can judge what is moral or immoral by whether someone is helped or hurt.

Of course, it is true that what might help someone in one situation might hurt someone else in another. Extreme anger, for instance, would usually be considered hurtful when directed by parents to children. Yet there could be a time when a parent's anger might motivate and help a child. There could also be a time when an intention to help could cause harm. Much of what we do to help people is based on individual choice, relative to a specific situation. Thus, teaching morality to our children requires us to teach them how to interpret many situations so that they can decide how to help and avoid hurting themselves and others.

A mother was informed by school authorities that her seven-year-old son was a "behavior problem." Instead of being concerned only about the child's misbehavior, she asked questions about when and where he misbehaved. She learned that he usually misbehaved around 10:00 A.M., during reading. So, one day she went to school and observed the teacher organizing small reading groups for students to read aloud. She immediately knew why her son was misbehaving. When he was a baby, fluid in his inner ear had affected his hearing and therefore his ability to learn to speak clearly. He was embarrassed about his handicap, and rather than read aloud, which was expected in the reading group, he disrupted the class. When he was given an opportunity to practice reading another way, his misbehavior ended.

This mother wisely recognized that she should understand her child's behavior by learning about the circumstances in which the actions took place rather than think about the child as "good" or "bad" because of an identification made by someone else. We would be wise to think about moral behavior as it is expressed in contexts of time, place, and company. That is the sense in which morality has a relative meaning. If we are to help our children learn to live moral lives, we must prepare them to adapt to many situations and act appropriately in them.

How the Definition Helps Us

For some people, this will be a new way to think about morality. Traditionally, morality has been thought of as obedience to a set of rules or laws transmitted by God, governments, or parents. Although important and useful in many ways, this definition is limited. In teaching children, for example, when we think about morality just as a set of rules they must follow, we place limitations on them that may prove a disservice to them. Learning obedience is important, but there are times when children might have to disobey a rule in order to be moral—for example, they must break a rule at school in order to help someone in need. Teaching children to focus just on the rules or laws does not prepare them to be as adaptable as they will need to be in order to act morally in a variety of situations. Such a focus also inhibits the development of moral independence, leaving children feeling a need for permission from someone before they act.

Another disadvantage to a view of morality as only a set of rules is that it can leave us without good answers when we discuss moral questions with our children. They deserve explanations when we tell them what to do and what not to do. "Because I said so!" or "It is the rule, and you know it!" are not effective defenses of a moral position. Our position is made stronger by an explanation that some act, some event, some people could help or hurt our children.

Further, the idea of helping and hurting lets us teach children about the consequences of *their* actions. In explaining to one of my own children about the reasons for telling the truth, I mentioned that lying would hurt him. Seeing I had his attention, I pointed out that a person who lies is cowardly—he avoids telling the truth because he is afraid of punishment or other consequences. If a time came when he needed courage to do something, he might be afraid instead of brave. He and I were both satisfied that he had learned an important and useful lesson.

Finally, by thinking of morality as helping someone and immorality as hurting someone, we can more effectively teach children the balance between responsibility for themselves and responsibility for other people. If it is immoral to hurt others, it is also immoral to hurt ourselves. In order to lead moral lives, then, children need to learn to help themselves and to help others.

Morality and the Moral Circumstance

Developing morality is a lifelong process. It takes a long time to become capable of acting morally in a great variety of circumstances. We all continue to face some situations in which we are prepared and able to act morally and some others in which we are not so prepared and able. That should tell us that we cannot teach morality unless we also understand something about the situations in which moral actions occur. Besides learning moral principles, then, children must learn to recognize the difference between a situation that involves moral choice and a situation that does not. In some situations, helping or hurting someone is not ordinarily a matter of much concern. We do not, for example, usually think of eating, exercising, studying, or walking to school as requiring moral judgments. We refer to these situations as nonmoral or "conventional" because they usually do not involve helping or hurting.

Suppose, however, that one of these ordinary situations changes—an argument starts between two friends walking to school. Now the idea of helping or hurting becomes relevant. Or, suppose that a child is faced with decisions about dating, going to a party where alcohol is available, or joining a youth gang. Such situations have greater than average potential for helping or hurting. If we think a particular activity or situation is likely to help or hurt someone, then we think about it in a moral sense. As parents, we might want to know who will be there, what they will be doing, who is in charge, how long the activity will last, or how people will get there. We want to know all of these things for ourselves and for our children because we recognize the potential for someone's being helped or hurt.

Children are more likely to be moral if they can tell when a conventional situation is changing into one in which someone could be helped or hurt. Teaching our children morality, then, requires, first, that we teach them what helps or hurts, and, second, that we teach them to recognize circumstances when helping and hurting can take place. In other words, we must teach children about moral circumstances at the same time we teach them about moral principles.

For example, when we tell our children that stealing is wrong, we should also tell them that they might find themselves needing to avoid stealing something in a department store when other children may be encouraging it. Obviously, this is more complete than the moral imperative "Do not steal." We might explain, "It is harder to be honest if you are afraid that you will be laughed at, but you can still do it."

Teaching Morality Is an Everyday Opportunity

I have often been asked what can be done after people have been hurt by what has happened. Attempts to help someone recover from immorality can range from a short and somewhat mild effort to an enormous, long-term struggle. In the case of one woman I know who was abused by her father, the effects of his immorality have extended into her marriage and family life, continuing for many years. Her efforts to develop a belief in love that could replace her fear will require many more years, even though she has already worked at it for some time. Knowing something about her father, I can understand with some compassion that he, too, is the product of immorality and, as many parents do, has passed on to his daughter what he has learned.

As a way to prevent such misery, the demanding task of teaching morality to children in the small moments of family life seems well worth the effort. In my opinion, teaching children to be moral provides the greatest joys of parenthood, the most fun, and the greatest satisfaction. It also produces the most lasting rewards.

CHAPTER 2

HOW MORALITY DEVELOPS

We are used to the idea that children improve their abilities as they grow, and so it makes sense that children will understand more and be able to handle more complex situations as they mature. Yet, we have not had much understanding about how morality develops. Some have thought that morality develops along with children's abilities to reason and think. (Kohlberg, 1969.) Others have suggested that morality develops along with children's abilities to communicate socially, to act out examples they see, and to carry out instructions or rules. But these proposals, and others like them, do not give us much useful information when we are responding to a child and his or her moral development is at stake. We want to know what will work and, because we love our children, we want to know what will yield enduring results. That view in itself is the best one I know of for promoting the moral development of children: morality develops over a long period of time, and parents must continually be a part of it.

Furthermore, the key to moral development is in the process of mental and emotional *synthesis,* or *integration.* In other words, as children mature they are able to synthesize, or integrate, more completely what they know about themselves with what they know about rules, work, people, and situations. When we promote our children's ability to integrate, we are promoting their moral development. When we neglect to nurture that ability in our children or stunt its development by our ineffectiveness in parenting, then we are also slowing or hindering the moral development of our children.

Children and the Moral Circumstance

Much evidence shows that maturity and experience increase children's ability to reason. Yet even young children are capable of acting on high levels of morality in specific instances for reasons as sophisticated as those attributed to older, more mature people. And of course, adults can be both moral and immoral, mature and immature.

We tell our children what to do and what not to do. Sometimes they obey, and sometimes they do not. Having told them something, we think they understand it and know what to do. We are chagrined if they fail. Expressing frustration at their disobedience might relieve us and perhaps make a more dramatic point with them, but it does not explain why they failed to do as we asked. Were they simply immature? Is something wrong with their personality?

As parents, we want to know in specific terms why children cheat, steal, or tell lies instead of doing something better. We want to know how to teach them to help people and to avoid hurting people, and when a moral situation arises, we want them to act as we have taught them. We may emphasize compliance to rules, maintaining good relationships with others, or achieving goals and working hard. In doing so, we try to develop control or teaching strategies that will influence children to be more moral. The result is that we miss teaching them how to integrate all the aspects of the situation we are calling *the moral circumstance*. Even though parents have taught their children what to do, and even though children have "learned" what the parents have taught, if children do not understand the moral circumstance and how to adapt to it, they still might not act morally.

To help them integrate the parts of a moral circumstance, it is useful to define three integration tasks our
children face:

1. To appraise a moral circumstance, identify its purpose, and decide what can be done to help and not hurt;
that is moral reasoning.

2. To choose to help and not to hurt in this situation;
that is moral judgment.

3. To act as reason and judgment require; that is moral
conduct.

When children fail to act as they have been taught, the
failure could represent inadequacy at one or more of these
tasks. Their failure might mean that they are uninformed
about what is going on. Or they might misinterpret a situation and not recognize that someone could be helped
or hurt. Even after they recognize that help is needed, they
might be unable to decide what to do to help. Or perhaps
they have interpreted the situation correctly and have
made good choices but still fail to act. We must teach our
children to integrate the parts of a moral circumstance in
which they might find themselves as well as about the
moral principles we want them to learn. Otherwise, they
may know what to do but not when and how to do it.

Ellen, a teenaged girl, wanted to be popular. She was
thrilled when some popular girls invited her to a slumber
party. During the evening, she found that Gail, one of her
best friends, had not been invited, and the popular girls
made several critical comments about her. Although some
of the girls seemed to like Gail, Ellen saw that the group
intended to exclude Gail. Ellen left the next day with mixed
feelings—wanting to be liked and included by the girls at
the party but feeling friendship and loyalty for Gail. If she
spent time with the group who did not want Gail, Gail
would be excluded. If she kept her friendship by spending
time with Gail, she might be left out of the group.

Distinguishing a moral circumstance depends on identifying the purpose or tasks of the situation. Most of us

learn from an early age to gauge the purpose of social situations so we will know how to act. When we do not know the purpose of a situation, we may feel uncomfortable and confused. Suppose we enter a room uninvited and find it filled with people standing and talking with one another. We do not know immediately whether this is a family gathering, a business meeting, or a party. Our first reaction is to gather information so that we can decide what sort of meeting or gathering is taking place. If we learn about the purpose of the meeting, then we will know what to do there. Sometimes we identify a purpose of a gathering by identifying the people who are present. If the mayor is in the room, for example, we might conclude that the meeting has something to do with city government. Sometimes we can learn a purpose from some other aspect of the situation. The presence of food in the room tells us something about the meeting, and its arrangement tells us even more. If the food is arranged on a long table with paper plates and plastic utensils at one end, we can probably assume that it is an informal buffet and that we are free to help ourselves. If the food is placed on a table where individual places have been set, we conclude that it is a formal dinner, and we will probably wait for an invitation to be seated. Teaching children to appraise situations in this way will help them decide whether or not the purpose of a situation is to help or hurt someone. So our young friend Ellen must first discern the purpose for this gathering of "friends." Having thought about that, she makes an evaluation: Can this purpose help or hurt someone? Yes, it can. She has found herself in a moral circumstance. Now she must decide what she will do.

Ellen is a *moral agent,* with personal desires closely tied to all the experiences she has had. What she *wants* to do will greatly influence her choices in this situation. Since she is in her early teens, she might *want* to go with the popular girls and exclude her friend Gail. But she also has some knowledge of moral standards—what she thinks she *should* do—and these standards will also influence her choice. The final component of this moral circumstance is the other girls, including the absent friend, Gail. Moral circumstances almost always involve *other people,* who may or many not be physically present. What Ellen thinks about Gail and the other girls will influence what she eventually chooses to do.

The child. The person brings into the situation his or her experience and character traits. In a moral circumstance, the child will be faced with three moral tasks: first, interpreting the situation and evaluating the possibilities for helping or hurting (moral reasoning); second, deciding what should be done (moral judgment); and third, acting to help and not hurt (moral conduct).

Moral standards. The moral standards are the rules known to the child and others about what helps and what hurts people. Moral standards include and involve many types of knowledge.

The purpose or tasks to be performed. A moral circumstance is a social situation, meaning that people are together. Any situation may have several purposes, each of which must be discerned and evaluated by the child to see if it can help or hurt someone.

Others. The others in the moral circumstance are those, present or thought about, who influence the moral decisions of the child and who may be affected by them.

All the elements of the moral circumstance come together in the example of Tommy Edwards. Tommy was popular at high school. He was a star player in football, basketball, and baseball. He was also a student-body officer. After the last football game one year, most of his teammates decided to have a party to celebrate the end of the season. As a starting player, Tommy felt an obligation to go. He felt added pressure when some of his teammates stopped to talk about the party one day at school and wondered sarcastically if "Tommy the All-American was too busy to come to a little old team party." Tommy shrugged off this jibe good-naturedly and assured his friends that he planned to be there.

When he arrived, many of the other boys were already there and were sitting and talking. Each had brought some food, and, Tommy learned, some had also brought marijuana and cocaine and assorted alcoholic beverages. Tommy picked up some chips and a soft drink. His parents had taught him to avoid drugs and alcohol, and he had never used either. He had been to other parties and so was not concerned as he settled in to watch some reruns of old game films.

During the evening, several of the boys got drunk; others got stoned; some were using both drugs and alcohol. The others began to notice that Tommy was not joining in. At first no one said anything, but finally one boy, a bit drunk, said, "Hey, wait a minute! Our All-American wonder boy isn't drinking anything!" Several of the others stopped talking. Smelling some fun, they turned to join in. Soon all were kidding Tommy about being "churchy" or "too good for the rest of us."

The party had changed from a celebration of a fine football season to a confrontation between the values of one person and the values of the others present. For Tommy, a conventional situation changed to a moral circumstance. Someone could be helped or hurt—in this case, Tommy himself. Tommy has his personal desires and his knowledge of moral standards. Now he must interpret this situation, make a decision, and act.

With more experience, Tommy might have been able to see that from the beginning the end was probable. The sequence of events was predictable, from the pressure that was put on Tommy to go to the party, to the drugs Tommy noticed when he arrived, to the taunt of the first boy and the joining in of the group. If we want to teach our children to behave morally, we must help them see as clearly as possible and integrate all the elements of a moral circumstance.

Children and Moral Character

If our children's moral training is complete, it will include instruction in correctly integrating the parts of a moral circumstance. Even though we cannot teach them about every situation they might face, our own understanding of moral circumstances will help us prepare our children to know when someone can be helped or hurt, what kinds of decisions they will need to make, and what they must do to be moral.

Because our children are moral agents, they will need moral standards that can be followed in many moral circumstances. So we want to teach them standards of right and wrong. We also need to help them develop certain personality traits that will help them apply what they know. The term *moral character* implies moral standards expressed in personality traits (such as honesty and kindness) that are applied in many different situations. Developing moral character in our children is the purpose of all our teaching.

Children can be influenced, sometimes excessively, by people or situations. Helping them develop moral character is how we prepare them to withstand pressure and have confidence to choose and act morally.

As we watch our children, we can notice certain tendencies in their behavior. If they are often quiet in social events, for example, we might conclude that they are shy, retiring, or backward. If they persistently refuse to share or cooperate, we might think of them as selfish or stubborn. We usually do not apply the names of these traits to our children unless they describe frequent or typical behavior. Using such words can be dangerous because our children may assume that they are true. Once we have labeled a child, we may miss other aspects of his or her personality. If we label our children too often or too narrowly, our children will feel limited or misjudged. Then we may have difficulty teaching them to be moral. Not many children will let parents teach them moral behavior when they believe the parents do not understand them.

The words that describe character traits have other powerful effects. Heard from us these words stay in our children's minds; they are the words the children will use to understand themselves. We may call a certain action "kind" and use this word often to describe behavior we see, or would like to see, in our children. Then our children learn what *kind* means in their behavior. We can use words in this way to motivate children to acquire the traits we value. So we should use such words as *loving, kind,* and *thoughtful* as we help our children develop moral character and learn to describe themselves. And of course we should avoid such words as *liar* and *stupid.*

But we do not use trait words solely to describe how our children behave. We also use trait words to predict how children will act in situations for which we have not directly prepared them. When a child wants permission to do something new, we think about what kind of person this child is before deciding whether to give our permission; in essence, we review the child's moral character. If we think a child is predictably good or obedient, then we are more likely to give permission. If a child has frequently acted differently from what we had expected, then we consider the child unpredictable and are less willing to give our permission.

When we repeatedly use trait words to describe a child's behavior and to predict what he or she is likely to do, we help form the child's character. Thus, we can consciously help a child develop moral traits.

At first, it might seem naive to suppose that certain character traits are useful for every child; after all, every child is different. Yet, if we examine the lives of moral people, we discover that all moral people seem to have some common characteristics, which we want our children to develop:

Autonomy. Autonomous people have a sense of responsibility for self. They have the ability to pursue a course of action they believe to be correct and to withstand pressure to oblige.

The opposite of autonomy is *susceptibility*. In a moral sense, susceptible people are extremely reactive to external pressure.

Empathy. Empathetic people have a vicarious understanding of the feelings of another person, leading to compassion and a sense of caring. Empathy produces guilt, which can help prevent hurtful acts.

The opposite of empathy is *defensiveness*. Defensive people shift responsibility for their actions to someone else. This allows them to justify immorality by avoiding guilt. They hide their feelings and alienate themselves.

Activity. Active people have initiative, responsiveness, and an orientation toward achievement. The quality of activity leads them to perform acts of helpfulness and to find alternatives when judgment says that someone can be hurt.

The opposite of activity is *passivity*. Passivity prevents people from doing acts of helpfulness. Combined with susceptibility, passivity increases the likelihood of hurtful acts of omission.

Acceptance. Acceptant people have the ability to receive or accept what exists or is given. Acceptance is the ability and the willingness to understand instead of judging in a nonmoral context.

The opposite of acceptance is *prejudice*. Prejudiced people excessively judge others in nonmoral contexts, failing to distinguish between what should and what should not be judged. Prejudice can lead to insensitivity and hurtful acts.

Conversability. Conversable people participate in communication, which teaches, informs, and promotes understanding about oneself and other people.

The opposite of conversability is *social isolation*. Socially isolated people fail to participate in conversations, which failure leads them to have inadequate knowledge about people.

Emotional competence. Emotionally competent people regulate their moods to maintain positive emotional states. Their positive emotional style increases their alertness to their surroundings and aids them in resisting temptations.

The opposite of emotional competence is *emotional incompetence.* Emotionally incompetent people have a negative emotional style, a tendency toward extremely negative or changeable moods, which reduces their awareness and weakens their ability to resist temptation.

In Stanley Milgram's famous study of moral behavior, subjects were told that they were participating in an experiment about the effects of punishment on learning. They were asked by a scientist to operate a machine that supposedly applied shocks to a "learner" whom they could see through a one-way mirror. Unknown to the subjects, the learner knew the truth about the experiment and received only a mild shock.

Actually, the experiment was about compliance with authority. Even though the subjects exhibited stress, a large percentage of them followed the instructions of the experimenter even when they were asked to administer a "lethal shock" to the learner. This classic study illustrates that obedience to authority is a powerful motive, especially if someone believes the one in authority will be responsible for what is done.

This explanation is not all we need to understand what is happening here, however. We want to know about the people who did not comply with the experiment so that we can understand what makes a person likely to act morally instead of immorally.

The people who gave what they thought to be lethal shocks to another human being lacked the ability to resist the demands of authority: they were susceptible to the pressure they felt from the experimenter. These people lacked *autonomy,* which is a sense of responsibility for one's actions and the ability to act without being unduly influenced by others. Thus we can say that autonomy is perhaps the first prerequisite to moral behavior.

The role of autonomy in moral action has been the subject of much study. Autonomy exists in children when they are able to understand the consequences of their behavior for themselves and for others and when they know how and when to exert self-control to produce certain consequences they desire. (Morrison, Siegal, and Francis, 1983.) Autonomy is also described as self-control achieved when children have mental plans they talk to themselves about. These plans help children regulate themselves during times of temptation and when they do tasks and anticipate rewards. Without such plans, children are more susceptible to distractions, including temptations to disobey instructions. (Patterson and Mischel, 1976.)

Children have low esteem and are more susceptible to distractions and pressure when they compare themselves unfavorably with other people or feel nervous about performing some task. Children who have previously been neglected or rejected report more often than other children that they are worried their friends will leave them. These children more often do what their friends want than do children who have known more emotional support. (Shannon and Kafer, 1984.) Children made vulnerable by various negative life events—such as poor parenting, illness or injury, and divorce—are less likely to develop competent social functioning than are children not made vulnerable by these events.

We conclude that a child's having a sense of self-control, an understanding of the consequences of behavior, and the ability to resist pressure in order to obey a rule or finish a task will increase the likelihood of that child behaving morally. A person capable of this kind of behavior is autonomous. A susceptible person, on the other hand, is unusually vulnerable to outside pressure. Autonomy enhances moral behavior; susceptibility undermines it.

A second characteristic that contributes to the likelihood of moral behavior is *empathy*, the ability to sense vicariously the emotions and needs of other people and to help them. Research informs us that children display a kind of empathy from birth. (Hoffman, 1982.) If they have adequate examples, discussion of their feelings, and praise, children expand their empathy for others as they mature. Vicariously feeling what someone else feels is the basis for compassion, for sensitive attention to others. In addition, children who feel empathy for others are more likely to feel guilty when they fail to act morally. Empathy helps children sense when help will be needed, and guilt helps children avoid hurting themselves and others.

The opposite of empathy is *defensiveness*. Defensiveness is shown by an inability to express feelings and thoughts, excessive fear of the disapproval of others, shifting responsibility for one's actions to someone else, avoiding new or strange situations, aggression, and insensitivity to the feelings of others. Many of these conditions in the behavior of preschool children show that assertiveness and defensiveness were influenced by children's racial background and by divorce. (Weigal, 1985.) Defensiveness appears in children as early as four years of age and increases as they get older. (Brody, Rozek, and Muten, 1985.) Defensiveness increases with the pressure children feel to control the expression of their feelings. Boys, because they receive more social pressure to control their emotions, are generally more defensive than girls. Shannon and Kafer reported that young children who felt vulnerable to the influence of others felt more distance between themselves and other people. Interestingly, the most vulnerable were also the most defensive. They did not value trust, nor did they believe it to be a part of friendships.

In summary, then, empathy, the sensitive concern for other people, promotes moral, responsible behavior, while defensiveness, marked by emotional distance and fear, contributes to immoral, irresponsible behavior.

A third trait moral people have is an *active* orientation toward achievement. Active people tend to set long-term goals and work toward them. Passive people do not tend to have long-term goals or to work consistently toward achievement.

Researchers have found that children who scored higher on measures of achievement motivation and who did actually achieve were less easily persuaded than children not so oriented. My own research also showed a connection between moral behavior and achievement. (1988.) I submitted questionnaires to 1,457 young adults, asking them to rate themselves in certain areas of personal achievement and in their success in dealing with such problems as excessive drinking, drug use, early sexual activity, and conflict with parents. I also asked for certain biographical data. The responses showed that young people who were most successful in avoiding harmful practices and conflicts had committed themselves early in life to values and goals and were working toward those goals. Those who rated themselves less successful reported that they had been more aimless, noncommittal, and passive.

A fourth trait moral people share is *acceptance*. They have the ability to distinguish between moral and conventional standards and they understand the value of the ideas, values, and traits of others, even though they may differ from their own. If children understand when moral judgment is required and when it is not, they will be less likely to hurt someone. A prejudiced person, on the other hand, makes a moral issue out of a nonmoral condition, such as a person's religion, racial or ethnic background, or appearance.

A fifth characteristic of moral people is their *conversability*, which includes a willingness to discuss morality. Their vocabularies may include such words as *honesty, fair-*

ness, sharing, and *unselfish.* Conversation is important in resolving moral issues. It is especially important in resolving problems between friends, learning about the intentions of others, and arriving at a moral decision that involves other people.

Henry (1983) has shown how moral development results from communication that helps children identify with their parents. Grando and Ginsberg (1976) studied the effects of a communication program on father-son relationships. Prior to the program, sons and fathers reported anger, difficulty in sharing, and difficulty in disclosing their feelings. Afterward, through improved quantity and quality of conversation, these conditions were decreased.

Clinical reports show that children are more likely to be self-destructive (anorexic, alcoholic, drug addicted) when they spend little time communicating with friends and family. In many dramatic cases, criminals felt isolated from others for many years before they committed a crime. Conversation skills help children learn morality and behave morally. Social isolation, on the other hand, prevents children from learning morality and may be related to self-destructive acts and criminal behavior.

The sixth characteristic moral people share is *emotional competence.* They can regulate their emotions. Children who are generally happy, content, or calm are more likely to behave well than those who are irritable, depressed, or moody. One study found that children were less able to resist the temptation to eat candy when they were sad than when they were happy. Children who were happy were more alert to their surroundings; they were better able to delay gratification. Positive moods (happiness) strongly correlated with achievement activity, social ability, and lack of hostility. Depressed people were less active, more isolated, and more hostile than happy people.

Mood, then, seems to play an important role in maintaining self-control. Fortunately, children do not have to

be prisoners to bad moods. They can learn to control their
emotions and be happier.

Integrity and Internalizing

As children mature, they grow in understanding and
experience, which helps them better interpret an ever-in-
creasing number of situations and more fully develop the
six moral traits I have described. Even young children do
moral things. They sense right and wrong. They recognize
in a basic way what helps and what hurts people. But most
children get better at morality as their abilities improve and
their experience broadens.

In the early stages of their moral development, children
explain that they behave morally to avoid punishment, to
obtain pleasure, or to win approval. We could say that
during these stages, children think about themselves and
their needs but do not necessarily think about others or
act morally even if they have been taught to do so. In the
later stages, children are motivated to moral behavior by
their knowledge of laws (moral standards) and eventually
by a consideration of their relationship with others.

Whether children can use their increasing knowledge
in their reasoning, judgments, and actions as they mature
depends on increased intellectual and social awareness.
Since such awareness can be taught, we need not think
that children are unable to learn morality while they are
young. We can teach them by helping them increase their
understanding of all parts of the moral circumstance and
by helping them think about and *integrate* each part with
the others.

The ability to integrate is important for parents, who
are the primary means by which children learn awareness
of moral circumstances. If we fail to teach all aspects of
the moral circumstance, or if we emphasize one aspect
over the others, children will follow us, focusing on just
that one part as they face moral dilemmas. Many parents

emphasize rules or laws, and this can lead to a neglect of
people and their needs. Other parents stress getting along
with others to the point that moral standards are neglected.
A preoccupation with the purpose of a situation could lead
to a pragmatic focus about "getting the job done" that
ignores both people and the appropriate moral law.

Because we love our children, we want more for them
than just an ability to think about lofty moral ideas: we
want them actively to avoid hurting themselves and others.
So, we are interested in the best way to teach. We want
to be assured that we can do it. We want to know that it
will work. Then we want to see results.

The better children understand the elements of a moral
circumstance (other people, themselves, purposes or tasks,
and moral standards) and see relationships between these
parts, the more likely they will act morally. When they act
morally, they develop the personality traits that eventually
form a moral character.

As children grow, they can understand more about
purposes, people, and moral standards. Further, they can
understand more about how to relate concepts to themselves. For example, young children may help others without fully appreciating the idea that they are also helping
themselves. Also, a person's ideas about helping someone
will change from sharing a toy as a young child to giving
complex emotional support as an adult.

We grow in understanding throughout our lives. When
facing a moral dilemma, more mature individuals usually
take more rather than less information into account when
making judgments. They are more likely to know what
will help or hurt people under many conditions, and they
come to see moral standards as complex principles rather
than as simple rules. As Piaget (1965) noted, what children
think about morality changes and becomes more person-
oriented as they mature. As children learn more about
people and how to help them, they grow in moral char-

acter. This progression can be observed in five stages of moral development.

Discrimination and intention. During the first three years of life, children coordinate their senses and explore the world. Changing vision, hearing, and movement helps children identify the parts of a moral circumstance. They identify a sense of self, develop intentional behavior, and learn to understand the concept of purpose. Further, they discover much about other people and show a basic ability to evaluate people's actions or objects as good or bad. During this time, children display empathy, an emotional style, and the beginnings of autonomy. The synthesis between a child's behavior and his or her knowledge of situations is now possible.

Adapting self to others. Once children have identified the parts of a moral circumstance, they adapt to different situations according to the approval or disapproval they receive from others. These responses stimulate them to search for cues about how to adapt successfully. During this second stage, children use conversation skills to help them adapt. They talk to learn how to adapt or to explain why they did not. Children deepen their understanding of other people and of themselves. Most important, they recognize that situations require certain behavior. That is, how they act is governed by the rules of a situation. The rules may be those of a judge's gavel, what parents say, or how to choose the sides of a team. This adaptation may be observed when young children practice going to school, going shopping, and other adult activities.

Applying moral standards to self and others. In adapting to different situations, children discover that rules exist for each situation. Examples include admonishments to share, take turns, say only nice things, and so on. These early admonishments related to social conduct become moral standards when children evaluate whether people have been helped or hurt by their actions. As a result, in the third stage they learn to distinguish moral standards from social rules. Children learn it is they who must choose how to apply a moral standard so that no one gets hurt. Children have by now made many choices, some of them about moral issues. A child becomes a moral agent who is responsible for what he or she does or does not do rather than merely being controlled by external forces.

Self-interest and responsibility to others. In the fourth stage, children face what seems to be conflict between promoting their own interest and acting from their sense of responsibility to others. Throughout adolescence, children may hurt others through selfishness or help others selfishly (with an ulterior motive). During this stage, children are developing morally if what they do for themselves does not exploit anyone else. They also develop a sense of affiliation with others, believing that others may be helped or hurt by what they do or do not do.

Internalized moral character. In the fifth stage of development, children attempt to make their actions coincide with their beliefs. They look sensitively at situations to see if someone can be helped or hurt. They attempt to help people by volunteering time, energy, and resources. Such individuals recognize situations when someone can be helped or hurt. They understand moral standards and usually act morally.

Understanding the course of moral development can give you a perspective of where your child might be at a given time. Further, it can help you identify what children need to help them progress. Moral development is not inevitable. Children must be taught, and we must identify the most effective way to teach them.

Integrating the elements of a moral circumstance can be done by teaching children how to reason, judge, and act morally. That is the beginning. The end is the formation of their moral character.

CHAPTER 3

MORAL REASONING: LEARNING WHAT HELPS AND WHAT HURTS

Moral reasoning is a way of thinking about moral circumstances that enables us to consider all parts of a moral circumstance, understand their relationship, and make judgments that result in moral behavior. If children see themselves as moral agents, if they can think compassionately about others, if they understand the moral tasks facing them, they will be more likely to behave well when morally challenged.

Children do not automatically think that way. Parents who want their children to behave morally must teach them moral reasoning and look for opportunities to do so.

One mother sent her young son to buy a loaf of bread and a dozen eggs. She gave him enough money for the groceries and for a treat. She coached him about how much the eggs and bread would cost and about how much he would have for a treat. When he returned, he had the eggs but no bread and no money. She asked what he had done, and he confessed to spending the bread money on candy. Then the mother did something that seemed unusual to the neighbors who heard about it and discussed it later. Instead of punishing her son for disobedience, she punished him for thinking incorrectly. She asked him to think about why he did what he did. Then she explained that he had thought only about what he wanted and had failed to think that his family needed bread to eat. His thoughtlessness hurt others. She explained that he must, in the future, think about other people as well as himself.

The neighbors were somewhat surprised that this mother did not place more emphasis on the boy's disobedience. But she knew that what we emphasize is what our children will learn. If we recognize obedience to authority as the most important aspect of morality, then we will find ways to get children to obey us. But focusing on obedience instead of on how children think limits what our children learn to notice and respond to. If we teach only obedience, children will look for the rule or law to obey, but they may not see all the aspects of a moral circumstance and be able to evaluate them.

Children need to think about their own intentions and behavior, and they must understand the effects of what they think and do on themselves and on others. Children also need to understand the needs, intentions, and behavior of others. They must learn both to observe and to understand what they have observed. They will do that as they mature mentally, as their ability to use language develops, as they gain experience, and as we talk with them about moral issues—as did the mother whose son failed to bring home the bread.

Talking about Moral Principles

As children grow, they want to stay close to their parents. They soon learn that the most effective tool to help them do this is language: it works because parents respond. Thus, children are motivated to learn language and use it in conversation. Moreover, children learn by their conversations with us what we think is important to talk about, and these things will probably become important to them, too. They will also learn to use conversation as we do. If we "talk over" and resolve problems, they will learn to do it, too.

Parents who want to help their children grow into

moral adults can teach them three important things: how to talk about moral issues, when it is important to talk about them, and when conversation is necessary to resolve moral problems or to act morally.

We teach children how to talk about moral issues when we ask them to talk about themselves. "What are you feeling?" "What do you think you like?" "What do you want to be?" "Why do you think you did that?" As we ask our children about their feelings and listen carefully to what they tell us, they will come to understand their own motives, feelings, and desires. At the same time, we can encourage them to talk about and understand others. "Why do you think that woman was angry at her son?" "What do you think your sister is feeling just now?" In that way we help our children learn empathy, and we also give them a set of "people" words—such as *woman, son,* and *your sister*—to think with, so that they can understand ideas about morality.

As we guide our children through this process, we express our own opinions about the behavior we have observed together. We teach them that other people have real feelings and real needs, that they need recognition, attention, and love. We show our children how people are motivated by these needs or by desires for money or popularity and how these different motivations result in certain kinds of behavior. We can find ways in our daily conversations to make what we know come alive in our children's experiences.

I once spoke to a class of twelve-year-olds, one of whom was my son. Many of the children excitedly asked questions, talked out of turn, cracked jokes, and interrupted one another. As it happened, a few days later this son took two or three matches to school. He was playing with them and accidentally lit them. His teacher took him to the school office. The vice-principal imposed no punishment, but he did send home a note. It was easy to help this child understand that in taking these matches to school, he was seeking recognition, much like those in his class who had talked out of turn. We talked about finding better ways to achieve recognition than by taking matches to school.

The "people" words associated with motives, feelings, and goals become the basis for helping children understand how others can be helped or hurt. We can help people by learning how to understand them, by acting so that they will have good feelings, and by contributing to their worthwhile goals. We can hurt people by failing to understand the reasons for their actions, by ignoring or hurting their feelings, and by distracting them or preventing them from achieving their goals and desires.

While we are teaching children such words, we can also teach them when to talk about moral concerns with others. Furthermore, we can teach them that conversation is often necessary to ensure morality.

The following example shows how refraining from talking hurt someone when talking could have helped.

Janice and Rob met during ninth grade. A year later they found themselves in the same high school. They got along well and began to date. After a few dates, things were going so well that Rob suggested they go steady. Janice agreed. From then on they talked often on the phone, and they went out at least once a week and sometimes more often. During their junior year they scheduled as many classes together as they could. As the year progressed, however, they had differences and arguments. Even though they spent much time together, they sometimes found it difficult to get along. Finally, after an argument one evening, they parted angrily and both went home unhappy. Janice went to school Monday expecting to see Rob and smooth things over. He wouldn't talk with her. She tried several times, and still he brushed her off. Later that week, she learned that he had a date with someone else.

As time passed, it became obvious that he did not

intend to make up. They sat in their classes in stony silence and passed in the halls exchanging cold looks. She could not find out if she had offended him or if he just wanted a change. The hurt she felt lasted a long time. She was not willing to trust any boy for a while.

Janice and Rob had come into conflict because of their immaturity and inexperience. Perhaps a breakup and some pain were inevitable. But Rob's refusal to talk to Janice hurt her unnecessarily. If Rob is unable to understand the importance of conversation in such a situation, his behavior will continue to hurt, not help, himself and others.

Researchers have examined the connections between conversation and moral behavior. Damon (1984), for instance, showed the role of conversation in achieving justice. He wrote of giving an assignment to children that required them to distribute three candy bars equally among four children. He described how these children were able to accomplish this by talking about ways to divide the candy and by considering together what would happen if the candy was divided unequally. Damon found that ten-year-old children were better at this task than younger children were, largely, he suggests, because their language and conversation skills were better.

Conversation is the means of establishing morality in relationships between people. Selman (1980) described how children change their perception of friendship as they grow older. He considered the situation in which one child might offend another and described what children would do to resolve this problem. He proposed that the more moral children became, the more likely they would be to talk things out. Young children, he wrote, do not talk because they do not recognize the need. As they grow older, however, children make excuses to justify themselves. These excuses are followed by conversation that explains their actions or asks for forgiveness. Finally, the most morally mature children use conversation to solve

problems and to reassure one another of the importance
of their friendship.

If conversation can be used to create morality, conversation itself can be moral or nonmoral. If our children
need to know "people words" so that they can participate
in moral discourse, they also need to know that words
themselves can hurt or help. Parents with younger teenagers often watch their children adopt a new vocabulary
that includes insults. These words often appear in children's vocabularies when they are self-conscious about
how they look to others. This attention to themselves often
coincides with selfishness and a lack of compassion for
others. Self-conscious children don't see the need to help
others, or they lack the willingness to act because of their
concern about what others might think. Many children
this age are hurt by the insensitivity of others, and they,
in turn, hurt others.

But parents can help their children through this difficult
stage of development by helping them learn words that
reflect greater consideration for themselves and for others.
One father overheard his son refer to an acquaintance as
a "nerd" and a "stupid jerk." This father asked his son to
explain why he used such harsh words. After hearing his
son's description of a recent incident, the father asked,
"Why do you think someone would do that?" "Because
he is a jerk!" the son exclaimed. The father continued
calmly, "There are usually reasons why people act as they
do. We need to learn these reasons before we judge someone." As they talked about the whole situation, the son's
attitude toward the other boy softened.

The father then spoke to his son about using harsh
words that reflected his insensitivity. They talked about
how using these words showed the boy to be a shallow
thinker. "Don't use such words," his father advised.
"Learn to say instead, 'What this person does makes me
angry.' If you cannot understand why the person does
such things, say, 'I cannot evaluate another person because

I don't have all the information.' " Because using negative words had become a habit for the son, the father stopped his son each time he heard him use the words and talked with him about why he had used the words until the father felt confident that his son understood the reasons for refraining from using them.

Words represent thoughts, and thoughts usually lead to actions. If we want our children to learn morality, we can help them learn to use the language of understanding and compassion. To be motivated to accomplish this task, we need only remember the great destructiveness to human life associated with the use of such negative words as *nigger, chink, wop, jap,* and *honky.* In contrast, the use of such positive words as *child of God, brother, sister, love, unselfishness, helping, sharing,* and *kindness,* may lead to improved moral behavior.

Learning about the Intentions of Others

Because understanding what other people intend by their actions is essential to being able to recognize and deal with moral circumstances, we need to teach children about intentions. The first step is to teach them to observe carefully.

Observation skills can easily be taught in family life. For example, we can teach our children to pay attention to facial expressions by playing a game of "stop, look, and think." In this game, young children can be taught to stop, look at people's faces, and think about what different facial expressions might mean. Facial expressions show emotions and are of great importance when trying to understand someone. Listening to voice tones is another important observational skill. We can point out the tones associated with anger, kindness, love, surprise, disgust, sadness, joy, or any other emotional state.

Gestures and posture are also important to observe. Children can be asked to think about the excitement displayed by rapid hand movements or the fatigue shown by slumping over with head down. Our attention and praise reinforce our children's learning to notice facial expressions, voice tones, and gestures. They will develop a selective attention to these cues to the meaning of the behavior of others. In other words, they will begin to understand what other people intend.

We also teach children about intentions by teaching them to observe sequences of events or actions. We can ask, "What happened here?" "What happened first?" "What happened next?" "Then what?" when we are discussing the plot of a story, evaluating a neighborhood event, or just helping children think about what they did to produce some result. Asking these questions helps children learn to feel, think, and act in a sequence.

In my community a man confessed to the police that he had sexually molested several young boys. To help people in the community learn how to protect their children from becoming victims of such activity, I was invited by the police and school officials to meet with the parents of the molested children. We discussed what this man did and learned that it involved several steps. First, the man walked by the school. He greeted the children a few times. Then he engaged them in conversation. He joked or played with them. Then he invited some of them to go for a ride with him.

After learning about this sequence of actions, I explained it to my own children, explaining that people do things step by step. I told them, "You can learn what people intend to do, good or bad, if you know what to watch for." Together, we practiced watching people in a grocery store and in a shopping center to see the sequence of their actions. While we were watching, we noticed a young boy steal a candy bar. We watched his manner as he approached the candy display, looked to see if he was being watched, and put the candy into his pocket. His behavior was different from the behavior of people who took things with the intention of purchasing them. Observing this difference, my children learned an important lesson about sequences and intentions. They learned another lesson when the boy with the candy bar saw us watching him and put the candy back.

Helping Children Reason about Themselves

Of course, it is not only the intentions of others that might be moral or nonmoral. Our children will have their own moral or nonmoral intentions. When children understand their own thoughts and intentions, they will be more capable of mature moral reasoning. Autonomy, a characteristic of moral people, can exist only if people are aware of their own intentions. If children know more about other people than they know about themselves, they are more likely to be influenced by other people. This lack of self-knowledge creates excessive vulnerability to external influences. In contrast, if children become more aware of their own motives and intentions, they will be more likely to maintain their own values even if pressured by others.

At first consideration, it might seem easy for us to identify our own intentions. In truth, however, most of us have more than one intention for almost everything we do. We can thus appreciate that our children may find themselves with mixed intentions, trying at the same time to please their parents, satisfy their friends, and fulfill their own needs. It may be difficult for them to sort out these intentions to discover which is primary at any given time. It may even be difficult for them to see that they have conflicting intentions.

It can also be difficult for us to understand our children's intentions. When children are young, their intentions are usually transparent to us because we can see their objectives. We watch, for instance, when a young child sees some cookies on the kitchen cabinet and moves a chair closer to reach the cookies. We accept moving the chair as evidence of the child's intention to get some of the cookies. As children grow, however, it is less easy for us—and them—to identify their intentions because their purposes are not as obvious.

But for children to reason morally, they must know how to identify their own intentions and think about them, so we find ways to help them do this. They may require much help even in coming to know what they intend. We can recognize, for a beginning, that children often confuse their own intentions with those of others. "Well, *he* . . . " a child might automatically begin when confronted during an argument with a friend or brother. "I didn't do it," a child might say in response to an accusation. Or, in explanation of poor performance at school, "The teacher does not like me" might be offered. "They are all doing it" might be a child's attempt to get some privilege from us. Reasoning about intentions depends on a child's ability to separate his or her own purposes and intentions from those of everyone else.

Being able to do that promotes autonomy, the sense of responsibility for one's actions. We can help our children develop this sense of responsibility by asking questions that focus the child's attention on himself. "What is *your* part in this?" we might ask. "What are *you* going to do?" or "What is *your* objective?" In this way we can help our children carefully and thoughtfully clarify what they intend both before and after they do something.

Interestingly, it is more common for us as parents to ask about something that has already happened than it is to ask about what is planned. But as children improve in their ability to talk with us, we can ask them to examine what they want to do or accomplish before they participate in some activity, as well as ask them what they accomplished or attempted to accomplish after some event has taken place. We might say, "Where are you going?" or "Who are you going with?" or "When will you be back home?" From the answers to these questions, we can get an idea of what our children plan. But to help *them* know their own intentions, we could also ask, "What do *you* intend to do?" or "What is *your* purpose in going?" After children have done something, we can ask, "What were you trying to do?" or "Tell me what your plans were." If the children cannot give us answers to these questions, it may be because they are not fully aware of what they intend. Our job now is to tell our children what *we* think their intentions are, and often they will accept our statements as accurately applying to them. In this way they come to know themselves as they believe we know them.

Two brothers began a mild argument. Sensing that it would soon erupt into something worse, their mother intervened by stating a purpose for their behavior. "I know that you both want to be understood," she said. "Let's start over and see if each of you can find out what the other wants." She then had one boy talk while the other listened. By acknowledging what was probably the best of their possible intentions, the mother taught them a way of learning about one another and of avoiding what else was brewing inside them.

A father took his two sons fishing. He carefully explained how they were to sit in the canoe and why they should not make sudden movements. A while later, one boy placed a can of bait near the edge of the canoe. A sudden swell in the water forced the can off the edge. As it began to fall, the younger brother lurched forward to catch it and fell against the side of the canoe. The additional weight on one side caused the boat to tip over, even when the father tried to steady it. After they surfaced, surprised and afraid, the younger boy called, "I'm sorry, Dad!" apparently thinking his father would be angry. Even without knowing about the bait can, the father said, "I know you wouldn't have done it without a good reason." Later, when the boy explained, there was a good feeling instead of an unhappy one.

If we supply our children with ideas in this way, they

will learn to believe that their intentions are good and worthwhile. Any child can be taught in this way that he or she is helpful, or kind, and so forth. In contrast, failure to focus attention on children's positive intentions, combined with blaming them for stupidity, can make them fear that they are not good and that their intentions are foolish and unimportant. These perceptions will lead them to believe that knowing about intentions is not important.

Besides telling children what we think their intentions might be, we can help further their knowledge by telling them of our own intentions. They watch us carefully. Children recognize that what we do is related intentionally to our objectives. If we say what we will do and most of the time do it, our children will learn to trust us. Then when we say, "I care about you" or "Even if you can't understand, do what I ask anyway," our children will believe our intentions are to care for them. Our hypocrisy, on the other hand, makes it difficult for children to recognize our intentions because of the confusion between what they hear and what they see.

Our children learn to reason about their intentions by learning how we reason about ours. A father once told me that he had taken three small children with him to do a few errands. After a while, the children were tired and irritable and started quarreling with one another. The father was about to yell, "Be quiet!" but instead he managed to say, "Look, I am tired, too. I have three more places I need to go, and then we'll be finished. I am trying to hurry. I hope you will help out by being quiet so we don't all fight with each other. Then we'll get some ice cream!" He was surprised, he said, to see these children understand him. After they knew that he intended to stop three times before getting ice cream, they knew what to expect, and they were quiet. Later in the week, one of the children was playing with a friend. The father overheard her saying, "I am tired of playing right now. I hope you will understand."

Family routines can help children learn to think about their intentions. Simple routines of getting up, making the bed, and getting dressed, which are a part of "getting ready in the morning," help young children predict what will happen and enable them more easily to discover their intentions. We can point out that these routines happen in a sequence. For example, after learning as part of a bedtime routine that dressing in pajamas is followed by brushing teeth, children begin to see dressing in pajamas as the intention for brushing their teeth. Sequences in other areas help children feel assured of what is intended because they can accurately predict what is going to take place next.

Security stemming from some routine in our families has an interesting, but often unknown, effect on children's moral reasoning. First, if children grow and live in a stable, somewhat constant environment, they will more likely learn to look for the routines and sequences in other situations. Second, if they are in a moral circumstance, children accustomed to stability can more quickly recognize the absence of routine and understand how the unexpected might bring hurt to someone. In contrast, when family life is chaotic, children come to expect no routine and may even resent or fear order. Life teaches us that immorality most often takes place in the absence of order. A certain amount of routine in family life, then, helps children develop an understanding of intentions and expand their capacity for moral thought.

If children have learned to be aware of their own intentions, their own contributions to the moral circumstance, they will come to understand that selfishness and excluding others hurt, and that kindness, acceptance, and sharing with others help. Understanding their own intentions can also help them discern the intentions of others. Generally speaking, if children understand what they hope to achieve at school, in sports, and in relationships with friends, for example, they will be more likely to be successful in what they do and will be less likely to be distracted by the immoral intentions of others.

Helping Children Reason about Other People

Often it is easy to recognize what other people might do. But sometimes moral circumstances can be so complex that it is not easy for children to understand whether someone intends to help or hurt them. Naive children are fortunate if they are in the company of people who intend to be considerate. But many children are hurt, and hurt badly, because they are unable to understand the intentions of others. Few children grow to maturity so insulated that they never hurt others or get hurt themselves. We want to teach our children to reason about the intentions of others to reduce the likelihood of such hurt.

Human ability to reason increases in sophistication with the growth and development of the brain. Parents can promote or retard a child's progress in learning to reason about other people depending on whether they know what to teach about it. It is obvious, for instance, that children's earliest family experiences exert influence on the attitudes they carry about other people. If children's families are loving, competent, and predictable, then trust of others develops, and children mature with more confidence in people than they do when their families are chaotic or abusive. As their language develops and experience expands, children come to recognize that not all people are alike. They begin to discriminate between those who intend to care and those who do not.

Before describing how we might teach children to reason about the intentions of others, I want to describe a type of reasoning that retards moral thought. Sociologists use the term *stereotype* to describe the failure to think about people as individuals. If we stereotype, we clump people into groups, that is, we speak of a person as a representative of a class of people with similar traits instead of as a

distinctive, individual human being. When we call someone a "blue-collar worker," a "yuppie," or a "punk
rocker," and assume that this says all there is to say about
this person, we have engaged in stereotyping. Once we
have applied a label to someone, we tend to neglect to
search for more information about the person. We may fail
even to notice obvious contradictory information because
we mistakenly believe that the label tells enough.

What we know about parental influence explains how
specific stereotypes can be transmitted from parents to
children. That is, our children will copy our language, will
refer to others as we do, will label people the way we label
them. But even more important than this, children will
copy our *style* of thinking. Children can also learn from us
to think about people in terms of group characteristics.
Parents who teach their children to think in stereotypes
are likely to teach their children prejudice.

Moral reasoning is quite the opposite of stereotyping.
Moral reasoning does not involve evaluating people according to the groups they may represent. It is, rather, a
way of thinking that considers each person as an individual, irrespective of station in life, race, family name, talents,
or religion. As we teach children to reason about what
others intend, we must emphasize thinking about individual behavior in a specific setting: "He seems to get angry
when someone differs with him," "She doesn't seem to
be very happy when her house is in a mess," "It seems
to me that he cries easily when he is embarrassed," "Look
how happy the baby gets when someone smiles at him."
We help children with this part of reasoning by teaching
them to collect information about personal attributes without comparing a person, favorably or unfavorably, with
anyone else.

Focusing on individual characteristics helps children
reason about the intentions of others in at least two ways.
First, we help children assume that the purposes or motives
of others could be the same as their own would be in the

same situation. We can ask, "What would you do if you
were in that person's situation?" This analysis might not
always lead to a correct interpretation of the other person's
thinking, but it is a good beginning to ask children to put
themselves in another person's shoes. Next, we can easily
teach our children that there is almost always a purpose
for the way a person acts.

Bobby was outside riding the new bike he had just
received for his tenth birthday. Four boys his age came by
and waved to him, smiling, calling out a friendly greeting.
Two of the boys were his good friends. The other two were
not such good friends. In fact, only a few days before they
had jeered at Bobby and ridiculed him for no apparent
reason while they were walking home from school. Bobby
saw that all four boys looked longingly at his bike—the
new chrome frame, special racing wheels, and pads for
handle bars and cross bar. Bobby stopped his bike at the
curb and let the two boys who had mistreated him have
a ride. Then he let his friends ride.

Bobby's mother had been watching all this, upset because she knew what the first two boys had done to Bobby
before, and she assumed that they were bullying him now
into letting them ride his bike before his friends did. Later,
she asked him about it. "Why did you let those boys take
your bike before your friends?" Bobby's answer surprised
her: "I knew they were being friendly to me today just so
they could ride my new bike, so I figured if I let them ride
it first, they would leave me alone and go home." Bobby's
correct understanding of the purposes of the boys who
greeted him enabled him to effect the result he desired in
this situation.

Children can learn about the purposes of others by
learning to observe the sequence of events in any situation.
That is not always easy to do, however, and sometimes a
more direct approach is useful. We can teach children that
when observation alone does not supply enough information, they can ask questions about what others are doing

and talk to others to clear up confusion. Many family and neighborhood situations present opportunities to apply these two suggestions. Children can learn to politely ask, "Excuse me, can you tell me what is going on here?" or "Could we talk about this, please?" Asking is a way to discover what others intend. We can also help children collect accurate information about the intentions of others by teaching them how people act who intend to help and how people act who intend to hurt. People who are honest and loyal, who keep promises and obey the law, are likely to be people who intend to be helpful. On the other hand, people who engage in malicious gossip, who tell lies and fail to keep promises, are likely to hurt others.

Our loving attention as we explore with our children these ways of learning to think about others is a wonderful gift. Children have many fears about others as they grow. We can see these fears when children meet a stranger (such as a new schoolteacher) or when they try to do something new. It is understandable that some children react to these fears by assuming that other people intend to mistreat them.

One morning my son Brett left home for the first day of third grade, grim and silent. When he came home that afternoon, he was exhausted and, uncharacteristically for an eight-year-old, took a nap. The next morning at breakfast he suddenly burst into tears, telling us that Mrs. Williams was mean. His mother asked, "What happened yesterday?" "Nothing," Brett replied. We waited. "Nothing—yet!" "Did someone tell you she was mean?" I asked. "Well, yes. Mike Jones said she was." This revelation let us help Brett examine why Mike gave him this unhappy news. "Maybe Mike thought she was mean because *he* was a problem," I suggested. We also talked about the possibility that Mike might just be trying to scare him. Later, we telephoned Mrs. Williams so that she could correct Brett's fears.

When we pay attention to our children's evaluations

of other people, helping to reinforce correct ideas and to clear up misapprehensions, we can ensure they will learn to think that many people intend to be caring and responsible. Without this attention, we risk our children's learning irrational fears of what others may do. Children who think that others generally intend to be helpful are more inclined to be helpful themselves. While we are helping our children develop an appropriate amount of awareness of the realities of the world they live in, we do not want to make them fear everyone.

Thinking about the Consequences

Moral reasoning involves thinking about intentions—our own and those of others. But it is more. It also involves thinking about the consequences of behavior. Parents frequently tell children, "Think before you act." But because all children tend to be impulsive, because they are immature, it is also useful to tell them *what* to think about rather than just leaving them with the general admonition to think. When we tell children to think before they act, they need to know that we want them to think about the consequences of their behavior for themselves and also for others.

Steve, an obviously obese boy, is walking from the school bus along the street toward his home. Two other boys, a year older than Steve, are walking behind him making comments about "fat" kids and how "stupid" they are. Steve notices but pretends not to, and he says nothing. The two boys talk louder and challenge Steve to a fight. Dave, another boy about Steve's age, sees and hears the taunting. What could Dave do? He could join Steve and even things up. If he is more mature, however, he might decline to fight and instead point out to the two boys the consequences of their actions. He might say something like this: "What you are saying would hurt anyone. Would you like someone to treat you that way?" He might then join Steve on his walk home, providing him "moral support" against any further insults by the other boys.

The ability to think about consequences of behavior is a characteristic of moral thought that usually improves with maturity. As we did with reasoning about intentions, we can help this process along by discussing consequences after they have occurred. This discussion cannot be to interrogate or punish. Rather, we will use this conversation to help children see that a thought, a choice, or an act is linked to a result that can either help or hurt someone. This conversation will add to the children's belief that they are significant and of worth.

Children are likely to hurt themselves and others if they do not see themselves as useful, helpful, or important. Parents who call their children worthless, stupid, or good-for-nothing are setting the stage for immoral behavior. Parents who tell their children they are helpful and important are building the possibility of morality. It is easy to emphasize the positive and point out when children help, when children serve, when children have done something of worth. They are more likely to mature as moral people when they think their actions produce helpful rather than hurtful consequences.

In a moral circumstance children will use what they understand about possible consequences. That is why we must give attention to the idea that consequences be linked in our children's minds with the notions of helping and hurting. What does happen when someone helps another? What are the many ways to do that? What are the consequences when one person hurts another? What are the many ways to do that? The only way children will know beforehand what might help or hurt in the varied situations in which they will find themselves is by learning to reason about the effects or consequences of what they do.

Children can learn a reasoning process as they would any style of thinking, just as they learn the reasoning involved in chess or math or their favorite computer game, just as they learn to convince a parent to bake some cookies or take them to the park or let them use the car. Children learn what they are taught, what they experience repeatedly. If we neglect to give our children the opportunities and direction they need to learn moral reasoning, we can be sure that they will find themselves in situations where they will not understand how to help and how to avoid hurting themselves or other people. In other words, they will find themselves behaving immorally, whether or not they "know better." We all learn by trial and error, but children with limited knowledge of potential consequences learn mostly from error.

CHAPTER 4

MORAL JUDGMENT: CHOOSING TO HELP AND NOT TO HURT

Living a moral life sometimes requires us to exercise our freedom to choose to help ourselves or others. We are never free from the freedom to *decide*. It is possible, of course, that we may not recognize a situation as a moral circumstance and think that no decision is required of us. If we make that mistake, the resulting inaction may hurt someone. A decision is always necessary in every circumstance in which people may be helped or hurt. Moral judgment is the process of making the choice to help or hurt after we recognize that either may happen. If our eventual choice, or decision, is moral, then we decide to help rather than to hurt. If we choose to do what hurts ourselves or others, our choice is immoral.

It is not natural for children to know how to decide well. Although the basis for making choices is an inherited function of the brain, much about deciding is learned. For example, most of us learn as we mature to suspend making decisions until we have searched for relevant information. We learn to compare pros and cons in order to make a better decision. We also learn to make a decision at a certain rate or within a certain time. Some of us are impulsive deciders, others are extremely deliberate, and most fall somewhere in between. Some even try to avoid decisions, fearing that anything they do might bring them harm. For these people, a moment of decision is agonizingly difficult.

One of our tasks as parents, then, is to teach decision

making to our children. But we want to teach more than a general form of deciding: we want to teach moral judgment, which means identifying a moral circumstance— when someone can be helped or hurt—and then making the correct decision when it needs to be made. Some of the judgments will be easier than others to make, especially when it is clear that one course is obviously better. At other times children will have to judge between doing what is right and having such things as other people's approval. Sometimes children will be required to make judgments when it is not clear what to do or when two or more alternatives look equally good. Decision making is a complex task, so, to simplify things, part of our teaching is directed to helping children understand the difference between moral choices and conventional choices. Then we can focus on the moral choices.

Whether automatic or involving thoughtful consideration, moral judgment is an essential part of morality, and in some ways it is at the very heart of it. Moral decision making is learned, and therefore it is up to us to teach our children to do it well.

Moral and Conventional Choices

Teaching moral judgment should include teaching children both what is and what is not moral. There is much about human behavior, for example, that should not be judged, only understood. *Acceptance* is the term we use to describe nonjudgment. Acceptance is one trait of a moral person. Being accepting means we acknowledge that we wish to understand rather than to judge. There are many different but equally acceptable ways to talk, dress, believe, socialize, marry, give birth, practice religion, and express opinions. All deserve to be understood rather than judged as moral issues.

Prejudice is the opposite of acceptance. This attitude exists when children fail to understand other people and their circumstances and then make judgments about them from ideas based on limited experience, learned at another time or from someone else. Prejudices are usually family traditions, not a result of firsthand personal experience, and are often learned by children because of harsh disapproval they receive from others. That disapproval creates fear, the root of prejudice. If we react in an overly intense and angry way when a child thinks or acts in a way that we parents do not, our children may believe they are required to think as we think. The absence of our acceptance makes our children's fear of disapproval so intense that they hide their thoughts and emotions to avoid exposure. Unfortunately, this reaction reduces their ability to understand others accurately, and instead they learn to disapprove without knowing much more than the briefest and shallowest information. They have learned prejudice.

Teaching children to be accepting also helps them distinguish between social conventions and moral concerns. Social conventions include etiquette, or customary behavior we may think to be important socially, but social conventions are not the same as moral judgments. Children ranging in age from seven to nineteen were asked to read a list of three types of social transgressions, classify the list into three groups, and indicate which, if any, of the items on the list were wrong. The list included such moral issues as cheating, lying, and stealing; conventional behavior such as styles of dress and table manners; and personal choices such as selection of friends and joining clubs. Children of every age were able to distinguish moral behavior from the other two. They were also able to identify immoral behavior. (Nucci, 1981.)

Significantly, the children assumed that everyone agreed with them about what is right and what is wrong. The study suggests that, distinguished from social conventions, children know that moral judgments focus on issues of right and wrong. That means we can teach children to distinguish between the two by teaching them to

accept and understand social conventions and to judge
only in situations when someone may be helped or hurt.

Knowing Right and Wrong

It is essential for us to recognize that knowing both
right and wrong is necessary. One tells us about the other.
Sometimes, especially for children, *right* is what wrong is
not; however, the importance of teaching both right and
wrong is often lost in the challenges of routine child management. Most of our disciplinary methods, for example,
emphasize responses to mistakes children make rather
than point to the right choices available to them. Reacting
only to correct wrong behavior creates an imbalance unless
we give equal emphasis to teaching children the correct
thing to do. The most common measures of restricting
privileges, yelling or scolding, spanking, or isolating children in their rooms seldom teach what is correct. The very
best punishment for misbehavior is to require children,
whenever possible, to rehearse what would have been
correct but what was not done in the misbehaving situation. Children who argue can be expected to do something
cooperatively. Children who hit can help someone. Children who can't get home on time can be given a watch
and told to go outside and practice coming in "on time"
before they are allowed more extensive time away from
home. If we explain to our children what we think is wrong,
require them to practice what is right, and use positive
reinforcement, they will learn about both right and wrong.

Another idea that deserves emphasis is the connection
between the judgments children make and the actions they
subsequently choose to take. We, of course, want our children to do more than be intellectually aware of what is
right and wrong. We want them to make moral judgments
that lead to moral acts. In some situations, there is a connection between children's judgments and their actions,
but at other times there appears to be no link between the

two. (Blasi, 1980.) Obviously, then, we need to identify what makes moral actions follow moral judgments.

I believe that whether children act morally after making a correct decision depends on how they learn about making moral judgments in the first place. If we teach only by telling, lecturing, or practicing, for example, children may develop definite ideas about right and wrong, good and bad, but they will not have clear connections between the ideas and what actually to do. Moral judgments that lead to moral acts cannot be considered just a mental exercise.

How Children Learn the Concept of Moral Judgment

Recent findings about the human brain indicate that some conditions appear to be present in the human personality without having to be learned. Our concepts of time, space, numbers, and language appear to be a few of these. (Restak, 1984.) Another of these inherited characteristics is the basis of evaluation. It appears that every human mentally evaluates ideas in order to understand them. (Arnold, 1960.) Further, we evaluate an idea or an object in terms of its being good or bad. (Osgood, May, and Miron, 1975.) Whenever we are confronted with something new, our first evaluation is between good and bad, to see if the object, person, or idea is a threat or is not a threat.

The basis of moral judgment (evaluation) is present at birth, a natural condition of all human beings. The ability to discriminate between what is good and bad, right and wrong, is important to our survival, our intellectual development, and our social relationships. Beyond that innate ability, what we believe about morality and teach to our children comes from a shared understanding called a moral order, which embraces the standards of conduct that promote the welfare and unity of a given group of people. Such standards are called "community standards." They are based on values about human behavior held in common by all in the group, values derived from religion, traditions, and family rules.

Sometimes the shared ideas that unify one group hurt others. For example, Nazi harassment and killing of Jews may have unified some groups in Germany. In such a case, of course, the community standards and the moral order are no longer moral in the true sense. As parents, because we want our children to be truly moral, we teach them the personal and community standards that guide them to help and to avoid hurting themselves and others.

For the most part, children's first acquaintance with community standards is through the approval or disapproval they receive from parents. Ours are the first judgments children experience. Approval may include praise, rewards, attention, warmth, and social station. Disapproval may include such responses as spanking, criticism, shunning, shaming, and punishments.

From approval and disapproval, children learn to discriminate, or judge, what is right and wrong or what will be approved or disapproved. Just as important, however, they learn a style of making judgments, which they tend to use thereafter. The way we judge children will generally be used by them to judge themselves and others. Parents who harshly and punitively judge will often produce the tendency in children to make judgments with the same negative intensity. Parents who seldom approve or disapprove may teach their children there are no judgments to make, because children cannot identify what is moral from what is not. Parents who give both approval and disapproval, considerately and consistently, will teach children this style of judgment and also to judge between right and wrong, good and bad.

After learning what will be approved and what will be disapproved by their parents, children will usually test their knowledge in public. When and if they find that other people outside the family also approve and disapprove, children confirm their knowledge of what is judged and also the style of judgment. Thus they learn community standards. When children find that their parents differ from other people in what they approve or disapprove, the children often have difficulty establishing standards for themselves. The conflict between parents' standards and the standards of others is often associated with children's delinquent behavior.

To avoid that situation, some parents of teenaged children formed neighborhood groups to make common rules about curfews, dating, and activities their children could participate in. Later, when they informed their own children about these conditions, the children were unwilling to comply with the rules until they learned that their friends were affected the same way. Children accept their parents' right to make judgments and are willing to learn the behavior that would be approved or disapproved when the children believe their parents' standard to be shared by others—a community standard.

Children also tend to believe that their parents' judgments and their own are similar to others' standards. Nisan (1984) suggested that children learn moral standards from their culture. Children think these beliefs, or standards of right and wrong, are agreed to by others. Thus in a moral circumstance, children's judgments are based partly on what has been taught them and jointly reinforced by parents, schoolteachers, church leaders, and so forth.

Sometimes children find that choosing to do right brings the approval of some and the disapproval of others. If children try to make judgments that satisfy other people, then how can they be helped to choose what is right if they know others will disapprove? I suggest that children have several "reference" groups, and disagreeing with one may bring the approval of another. That is why parents who establish a warm and communicative relationship with their children are usually rewarded by the children making judgments that agree with their parents' rather than someone else's. If children have such a relationship

with their parents, they can more easily make right decisions that result in the disapproval of someone else. When
children do not belong to a reference group, or if their
group has immoral standards, they are likely to decide to
act immorally themselves.

Research has demonstrated that by age five, children
identify two ways to be moral. One is to help by being fair
or just, and the other is to help by regulating how they
themselves act in order to promote the welfare of themselves and others. (Turiel, 1979.) Both of these judgments
are influenced by what children think others expect. This
finding suggests that children will learn to be fair and just
and to attempt to regulate themselves, if they believe others
will approve if they do.

To teach our children to have moral judgment, we must
give them numerous examples and opportunities both of
judging how to help and of having the courage to trust
their judgments and act on them. If we always tell our
children what to do or prevent them in other ways from
choosing themselves, they may be less likely to make moral
choices when it is required of them. Whether alone or in
the company of others, our children must be able to judge
whether to help or to hurt and then decide how to do it.

In summary, then, children must first know right from
wrong and, further, be able to make judgments that lead
them to do moral acts. Children must be able to judge
whether a situation requires them to decide to help or to
hurt and then to decide how to help. What children decide
to do will be an attempt to satisfy the moral requirements
of their community (family, friends, town, or nation) by
regulating themselves to promote the welfare of themselves or others or by seeking justice and equality. These
ends can be accomplished in many ways and will vary
according to the situation.

The Role of Emotions in Moral Judgment

One part of the human personality lends itself in an

exceptional way to the development of moral judgment. Although the emotions are not as well known as some other parts of us, it appears that they, combined with moral instruction, are the means by which children learn moral judgment. First, emotions are "action tendencies," which are the motivation for action. When we influence how children express themselves emotionally, we are teaching them to act upon their judgment. Second, children learn two sets of emotional responses about themselves and other people that are related to morality. One set is the positive emotions (love, joy, caring) that are related to actions that promote the welfare of people. The other set is the negative emotions (anger, fear, disgust) that are related to actions that hurt people. And third, children learn to express emotions in specific situations according to cultural expectations, and they display or express emotions in ways they believe other people will understand and approve.

We can see how close the relationship is between the display of emotions and moral judgment when we recognize that the outward expression of emotion is part of the basis for the judgments we make about ourselves and others. For instance, we watch facial expressions to identify the emotion (smiling and happy, or frowning and discouraged). By observing voice tones, posture, and other physical movements, we judge how intense the emotions are. We rely so much on these cues that should the person's words contradict the emotions displayed, we rely more on the behavior than on what is said to make our judgment.

In addition, we evaluate the emotional display of one another in a moral sense. Our society usually considers it good, for example, if we are able to control or regulate our emotions to some degree and are not too extreme or exaggerated. It is considered "bad" or "wrong" to be "out of control" and display emotions too intense or otherwise inappropriate for the situation. A person might apologize for crying or for losing control of his or her temper.

The role of emotions in moral judgment and human behavior is illustrated in a story about the great athlete Jim Thorpe. An American Indian, he was reared according to his tribal customs. Then his accomplishments in sports brought him into contact with people and customs new to him. One of these customs involved displaying emotion. One day some of his friends were good-naturedly kidding him and being mildly sarcastic. To them he seemed to smile in response. Thinking he was not offended, they continued. His smile became even broader as they continued to tease and laugh with him and at him. Suddenly he became angry, pushing and shoving some of them. They, of course, were shocked at what seemed to be anger. After the ruckus died down, he explained that their "kidding" was insulting to him. He had been trying to get them to stop by showing his teeth—a gesture, or emotional display, that to him meant displeasure. Of course, the others had not interpreted or judged his display correctly because they had thought it to be a smile.

Similarly, we evaluate emotional displays as good or bad, helpful or hurtful. We express emotions according to what we believe others approve of, just as with making moral judgments.

Emotions are the bridge between thoughts and acts. If individuals display emotions correctly for any given situation, they are likely then to act correctly.

Learning moral judgment requires learning emotional skills in combination with learning moral knowledge about right and wrong. Knowing moral principles, without having emotional skills, is the same as knowing what is right and failing to do it.

As parents we can teach our children about emotions, and we can teach them how to express both the positive and the negative emotions related to moral behavior skillfully and accurately. Having these skills will help them make moral decisions and then act to help and to avoid hurt.

These objectives require us to teach our children to recognize and feel a variety of emotions and to express them in many different moral circumstances. Because emotions are related to the ways they are expressed with moral judgment, we need to teach children the skills of regulating and adapting emotions and behavior to the requirements of moral judgment. In other words, we need to teach our children to make judgments that are understandable by others in our moral community, to regulate their emotions and adapt their behavior to promote the welfare of themselves or others or to achieve justice for themselves or others, and to make judgments that they will act upon, not just think about. We teach them to recognize and feel a variety of emotions, to regulate the intensity of their emotional display, and to adapt their emotions to many situations.

A Variety of Emotions

Because we want to help our children make moral judgments that lead to various helpful actions in many different situations, we need to teach them a variety of emotions related to moral behavior. In conversations with our children, we can introduce the names of emotions — *trust, love,* and *generosity,* or *shame, envy,* and *greed* — and relate these names to moral behavior. When we use such words as *happy, loving, calm,* and so on, children tend to use them also to communicate with us. The next step is to link the word to the action by pointing to the child's action and using the appropriate word: "You seem happy" or "You seem jealous" or "You seem to be feeling nervous or guilty about what you did. This tie between word and act is solidified by reading and telling stories. When words and actions are related in these ways, children remember the associated emotion. My mother told marvelous stories about people, their sadness, and what made them happy. She often became so involved that she displayed the emotions that the people in the stories must have felt. She wept at sadness or tenderness and laughed at fun or joy. As a result, stories and feelings are inseparably connected in my memory. I soar with the triumph of others and feel some shame at the mistakes of others.

Consider how empathy, a characteristic of a moral person, is learned. Children have empathy from birth and develop it further unless they are mistreated. *Empathy* is vicariously feeling what another feels and then being willing to help without expecting a reward for doing so. When we do not feel empathy, we are indifferent to others. That indifference may show up as *defensiveness,* which is such intense concern about our own welfare that we worry excessively about making ourselves look good and shift responsibility for our actions to other people.

Learning empathy reduces defensiveness. More importantly, helping children learn empathy also teaches them faith in a sense of moral rightness.

The Hendersons were concerned about comments their son Rob made about a boy at school. One day after Rob spoke harshly and critically about this boy, Mr. Henderson asked Rob about him. "Well," Rob began, "the other day in class, I was talking and he made fun of what I said. Then, a group of us were standing in the lunch line and he jumped in front of me, saying he was late for class. He is so stupid!" Mr. Henderson asked, "Do you know why he acted that way?" He knew that the other boy's parents were divorcing. He asked Rob if he knew. "No," Rob replied. "I wonder if that would make him feel strange enough to do what he did," the father suggested. "How do you think children might feel when their parents get a divorce?" Mr. Henderson could see Rob's feelings soften somewhat, and he asked, "Do you think there is any way to help him?" They continued talking until Rob recognized that the other boy might benefit from some friendly attention.

Susan was ten years old and planning a birthday party.

She wanted to invite her friends. A new girl had recently moved into the neighborhood. Susan and her friends did not yet know her very well, and Susan's shyness made her resent the new girl somewhat. When Susan asked her best friend about inviting the new girl to the party, her friend said, "Don't invite her. Just have our friends come." When Susan and her mother were preparing the invitations, her mother suggested that Susan invite the new girl. "I don't want her to come," Susan replied. "Why not?" her mother asked. Feeling accused, Susan retorted, "Shelley doesn't want her to come either." "Hmm," her mother said, "do you remember how lonely you felt when we first moved here and how happy you were when Heather and Tami brought over welcome gifts?" "Yeah," Susan said. "Well," said her mother, "don't you think we should help this new girl feel welcome too?"

These parents were teaching their children to go beyond the obvious to gather information about the other person, who was being judged too quickly and defensively. The children were asked to understand by comparing their own feelings with those of the other person. Then they were asked to do something right to try to help. No reward was mentioned, nor was success guaranteed.

Our children must be familiar with many emotions to understand what others may be feeling in various situations. Rob was asked to understand frustration, anxiety, and anger at a hidden enemy so he could have sympathy for someone whose parents were divorcing. Susan needed to know what loneliness, rejection, and unhappiness felt like in order to feel what might happen if she did not invite the new girl to her birthday party. The more emotions children understand, the more likely they will be able to sympathize with others in varied situations. A lack of familiarity with various emotions suggests that sympathy will be limited and defensiveness more pronounced.

Another way for children to learn a variety of moral emotions is to practice and rehearse their appropriate display. That is done routinely in real-life situations through imitation. Parents can do more than that, however. A family game that my children like to play is based on the idea that names of emotions need to be linked to actions.

To play the game, write each of the following words on a small card. Shuffle the cards and give five to each family member. Taking turns, each player has forty-five seconds to pantomime the actions (gestures, facial expressions, etc.) associated with the word on the card. Score one point for each emotion correctly guessed. After each person has a turn, shuffle the cards, distribute five to each person, and repeat the process until someone scores twenty points. Eventually, children will learn how to display these emotions and many others as they are taught. They will recognize them in others, too.

love	activity	tempt
care	freedom	spoiled
concern	self-control	defensive
thoughtfulness	passivity	cooperate
kind	reliance	share
appreciation	respect	equality
trust	reliability	fairness
cheerfulness	autonomy	honor
optimism	slyness	sham
nice	spitefulness	just
helpfulness	bullying	sorry
empathy	stealing	foolish
affection	meanness	shame
calm	lying	unequal
forgiveness	exploitation	rude
gratitude	hurt	hate
serenity	anger	annoy
warmth	rage	ridicule
interest	revenge	cowardly
loyalty	jealousy	greedy
friendliness	envy	disgust

tenderness	contempt	remorse
gentleness	flattery	resentful
sensitivity	guilt	unfair
esteem	selfishness	using
responsibility	unfriendliness	destroy
courage	taunt	insensitive

Helping Children Regulate Their Emotions

There are many ways to characterize emotions. One is intensity, shown in loud talking, flushed or pale skin tone, and other nonverbal cues. In our culture, most people expect and are expected to regulate the amount of intensity they show in their behavior. Too much excitement, anger, aggression, pouting, or sulking usually results in disapproval. Too much passivity, boredom, or indifference is considered negative, too. When we act in these ways, we are told to "calm down," "grow up," "get moving," or "do something useful." We are patient with young children's emotional excesses, but as they grow we expect them to exercise more and more control.

Children who are less able to regulate their emotions are more vulnerable to pressure from others, temptations, and distractions. Their vulnerability, in turn, makes them less reliable in their moral judgments. In contrast, the ability to regulate emotions is a major component of autonomy. In fact, helping children to regulate their emotions is a chief means of helping them develop autonomy.

Being able to regulate their own emotional intensity, or becoming autonomous, does not mean that children are inhibited or overly restricted. It simply means exercising self-restraint according to a set of personal standards to prevent themselves from being overwhelmed by a situation. Moderating the intensity of anger is one example of regulating emotion.

The ability to regulate the intensity of emotions generally and naturally increases with maturity. The human

brain acquires new abilities because of practice and increased effectiveness. Parents can help the process along.
One technique is to let children be responsible for being
in control of themselves. If they are irresponsible—by having a tantrum or by being oppositional and refusing to
obey—we can calmly say that we are sorry they are out of
control and they will have to sit on a chair until they control
themselves. When I suggested this procedure to one
mother, she said, "What if he won't stay on the chair?"
"Sit on him (without hurting him)," I suggested. She reported later that it took two sittings before the boy learned
to sit on the chair until he got himself under control.

We can also teach our children cognitive techniques to
regulate their emotions, such as the old tradition of count-
ing to ten before speaking. These work best if we teach
the children to recognize situations in which such techniques will be helpful. First, *keep a record* of the times and
places that the child is not in emotional control. Second,
discuss the situation with the child and ask for an explanation
of what happened. Third, *reconstruct the situation step by
step,* until the point is reached where the child's emotions
were too extreme. Fourth, have the child *practice a self-
command* that we whisper with them ("be calm"), or develop a distraction (thinking about a favorite movie) that
the child will use when the situation happens again. These
techniques have been used successfully with touchy children to help them regulate their emotions. (Douglas, 1972;
Varni and Henker, 1979; Cameron and Robinson, 1980.)

Although these and other techniques may be applied
with success, parental example is the most influential
teacher over the long term. Parents with tempers, for example, actually teach children to be violent. Parents who
regulate their tempers can help their children do the same.
The importance of regulating our own emotions is made
very clear when we remember that such significant moral
concerns as sexual opportunity, chemical abuse, and

aggression are closely linked to children's inability to regulate their emotions.

Helping Children Adapt Their Emotions

The ability to adapt or adjust emotionally is as important for moral judgment as learning a variety of emotions and regulating them. There are two kinds of adapting or adjusting. One is to alter an aroused or excited state by making a moral choice in order to feel more at peace. To be able to do that, children must be taught that contentment, calm, peace of mind—"feeling good"—are related to choosing and doing the moral, or right, thing. The second type of adapting is to alter feelings to match the behavioral requirements of a given situation.

Moral choices are often difficult because of a conflict between two or more things. Children may be torn between what they *want* to do and what they believe they *should* do—for instance, between wanting to do what their friends are doing and knowing they should not. And even if children decide to do the moral thing, they must further decide what to do to help. That is often not clear. Quite frequently, children must decide and act, hoping, but not knowing, whether anyone else will agree with them or support them. In some cases, they may think rejection will be the only reward they receive for making the right choice.

Many moral decisions are difficult because the stakes are high: what eventually happens will either help or hurt human beings. In a moral circumstance, anyone—except the naive, the crass, the insensitive, or the hardened—can appreciate what might happen to others. Further, those threatened by the immoral intentions of others can feel the challenge or risk of the threat. Moral judgment, therefore, may be highly emotional.

Let's consider two different situations. Suppose one moral circumstance involves a decision to steal or to refrain from stealing something. Most children will have been taught repeatedly that stealing is not acceptable and will know without much deep thought what the choice ought to be. If the object to be stolen is highly desired, or if friends apply pressure, an individual child may feel forced to make a choice between doing what is right and yielding to other competing pressures.

In the second moral circumstance, suppose a child knows a friend is about to do something wrong and is faced with the choice of telling someone (in order to prevent the friend from hurting himself or others) or keeping quiet in order to be loyal. The child has not repeatedly been taught about such a case and does not have a ready idea about the "right" thing to do, yet feels caught between two conflicting feelings.

In both cases the children feel frustration, anxiety, and uncertainty. These feelings are unsettling and provide a motivation to solve the problem in order to get rid of them and feel calm again. Sometimes children think that a decision, any decision, is better than agonizing between two conflicting feelings. Yet at the same time they also understand that an expedient or immoral choice will not reduce the feelings of anxiety or guilt.

The connection between choosing morally and peace of mind can be taught to children. We can teach our children by telling them about the calm and contentment they will feel when they have made correct choices. We can discuss their choices with them and encourage them to make decisions rather than avoid resolving the difficult feelings involved.

A widow called the minister of a nearby church and complained that some young boys had been harassing her by throwing broken bottles in her driveway, piling rocks on her lawn, breaking an outdoor security light, and throwing snowballs at her house. The matter was announced in church so that the neighbors could be made aware of the situation and help out. After church, one father asked to see if his son knew anything about the matter. The son's claim that he knew nothing was a little too quick and a little too certain. A few minutes later the boy was on the phone to his friend, having a quiet, guarded conversation. His dad correctly interpreted this to mean that the boy did know something about it. The father asked, "Did you do anything to this woman?" The son answered no. "Do you know who did?" his dad continued. Then he confronted his son with his knowledge of the phone conversation. The boy finally admitted he knew who had harassed the neighbor but claimed that she was not telling the full truth. The father asked, "What are you going to do about what you know?" "I don't know," came back the not-so-calm reply. "Well," the father said, "I think you have a problem. Because you know who is doing these things, if they do anything more, you are partly responsible."

During the days that followed, the father pointed out in other conversations that the boy would feel at peace only after he made the right decision. The boy just wanted to drop the whole matter, but his dad wouldn't let him. Finally the boy said he would tell the minister what he knew. The father supported his son's choice, accompanying him to his interview with the minister. Afterward, the minister called all the boys in, listened to their side of the story, and worked out a solution with the woman.

Resolving dilemmas by making moral choices is a necessary part of moral judgment. Our children have learned this principle when they know that regardless of whether the moral circumstance is an easy situation or a tough one, the moral choice will produce a sense of rightness or peacefulness. Through repeated practice or sensitive concern we can point out to our children, "Look how happy you feel," or "Don't you feel good when you have done something right?"

The second form of adapting that is necessary to making moral judgments is learning to alter the display of an emotion to fit the demands of the situation. For example, certain emotional behavior is more appropriate on the play-

ground than in church. What children feel and express
appropriately during meals with the family may be different from what is appropriate for a public speech.

We recognize the need to adapt our expression of emotions to situations when we teach our children about social
behavior. A mother has taken her three-year-old son with
her to the grocery store. He is happily calm until he asks
for some candy. She says no, refusing to let him have it.
He begins to yell and falls to the floor kicking and crying.
What are her alternatives? She might first try to regulate
him by telling him to "calm down" or "stop it." If that
doesn't work, she might get angry and threaten him with
a spanking or worse if he doesn't stop. Or, she might take
him from the store to calm him. (Some parents might even
give in and get the candy.)

In order to understand what she actually chooses to
do, we need to know that at home earlier in the day, the
boy wanted some cookies just before lunch. When he was
told "no, not until after you eat your lunch," he had a
tantrum, but his mother ignored it and walked out of the
room. He soon quieted and readied himself to eat. The
mother did not get angry, did not threaten, did not even
try to quiet the crying. Why?

In most cases the difference between her responses to
her child could be explained by the difference between the
circumstances of home and store. In the privacy of home
a young child's crying may be considered more appropriate, though an unpleasant experience for the mother.
Crying and yelling in the store, a public place, is not usually
considered appropriate by most. If his mother ignores the
child's tantrum in the store, she has to reason, "What will
others think?" So, if she is typical, she will do something
to quiet her child. If he stops yelling and crying, she might
also let him know his emotional response is now more
acceptable. Adapting her discipline to the emotional display of the child in several situations teaches him that he
too must adapt.

Attending school, church, and participating in numerous friend and family relationships, children learn to succeed in a variety of social contexts by adapting their emotional responses. We can think of many that are commonplace. Consider children working quietly in school. The bell rings for recess, and suddenly there is noise and tumult. After recess is over, they must adjust back to quietness. Or consider adjusting a modest display of affection for a neighbor to a more exuberant expression to a well-liked relative. Another example is the talkative expression of a teenaged boy with other boys that changes to reserved attention with a girl he likes. Still another is the smiling, chatter, and laughter that change to quiet reverence when children enter their church.

We should remember that some emotions, their expression, and the circumstances for expressing them appear at different periods of a child's life. Thus children are busy integrating emotion and context for several years. We seem to possess an internal cultural clock that helps us recognize that certain emotions will be of greater worth to us and must be fitted into situations according to our age and experience. It is widely accepted, for example, that toddlers will have a limited variety of emotions and not express them well in any situation. We tolerate that. During the "terrible twos," because of their new language skill, children demonstrate more anger and more autonomy. This period is followed by a social period when play and friendships involve sharing, cooperation, jealousy, loneliness, and liking. This period may be followed in our culture by a period of achievement and industry with accompanying emotions of hope, despair, fun, enjoyment. Then sexual emotions and friendships motivate learning an appropriate form of expressing sexual attraction, courtesy, self-consciousness, enthusiasm, affection, and warmth.

At first children try out an emotion in ways they have observed others use. We usually are more tolerant and patient if they fail at first to match the appropriate display to the situation. As time passes, we think the need for correct adaptation increases. Our approval and disapproval become stronger, and if children at a certain age still fail to adapt, our concern increases and we search for other ways to teach or pressure children to adapt properly. If they delay adapting, we call their behavior delinquent.

While children are learning to fit an emotional response to a situation at any stage, they also learn a sense of rightness or wrongness about each. That is felt as a moral requirement, or what should happen, at a given time and in a given situation. As an elementary student, I was walking toward the school door after recess and heard a boy say mean words to a girl and then hit her. I instantly felt he should not do that and told him to stop it. He replied, "Make me." I felt a real obligation to do so because I was bigger and what he was doing I thought to be wrong. Fortunately, as I moved toward him, fearful but full of a sense of right, a teacher appeared and saved us both. I wondered why I felt as I did until I remembered the many occasions my mother reminded me, appropriately approving or disapproving, until I began to show the responses of respect she thought a boy should use toward a girl.

We must teach our children to adapt to moral situations within their control. When they cannot adapt, we must remove them from the situation. Then we need to show them how we want them to act by modeling the desired behavior for them. This process helps children become skillful at adapting their display of emotion. As time passes, they repeat the appropriate expression for a given circumstance and find it approved. The response eventually becomes habitual, and they no longer are conscious of it. The skills of adapting emotional behavior allow them to enter into familiar settings with the confidence that they know what to do. As our children mature and are faced with something new, they apply their adapting skills to find the correct adaptation for the new situation.

Learning the appropriate emotional display for a given situation is the means by which children acquire social confidence and a sense of moral rightness. When children, as well as adults, express emotions inappropriately, a sense of rightness or wrongness comes into play. I remember treating a man who was a passenger on a commercial plane when an engine exploded and the plane was forced to make an abrupt landing, dropping suddenly from thirty thousand feet in the air to the landing strip. The next time this man went to fly he began to tremble and couldn't board the plane. Because he had his own pilot's license for small planes and had previously enjoyed flying, he wanted to overcome his fear. I asked him what he did after the explosion. He answered, "It was terrible. The room filled with smoke and the plane decompressed." Because he had not answered my question, I asked again. Again he avoided it and told about being able to see into the pilot's cabin. I asked a third time. Seeing that I would persist, he fell quiet and then told of the terrible fear he had felt. "I began to scream," he said.

This admission on his part helped us solve the problem. He was not so much afraid of flying or of planes. He was afraid of his own feelings, afraid of being unable to control them and failing to express them the "right" way in that situation. The sense of inappropriateness he felt and his fear that he would again do something he felt was inappropriate was preventing from flying. We talked about what was right or wrong about his feelings. With a few experiments to build his confidence, he began to fly again.

His experience tells us that we have a sense of rightness or wrongness about the way we express our feelings. If we display the right intensity or the right emotion for the situation, then we can expect to be more successful socially.

Adapting becomes very significant for our children the moment a dilemma creates a tension that impels them to judge. One feeling often has to be changed into another as part of the judgment children make. Twelve-year-old

JoAnn was walking home from school on the same route she took at the end of each school day. As she walked along the road, she saw a woman's purse. Opening it, she found a large quantity of money and also the owner's name and address. What had been a routine walk was now a moral circumstance. She found something belonging to someone else. She may have first felt surprise and excitement about the money that then was colored a little when she found the name and address of the owner. What is the right thing to do?

Intellectually, we know the purse should be returned. JoAnn's judgment, however, will be affected by her ability to adapt the emotion of excitement she felt when she found the purse. To do what is moral she will have to alter that feeling of excitement into one that includes a sense of right and concern for the individual who lost the money.

Consider another example. This time some high school boys were standing in the parking lot talking about a very disliked math teacher. Each had a separate story to tell about being mistreated. As they talked, their anger and frustration grew. Bill was angry, too, thinking of a recent unhappy experience. Someone spotted Mr. Taylor's car and said, "Hey, let's let the air out of his tires." Others moved toward the car, indicating they agreed. Bill walked with them. He began to think that it was not right, but he too was mad at Mr. Taylor. For Bill to be moral and not to hurt someone, he has to adapt the emotions of anger and resentment into concern about doing the right thing and concern for Mr. Taylor.

What determines whether these two children alter their emotions, make a correct judgment of what to do, and then act morally? Foremost, of course, is the skill of adapting that children learn as they grow. Those who understand they must adapt to some situations are more likely to adapt during a moral circumstance. JoAnn, for instance, could get a temporary excitement by never telling anyone and keeping the money she found. Bill could get immediate approval from his friends and a temporary satisfaction from letting the air out of Mr. Taylor's tires. But if they elect the moral option to help and to avoid hurt, they must alter their feelings into other feelings. They will be more able to do so if they have practiced this skill.

Another factor that helps determine whether Bill and JoAnn choose morally is a belief about what they would prefer to feel. In the last few years, behavioral scientists have demonstrated that many emotions are related to what we believe about ourselves and others. Is the excitement about the money and the satisfaction of getting back at a teacher better than feeling secure about doing what was right, peace of mind at doing something correct, and the warmth that results from concern for others? If Bill and JoAnn believe the latter is better for them, they will be able to make the choice to help and to avoid hurt. JoAnn will take the purse home, find the owner, and return it. Bill will be more likely to tell his friends he won't let the air out of the tires and he doesn't think they should either.

Adapting during a moral circumstance requires that children become aware of their own feelings and have beliefs about the more desirable feelings that will result from the moral choice they make. This skill is learned from a full exploration of the mistakes our children make while growing up to ensure they feel the negative emotions related to immoral choices and the positive emotions associated with moral decisions. We can recognize that mistakes are as useful to us as wisdom while we are teaching our children the process of moral judgment.

Lastly, adapting to make moral choices is affected by the idea of faith and hopefulness. Bill and JoAnn had no guarantee they would feel better if they chose morally than if she kept the money and he released the air in the tires. What makes them or any child do what is moral when there is no guarantee or even a possibility they will receive anything in return? They must make the moral judgment believing, hoping, but not knowing, that it is right. In the end, all moral judgments and the emotional adaptations that precede them are based on faith. Parents teach children faith when they teach them the worth of hoping and planning for a positive future. It may be religious faith, in which children are taught of God and his commandments. It may be faith derived from the confidence one gets from enduring hardship and achieving success. It may be faith in loving parents or in caring friends. Regardless, it is *faith,* meaning hope for some future possibility. If children lose faith, or have not had it at all, they have much less motivation to be moral. With faith, children are more likely to solve their challenges morally.

In all our teaching, we must teach by example, giving encouragement more than criticism. We must teach by optimism, by loving in abundance, and by involving ourselves with our children as they grow. They come to believe in us, and as we live and hope, so will they. When we rise from disappointments and help them, then they will believe they can rise from disappointments and help themselves and others. At that very moment, when our children are compelled to decide between right and wrong, it is practice, belief in something more desirable, and faith that enable them to adapt to the circumstance and choose the right.

CHAPTER 5

MORAL CONDUCT

Why do some people with good moral training act morally whereas others with similar training do not? Some believe that those who act morally feel a responsibility others do not feel. According to this view, those who do not act morally apparently believe that someone else will do what needs to be done. Others believe that those who act morally have more skill in interpreting complex situations than those who do not.

Lawrence Kohlberg (1969) proposed that moral deliberation develops and matures from one stage to another: first children are motivated by trying to avoid punishment, and then they are interested in seeking approval from others, in fulfilling expectations about what a good boy or girl does, and in following rules simply because they have learned the rules. Mature morality, according to Kohlberg, is displayed when children recognize their responsibility to others and accept a universal "truth" about the right thing to do. Jean Piaget (1965) demonstrated that moral judgment (deliberation) changed with the age and growth of children. Kohlberg's work helps us understand more about moral reasoning, and Piaget's work shows that moral perception changes with maturity and experience.

But these two popular descriptions lead to us to think of morality as an intellectual or a cognitive aspect of a person's life rather than as the representation of a whole human character. Obviously these descriptions of morality lack something: they emphasize *knowing* morally, not *doing* morally.

Moral conduct requires that children go beyond moral reasoning and moral judgment to actually doing something helpful. Those who teach morality to children only according to Kohlberg's and Piaget's theories might help children to know about right and wrong in a moral circumstance, but they may not help the children develop the skills to actually do what is moral. Because we know that sometimes moral actions follow moral reasoning and sometimes they do not, as parents we focus on moral action as the result of our teaching. We want our children to interpret situations to know what helps and what hurts people, and when they are confronted with a moral choice, we want them to choose what is moral and then do it.

Developing Moral Character

As parents we are interested in helping children develop a moral character rather than producing children who merely think about morality. We also want to help children become compassionate and flexible in their judgments rather than to behave like robots programmed with a "moral code." Such programming can result when our punishments and rewards are so strict that children are left with little room for initiative or with little sense of freedom. That is why we must teach them moral reasoning and moral judgment. These help us influence our children's thoughts and feelings, the parts of their personality that allow for uniqueness and freedom. If we try to control how our children act by using force or by yelling, anger, threats, withdrawing love, or bribery, we are actually undermining our efforts to teach them morality.

Helping children to understand their thoughts and feelings and then integrate them with their actions will foster in them a more complete system of morality. This total approach helps ensure that our children will demonstrate moral character by their actions.

Morality Is Active

Some actions, related to thoughts and feelings, are learned cumulatively. Each experience is added upon earlier ones until children have acquired a variety of actions they apply to a variety of situations. Some specific acts, such as telling the truth or demonstrating respect for property, may have to be repeated many times before they are a consistent part of a child's behavior. It therefore is useful to begin moral training when children are very young.

Children do not naturally know that they need to do something instead of being passive. They usually must be taught that there are times when they are to implement, perform, function, achieve, accomplish. We teach children when and how to do this by participating with them in many situations where they act rather than merely listen or observe.

Because children need to learn to be active rather than avoidant or passive, parents should promote rather than stifle active behavior. Children allowed to roam the house instead of spending excessive time in a playpen, for example, are likely to be more active. Too many restrictions by overly cautious parents may promote passivity. Excessive criticism or punishment of children may do the same.

Even television reduces the activity levels of children. In 1970 the average time children watched television was three and one half hours daily. In 1980 the average time had increased to five and one half hours. By age eighteen the average child will have spent more than thirty-six thousand hours being passively entertained in front of a television. When we consider that active experience is necessary for children to learn morality, we can imagine how detrimental these passive hours are.

Children cannot choose to refrain from doing something immoral unless they are active doers. The better we teach children to do things, the easier it will be for us to teach that there are times when it is useful to choose to be passive. In contrast, allowing children to be passive makes it more difficult to teach them to be doers. Passivity leads to more passivity, not to action.

Identifying Moral Acts

Children do not automatically know what moral actions are. We have to teach them what is moral and what is not. In order for them to learn morality, they must actually participate in the activities that will teach them. As we participate with our children in those activities and allow them actively to satisfy their curiosity about things, we can make sure that moral actions stick out and are noticed by them. We do that by our own example, by our approving of what they do well and by our disapproving of their mistakes. All three are essential for children to learn what is moral and what is not.

Any situation can be made a part of our children's moral education if we focus on what we do to teach them our standards. Unless we are consciously aware of the need to help our children develop morality, we might not see mealtime, for example, as a time when morality can be taught. But when we realize that any of our children's actions might lead to a certain character trait or type of personality that will continue throughout their life, then we will use any situation to teach.

Think of children who are grumpy or angry and who argue with others at breakfast. The mood, the noise, and the frustration prevent others from having a peaceful and pleasant meal. We can respond by (1) saying or doing nothing and allowing the disruption to continue, hoping it will pass, (2) becoming angry and yelling at the children to stop, (3) making the children leave the table because they are offending other family members, or (4) distracting the children by telling a story. These possibilities exist for every parent who eats with his or her children.

Let's consider what children might learn from each of

these four potential responses. Frequently allowing children to act angry and grumpy without regard to others' feelings might contribute to insensitivity and a lack of concern for other people. Ignoring how children act will not teach them anything moral or immoral unless they interpret our lack of response as approval.

Yelling at children will help them know that some behavior is not acceptable, but it may teach them to be considerate only when a strong authority is present to enforce the standards. This response may also present to the children an example of hypocrisy, a distinct difference between what we say and what we do—that is, we are yelling to get them to stop yelling. In most such cases, children will do what they see us do, not what they hear us tell them to do.

If we just send the children away from the table, saying they can return when their mood has improved, they will learn grumpiness is not acceptable because of our disapproval, but they will not learn what is correct behavior unless we do something else. That is true also of the option to distract the children by telling a story.

To teach our children correct behavior at mealtimes, we must set an example of the behavior we want our children to learn and then be willing to show approval (such as praise and affection, or returning the children to the table if they have been sent away) as well as disapproval. Another example will further illustrate. Two four-year-olds are playing in the bedroom. They play quietly at first, but soon we hear loud, angry voices, and soon the children hit each other. Both begin to cry. Our child comes to us, and we find out that our child would not share with the friend. Effective teaching suggests that we go into the bedroom, find out what was wrong, ask the children to explain how selfishness made them feel (unhappy), and then show them what sharing means. We might even practice sharing additional toys or make up a sharing game. When the children are able to share well, we might reassure them again before we leave them alone. By following this routine of teaching both moral and immoral acts, we can demonstrate our example of sharing with them (the correct behavior), our approval when they do share, and our disapproval with their failure to share properly. If we apply the same series of steps for many other situations where children participate, we will highlight moral concerns and moral behavior. Through this means, children will come to know that the requirement to act is an integral part of life.

Verbal Cues and Moral Conduct

As our children mature, we begin to use words to regulate them. We tell them what to do, we say "no, no," and give love or short explanations, depending on our inclination and their abilities to understand. We use this process to tie words to children's actions and to teach children to regulate their behavior by using key words. In one study, situations were identified in which impulsive children either did not act or did not act correctly. The children were given a cue word to whisper or to say out loud when they found themselves in these situations, words such as *go, walk,* and so on. This technique helped children learn what to do and how to control their actions. (Meichenbaum and Goodman, 1971.) The same thing ordinarily happens when we teach children, "Don't cheat," or "Stealing hurts someone," or "Tell the truth," or "Be kind." If we use words to name and describe moral and immoral possibilities, our children will use these words to guide their actions.

Moral Acts Are Governed by Rules

The next step in the development of moral conduct is to teach children about rules and about how rules govern their actions. How children learn rule-governed behavior is a fascinating story that shows us that children are observant, that as they mature they gain a greater and more complex understanding of the world, and they sense the need to adapt rules to a specific context or situation, much as they alter or adapt the expression of emotions. These characteristics suggest that the behavior of children is generally pliable and that we can reasonably expect varieties of positive skills, depending in part on the time and energy we take to teach them. Child psychologists generally believe that children's understanding of rules develops in the following sequence:

Experimentation, ages birth to two-and-a-half years. Infants and toddlers usually respond to their immediate surroundings. They experiment to learn how to fit physical skills—crawling, walking, and so on—with language and relating to other people.

Rules and actions, ages two-and-a-half to five years. Children discover that a rule of action applies to them. Their imitations of adult behavior, such as playing house or other childhood games, introduces them to the idea that they must learn rules about how to act; otherwise, they cannot successfully participate with others.

Rules for specific situations, ages five through nine years. Children learn that different rules for actions exist in many situations, such as games, school class, family situations, and playing with friends. As they learn to succeed in these situations, children usually believe the rules for each situation are fixed and cannot be changed. They evidence frustration and annoyance if someone fails to follow the rigid rules or attempts to change them.

Negotiating a change in the rules, ages nine through thirteen years. Children evidence more flexibility in their understanding of rules and recognize they must be willing to change them to fit a given situation—not having enough players to make up two complete basketball teams, for example. These changes, however, are arrived at by agreement among everyone concerned. Thus we see groups of children participating in "fair" strategies to "choose sides."

Adaptation: organizing a principle, ages thirteen years through adult. Children appear able to adapt a given rule to fit many different situations. This process involves trial and error, and occasionally mistakes are made—"We were just having fun and didn't think anyone would care." Children are expected to know how to act in many circumstances and especially how to adapt to changes. Those who fail at either of these will receive disapproval from others who share the situation and believe they know the rules.

The connection among rule-governed actions, situations, and morality is important. We want children to know that certain acts must be applied to certain situations so they will feel impelled to act and then be motivated to act morally.

Morality requires two sets of rule-governed behavior: (1) regulating behavior to help and to prevent hurting someone; and (2) promoting justice and equality. (Kurtines, 1984.)

Regulating behavior means that children will be able to help actively—that is, they will be kind, show charity, give love. Moral conduct requires children to regulate their behavior so that people are not hurt. Honesty, resisting temptation to cheat or steal, patience, and self-restraint help people. Lying, cheating and stealing, impatience, and lack of self-restraint hurt people.

Promoting justice and equality involves such things as learning to take turns, cooperating, sharing equally, and understanding social reciprocity. Social reciprocity means that in relationship to each other, both individuals give and both get something. Reciprocity establishes equality in that what one person gives another is equal to what he or she receives. Further, reciprocity is the basis on which justice is established. Justice requires that punishment fit the crime. People who have taken something from others "deserve" a just, or reciprocal, deprivation. Someone who has sacrificed for others to some degree deserves a just, or commensurate, reward.

Regulating behavior and promoting justice are the names for groups of specific actions we want our children to know. There are numerous ways to perform each action, and children choose these ways according to the conditions they find in the moral circumstance. At least one of these actions—regulating behavior and promoting justice—is involved in every moral circumstance, and sometimes children must do both to be moral. Teaching morality will require that we teach both.

Community Standards: What Children Are Expected to Live Up To

After we have helped our children identify what is moral and what is not, the next step in developing moral conduct is to help them expand their personal experience to include an understanding of the rules and laws of society and to make community standards (the requirements of the moral order) into a set of personal standards they can strive to live up to. In this way children begin to learn that regulating behavior and establishing justice have general social applications as well as specific personal ones. Parents, neighbors, television programs, schoolteachers, newspapers, books, and friends portray and teach common expectations about rules for regulating behavior and establishing justice.

Community standards shape the goals that children strive for and the ideals they live by in order to be like others. Children may, of course, encounter specific differences between the standards of the several communities of which they are a part. Religious standards, for example, may conflict with the standards of the team or the school. These differences, however, do not prevent children from learning a set of standards that are shared by others who matter most to them and that they are expected to live up to. Most people do find it easier to live in communities where people think and act as they do. That is why we choose to live among people who mirror our own standards of morality. We want our children to discover that they are to live up to the standards we find acceptable. There-fore, our neighbors, our friends, and our fellow church members are important. Children learn community stan-dards from several people, and we quickly learn that it takes many people to rear a moral child.

There are many ways to learn community standards vicariously as well as through direct experience. Children talk with their friends and learn about their friends' family rules. They may see their friends receive some form of approval or disapproval from their parents. And com-munity gossip can be an effective source of information about the approval or disapproval other people receive. Such gossip may include sensational events reported in newspapers as well as more immediate neighborhood events such as a divorce or an incident of child abuse.

We are wise, I believe, to recognize that gossip has its malicious side, which must be avoided if we want our children to be moral, but the informal discussions of other people's acts and their consequences are an effective way of establishing and reinforcing community standards. We often talk about others' proper or improper displays of character compared to the community standard. Usually gossip is about whether someone has failed to display the character trait—self-regulation, for example—that satisfies the standards. Children hear or participate in these dis-cussions, which adds to their information about what is right and wrong. (Sabini and Silver, 1984.)

Children learn another part of how to act in accordance with community standards from ceremonies and rituals. Community ceremonies that honor traditions—such as celebrations on Independence Day, Veterans' Day, or Pres-idents' Day, for example—teach children community stan-dards about those traditions. In addition, when children believe that everyone else maintains the community standards, they can develop a sense of "rights," which gives definition and direction to their actions. Our concept of fairness toward one another teaches us one of those rights. So does our idea of responsibility in the face of needs: if one person's need is greater than the need of another, the one with the greater need has the "right" to seek assistance from the other. (Harre, 1984.)

The "rights" shared by those in a given community are the spaces, the allowances, the opportunities, or the freedom for action in a moral circumstance. They are what people allow without disapproval. If everyone else does it, or should do it, then we assume it is within our rights to act the same way. Every parent hears children justify their actions by making the claim that "others do it." Another example of how our sense of rights influences us can be shown by comparing children's behavior in the classroom. In Europe children do not openly tell or correct a teacher about some irregularity because it is not considered a child's right to do so. In America children are more likely to make such comments because they assume they have the right to openly address or question authority.

Our culture-wide sense of rights gives children latitude to act in some situations and restricts them in others. The wider our children's exposure to people and situations, the clearer will be their concept of their rights. When children are brought into contact with different types of people, have experiences with many things a community deems to be of worth, and are exposed to many ideas, they will have a more elaborate sense of their own rights and the rights of others. Thus they will have greater freedom to act morally when a circumstance requires it.

Internalizing: How Children Form Personal Standards and Character

When children have learned to act, learned that actions are governed by rules, and learned what those rules and their applications are, children can internalize what they know and form their own standards of moral conduct. As children grow, their experience and knowledge will be varied and probably uneven; that is, they may have more experience in one area than in another. Therefore, a child may be better at being moral in some settings than in others. A child might steal, for example, but won't lie. Some cheat on tests at school but donate hours to a service organization. Some appear to be moral in public but engage privately in immoral acts, knowing they would receive disapproval if others knew. Such children may feel guilt for wrongdoing only if they are caught. Internalization is the process of testing what they have been taught against their own experience to see if it is emotionally true for them. Internalization smooths out the rough spots and inconsistencies in children's understandings and creates a more integrated moral character. This process in children implies that they have transformed ideas into actions. It suggests a strong sense of responsibility for self, so that they will adhere to standards even when pressure is exerted to prevent adherence.

Internalization is a complex of social, emotional, and mental events that usually take place during late adolescence, but they may begin earlier or may not begin until later in life. Some researchers have suggested that the notorious "midlife crisis" may happen because internalization did not occur earlier. In any event, when children reach a stage when they have had a variety of experiences with moral behavior, when the adults around them give them less supervision and external control, when they accept real responsibilities with real consequences for failure and success, then internalization takes place. The process of internalization usually has three stages:

Becoming private. Internalization requires that children's experience with a community standard become a private matter. To accomplish that, children remove themselves from those who represent the community, especially authorities; they might spend increased amounts of time alone, or complain that others are trying to control them, and they state, "I just want to be left alone."

To achieve a sense of privacy, children might also deviate from community standards just to see if they can get away with it. Many form a private life away from authority figures with friends exemplified by a vocabulary of new words, going to parties, and adopting rules in their group. These rules may or may not contradict community standards. Many children will privately violate some community standard, ranging from pranks and mild deviance to life-styles that are vastly different from the usual. Most prominently, children in this stage psychologically remove themselves from those they are intimately acquainted with in order to think and act alone without supervision. Many children will, eventually, quietly adopt the community standards as their own.

Integrating: forming a sense of individuality. The second phase takes place when children begin to participate in work, play, school, or personal activities without much supervision from others. The experiences they have "alone" are fit together with their knowledge of community standards. These standards are, in effect, tested to see if the child's experience will confirm the community standard as correct. When children succeed at doing this, they can better sense their uniqueness from others and will show improved ability to reason about themselves, recognizing they can acceptably differ from other people. They will understand what consequences their actions will produce for themselves and others, generally accepting some of their personality traits as permanent. Those who have deviated from the accepted standards and in the process have been alienated from others (having broken the law or some other standard) begin to return to the community because they discover that personal success requires a more conventional life than they have lived. Children sense a shift in the balance between emphasis on what others think and attention to their own choices.

Internalized personal standards are evident when children recognize that what they may decide to do may not be fully approved of by others. They are aware of and understand their personal beliefs as well as how others may think. During this phase children will show less fear of stating their opinions, values and standards.

Becoming conventional. The third stage begins once children have felt a sense of individuality and experienced some of the consequences of their own choices. Now, seeking to belong and succeed with others, they discover that demonstrating the conventional standards of the community improves communication and reduces the possibility of friction. Further, such demonstrations bring respect and approval from others. Economic and social success is often tied to a reputation of being a "good" person as measured by a person's display of the community standards. When opportunities permit, children with these personal standards will demonstrate their knowledge by adopting behavior accepted as proper by others, even if others might fail to demonstrate what is proper. Thus, children become conventional to be successful with others and because conventionality is consistent with their individualized set of standards.

After internalization, the children's moral character as represented in their personal standards is a demonstration of the community values. Standards are like traits, or behavioral tendencies. They include many ways to help by regulating or adapting certain actions or to help by seeking justice. Importantly, these traits are shared by other community members, thus making any individual a representative of what the community or society believes about how help is or should be given to one another.

Character is the understanding and interpretation of moral conduct shared by both the individuals and the other members of their community. If we now say our child is honest, then the way honesty is expressed by this child will be mutually understood by the child and other people.

Having a moral character means that our children have many ways to help, many ways to prevent harm, and the sense of responsibility to act when it is not clear that others agree or that what is to be done will actually work. The moments of moral courage when our children willingly maintain their standards are among the most important moments of their lives. Most of them will not be earth-shaking. They will not usually produce fame or fortune. But they will provide for our children many private moments of deep personal satisfaction.

A group of college boys in my dormitory formed committees to prepare for a coming Christmas party. The party was a success. The refreshments were delicious, the music was great, and the decorations were outstanding. Everyone enjoyed themselves. Later one or two of the boys on the decorations committee admitted they had stolen the decorations. The guilty parties feared getting caught, so a general meeting was called to help decide what to do. Since we were friends, it was understandable why the purpose of the meeting focused on "how to avoid getting caught."

"Let's not tell anyone," someone said. "We can keep it a secret." (A sense of privacy.) "Yea," another fellow replied, "but we would know." "Well," another stated, "it is not my problem. You guys should have thought about this mess before you did it." After a long pause, another said, "Why don't we take them back?" This comment was answered that someone stealing from people wouldn't take down the address. "Let's sell them and give the money to charity," another voiced. The chairman of the committee answered, "In the first place," he said, "we didn't keep records of where we got the stuff. In the second place, if we sell it, people might find out we took it." His comment was followed by a few nods of agreement.

In the midst of this discussion, one older fellow, who had been silent, now spoke. "I want you guys to know I won't have anything to do with something dishonest, and I don't think you should either."

I wished I had made that statement. All of us did. As a freshman and a friend of culprits, I was caught up in trying to find a way to prevent them from getting caught. The difference between the older person's comment and what I was thinking staggered me just a little. Why didn't I think it, or say it? He had internalized his standards and was less controlled by the situation he was in. I had not yet developed to that point, but on that day, I wished I had.

CHAPTER 6

SEXUAL MORALITY

Sexual experience in some form is a part of everyone's life. We may differ in the amount and the exact kind of our sexual contact with others; we may differ in the way we talk about sex, if we talk about it at all; we may differ in what we think about the appropriateness of certain sexual acts, or what we consider the proper circumstances and times for sexual behavior. So, we will differ in what we teach our children about sexual behavior. But we must all realize that every child learns something about sex; every child develops attitudes toward it; and every child participates in situations where sexual acts are possible. All children can be helped or hurt and can help or hurt others by sexual acts.

The pathway from immature child to sexually mature adult is such a natural part of human development that it is quite easy to notice the transformation in our children and not fully appreciate that sexual development can and ought to be accompanied by relevant moral education. As our children mature, we may teach them about their bodies; we may talk to them about human reproduction. They will also talk to their friends about sex, and out of curiosity they may experiment to find out more. Many of the sexual experiences our children have are simply motivated by a desire to learn.

It is possible for our children to go through this natural process without learning that they can be helped or hurt and can help or hurt others by what they know and do about sex. Unless we help them, they may not understand

95

that moral sexual development must be accompanied by awareness and mastery in many different situations. If we are interested in teaching sexual morality, we will want our children to be prepared to make decisions about the way they express themselves sexually, with whom, and under what conditions. If they are not informed and prepared to understand sexuality as involving decisions, they will be vulnerable to sensory pleasure and to impulsive violations of their own moral standards. Mature morality about sex includes active decision making, that is, making informed choices related to sex instead of acting impulsively.

Remembering our discussion of moral reasoning, we understand that it will help children if they know something about other people and how to interpret what these people do or intend to do sexually. How can other people be hurt or helped by sexual behavior? How can I? Being able to make these kinds of evaluations will help our children make correct moral judgments in moral circumstances involving sexual behavior. If they understand what helps and what hurts others in such a circumstance, if they have moral standards and know how to regulate their emotions in order to act according to these standards, then our children will also know moral sexual conduct.

Sexual Openness

Over the past few decades, sexual issues have gradually become more openly discussed in public. This increased openness has probably improved our general knowledge about sex and should be appreciated for that, but there are many things it has not accomplished. For one thing, we still do not have a clear-cut, accepted community standard about the way children are to learn about sex. Generally, parents are still not the primary teachers of sexual knowledge. If other people, such as school personnel, attempt to teach our children, we worry about what

they teach and whether they will teach them our standard
of sexual conduct. But many of us still assume, apparently,
that children will find out what they should know from
someone other than us. Our parents were often not our
teachers, and we are often unable to overcome their example. We should realize, however, that so many different
kinds of information are openly available to our children
that if we ourselves do not teach them what they should
know, they will not lack information, but they will at least
be confused and probably misinformed.

In my opinion, although our lack of involvement in
teaching our children about sex is a serious problem, a
greater failing is the continued societal confusion and disagreement about what is moral and what is immoral sexual
conduct. The absence of agreement in our religious and
civil communities makes it more difficult for parents in
individual families to decide what they will teach as moral,
and many, rather than stand alone, simply neglect to decide at all. What will children value if we, their parents,
are confused?

Since every healthy child develops sexual desire, and
all children grow up participating in situations where decisions regarding sexual behavior must be made, it seems
reasonable that by now the increased openness about sex
would have resulted in agreed-upon standards of moral
behavior that we could teach our children. In the absence
of such standards, however, I fear that many of us have
communicated to our children that their sexual conduct is
a matter not of morality but of personal preference. I have
interviewed many young people who began sexual activity
as a result of whims and experimentation. Sex is such a
profound part of us that our failure to help our children
understand the use of it as a moral issue places them at
great risk. Its great power to bring joy is accompanied by
at least an equally great power to hurt.

Making sex a moral concern does not mean that we
have to judge and disapprove or approve of every touch,

embrace, or kiss. But, as with any other part of morality, we want our children to know how to reason about sex, make appropriate moral judgments about it, and then act morally to help and to avoid hurting anyone. That will not be easily accomplished unless we make clear decisions about it ourselves. Using the guideline that moral is what helps people and avoids hurting them, I believe it is possible to come to a sound understanding of sexual morality and a clear distinction between what is moral and what is immoral.

Sexual Behavior: Seeking a Moral Standard

We usually evaluate a behavior as moral or immoral by examining its consequences. If someone is hurt, then we can, with hindsight, recognize it to have been immoral. If an act results in helping someone, then we define that act as moral. Then we apply these evaluations to future acts of the same kind. Using consequences as the only measure of behavior, however, makes it difficult to establish a definition of moral and immoral for some kinds of behavior. Sexual behavior is one of these kinds, because the consequences of sexual acts are not always immediate or readily apparent. We can easily recognize that rape is immoral because its harmful consequences are obvious and well known. As a community, we find it more difficult to reach agreement about the morality or immorality of premarital sexual contact from french kissing and petting to intercourse between consenting adults because it is hard to tell if someone is hurt by it. Thus we have a tangled growth of opinion seeded by religious belief, legal definition, personal preference, peer pressure, and the fashion of the day.

Some define sexual morality in relation to a legal definition of immorality as any act of sexual exploitation by one person of another. Examples of exploitation are child molestation and rape, including statutory rape (performed by an adult upon a "willing" but underaged partner). Others consider sexual morality to be behavior on one side of a "line" drawn through a list of possible types of sexual behavior—after a few kisses and caresses but before heavy petting, or after petting but before intercourse. Still others consider any sexual behavior with a loved person to be moral, while the same behavior engaged in randomly or casually, without love, is immoral.

It is easy to see why the diversity of opinion about so many types of sexual conduct confuses us about standards of sexual morality. It is also understandable that deciding about sexual morality seems such a large and complex task that we are reluctant to try to establish some common standard all can rely on.

The increasing incidents of sexual exploitation we hear about and the increasing sexual activity among young people should motivate us to try harder to arrive at community standards for sexual behavior. (Robinson and Jedlicka, 1982.) After our initial outrage at hearing a new instance of sexual exploitation, however, we seem to ignore the matter until the next dramatic case comes to our attention. Our collective efforts are like running from fire to fire, thinking that we are making progress against an epidemic of arson if we put out each blaze as it appears. And many have decided that sexual activity among young people is so widespread and inevitable that rather than trying to regulate it in any way, the best course is just to teach children to prevent some of its consequences. So, these people teach "safe sex," with prophylactics to prevent disease and contraceptives to prevent unwanted pregnancies.

Sexual exploitation and sexual activity among young people deserve our compassionate attention. Nevertheless, the urgency to respond to these concerns, combined with our confusion about sexual morality, tempts us away from confronting and accepting the obvious solution: the injuries and harm resulting from any inappropriate sexual behavior are virtually eliminated when people live the standard of chastity. This standard is gaining more favorable attention as it has become clearer in recent years that other sexual standards risk harm and misery.

For many years now, however, those who believed in chastity before marriage and sexual fidelity in marriage have felt they had to justify this position against the claim that anything is moral, or at least not immoral, if it does not hurt anyone else. Because it has been difficult to confirm that an obvious consequence results from some sexual acts (such as intercourse between consenting adults), the standard of chastity has been taught and lived in the faith that sex at the wrong time and place is harmful, even if the harm is not apparent.

Our culture's experimentation with varieties of sexual freedoms has not resulted in a better life and more happiness for those who have tried them. As parents teaching morality to children, we recognize the need for a community standard of sexual morality that is clear and understandable so that we can help our children learn and live it. The standard of chastity and fidelity, though still somewhat ambiguous, is at least more clearly defined than any other standard except sexual license, which is clearcut because it has no limits of any kind.

If it can be successfully argued, and I believe it can, that the role of morality is to preserve society and create unity among a people, then the far-reaching personal and social effects of sexual behavior certainly imply a demand for a sexual standard. And all sexual standards other than chastity and fidelity risk hurting or exploiting the people directly involved through emotional trauma and disease and also risk hurting the children their actions may call into being. And now, because of Acquired Immune Deficiency Syndrome (AIDS), an even wider group of innocent people can die as a consequence of other people's sexual acts. We live in a time when it is clear that society is faced with a serious struggle and disunity partly because of our lack of chastity and fidelity.

The advent of AIDS has brought many people to the realization that sexual acts can have life-threatening consequences. That innocent victims are vulnerable to AIDS has created a greater moral crisis and has helped fuel the search for solutions. The standard of chastity, however, need not be justified only by this terrible possibility. The past decade has yielded increased information about other effects sex can have on people. For example, we did not know a few years ago what we know now about the effects on the human personality of sexual exploitation. Chastity and fidelity do not exploit anyone and thus, according to our guideline, are moral.

If we truly understand the breadth and scope of the influence of sexual relationships in human experience, we can understand that sex should be more than a series of momentary pleasures from brief encounters. The true role of the sexual relationship is to bring a full and rich passion to life, to help us form a lasting emotional bond, to enable us to procreate, and to bring numerous other personal rewards. Sharing sexual experiences with the same partner, in the absence of fear and in the context of affection, allows expression of a person's deepest heartfelt impulses to give and receive love. This complete expression has been called, by those who have known it, the most wonderful experience possible for human beings. So we add to our definition of sexual morality any sexual behavior that promotes this outcome. Immorality, then, is anything that stifles and limits the full expression of sexuality in marriage.

The immorality of sexual exploitation and the morality of sex that builds love provides a rationale for chastity and fidelity as our standard of morality:

1. Sex with several partners may produce emotional alienation, reducing one's ability to form an enduring bond with another person. Although a temporary closeness may

be achieved through it, sex with several partners creates anxiety about one's lovability. Chastity increases confidence in one's ability to love and be loved.

2. The incidence of premarital sex has increased at the same time as the frequency of extramarital sex, suggesting a possible link between the two. Children who disregard and violate the standard of chastity may be more likely to participate in adultery.

3. When immature individuals participate in sex, the pleasure may lead them to focus their attention on this one aspect of a relationship, neglecting other aspects that are at least equally important. This restricted focus may lead to unrealistic and narrow expectations of marriage, increasing the possibility of marital discord.

4. Indiscriminate sex reduces the intensity of it. Individuals so engaged seek greater variety and more unusual sexual techniques in order to derive pleasure. This creates what Rollo May described as a "New Puritanism." The original Puritans had a great deal of passion but no sex. Nowadays, many have sex but no passion. We can conclude that chastity and fidelity may be the means of increased and enduring sexual passion.

5. Most sex-related diseases, usually acquired through promiscuous sexual activity, impair subsequent healthy sexual response. They may impair conception, interfere with prenatal development, and produce children afflicted with a disease. There is a sizable risk of hurting children when anyone violates the standard of chastity and fidelity.

Intimate premarital sexual contact alters our children's social perception and narrows their focus to finding sexual pleasure rather than forming friendships. According to our definition and rationale for sexual morality, sexual intercourse and all intensely intimate sexual contact between consenting adults before or outside of marriage may be immoral. The lack of an assured commitment between them will, at least in the long run, prevent them from a more total expression of love. Further, should a person have several partners, there is some probability of reduced ability to form an enduring emotional bond with another.

If there is no obligation or sense of responsibility for children born from the sexual union of uncommitted partners, the lives of these children, faced with uncertainty and potential unhappiness, may be evidence that sexual acts are immoral when people are unprepared to be responsible for the consequences. The immorality of adultery is demonstrated by the emotional pain often felt by both partners, and the terrible void it very often creates in the lives of others, spouses and children, which often requires years of struggle to overcome.

It seems obvious that teaching our children to be chaste is the one way to prepare them for future happiness. We can teach this standard of morality to children just as we can teach them not to cheat, steal, or lie. If we have decided to accept this standard ourselves, they will more likely learn and follow.

Children's Nudity, Curiosity, and Imitation

During the first five years of life, children learn much about sex. They gain impressions of their own bodies, they learn that two sexes exist, they understand that pleasure results from stimulating their genitals, they are exposed to our notions of modesty, and they will see other people engaged in some forms of sexual expression. They may also imitate what they see.

We can do several things while children are learning about sex to prepare them to be moral. For instance, we can help them learn acceptance, one of the moral character traits, by helping them think of their bodies as marvelous and beautiful. Warm touches and affectionate embraces create impulses of self-acceptance. If we praise their arms, their legs, faces, backs, and feet, we can help children form positive feelings about what they look like. Children with unhappy, negative feelings about their physical appearance are often more vulnerable when pressured or invited to engage in sex.

Sexual acceptance is also promoted when we tell them the names of their body parts as we talk with them about breasts, penis, testicles, vagina. Such matter-of-fact conversations help them recognize that differences between boys and girls do not make one inferior. Our ability to talk calmly, using sexual names and words, will also help them feel free to talk with us about their questions and ideas. Conversations about sexual topics are an important way to transmit sexual values to children as well as to prepare them to be moral.

A friend of mine and his wife were very good at talking with their children about sex. One day, my friend overheard a conversation between his five-year-old daughter and a neighbor boy. The boy asked her to take down her pants so he could look at her. "I will if you will," he said. "Nope," came the reply, "I know about that stuff, and it's no big deal." Talking with our children when they are young will make sex a topic easier to talk about when they are older, when the importance of talking is greater.

Many of us are concerned about our children's lack of modesty in running nude around the house or out-of-doors. Not having feelings of embarrassment, they go without clothes because they feel freer and cooler without them. They may also find that we run after them when, without clothes, they run away from us. Then it is fun. Most children develop a greater sense of modesty as they grow, and those who thought nothing of going to the bathroom with other boys and girls at age four or five will soon sense a desire for privacy and usually cover up. If we are uncomfortable about their nudity, or lack of modesty, it is usually our problem, not theirs. Mild reminders of getting dressed in private, accompanied by our example, will usually be sufficient. If we are too extreme and too restrictive, we risk making children feel that something is wrong with them.

Most children stimulate their genitals, usually before going to sleep when they turn on their stomachs and place their hands between their legs, or during bathing, or diaper changing. Occasionally, children will engage in prolonged stimulation. Girls, for example, will stimulate themselves with their hands or the corner of the bed or some other piece of furniture. Boys will stimulate themselves while going to the bathroom or while outside playing. In most cases with children under eight years of age, it is advisable simply to remove their hands without saying anything, or if that does not succeed, to talk with them about not touching themselves. Usually, the less said and done, the better, because too much attention could aggravate a situation that would have soon disappeared on its own.

In some instances, however, young children continue to stimulate themselves. Nearly always, masturbation over a prolonged period of time is an indication of some emotional disturbance. Childhood anxieties, including fear of parents or school or friends, may be involved. Or childhood masturbation may reflect molestation. In every case, we can further moral development by talking calmly with our children and frequently expressing our love and warmth. Their problems, though unfamiliar and discomfiting to us, should not make us withdraw our care and concern.

I have known parents who have become angry at their children for masturbating. Some have been repulsed and have withdrawn their affection. One mother, in contrast, sought counseling for a six-year-old daughter who frequently masturbated. After learning that emotional problems could be the cause, she kept records and discovered that her daughter stimulated herself after any intense or stressful experience. The mother participated in a program to reduce family conflict and to help her daughter learn another response to stress. It was not long before her daughter stopped masturbating.

Indifference is also generally the best first response

when children imitate a Hollywood kiss or engage in exaggerated forms of sexual expression; however, playing doctor and nurse to examine one another or displaying knowledge of petting or the positions for intercourse require something more than our indifference. Examining one another sexually is an experience that shapes attitudes and provides knowledge. Such experiences should always be followed by guiding conversations with parents. Finding out about a doctor-and-nurse episode, we should make it clear to the child that we want to talk about it. Curiosity usually signals a need to know. We could get some appropriate pictures of females and males, show them to our child, and begin to talk about what is in the pictures. Usually, in this context, children will become more open and will talk. If we are talking with our child about a simple experience that happened out of curiosity, we can ask, "What did you see?" "What did you feel when someone was looking at you?" "How do you feel now about what happened?" After helping the child talk about the experience, we should show appreciation for the openness and trust the child displayed in talking about the incident.

Talking with children about their early sexual experiences also gives us a chance to help them learn what to say and do in order to avoid such experiences. We can advise our children that if anyone wants to play a "game" again or look at them, to come immediately to us. We can role-play the situation and teach them to say, "No! I don't want to." And, we can remind them that whatever they want to know, they have only to come to us for answers to their questions.

We are currently much more aware of child sexual abuse than we have ever been, and this awareness has presented us with a dilemma. Do we teach our children that some people may hurt them and risk making them unduly afraid of everyone, or do we keep them uninformed and trusting? The risks of keeping our children naive seem too great, and we can choose to solve the problem by helping children learn to distinguish between those people who will help and those who might hurt. To protect their children against predatory people, parents must teach them specific skills:

1. Teach children through role-playing to say no if they are asked to take their clothes off, asked to enter someone's car, offered candy or invited to go anywhere with a stranger, or asked to go to the bathroom with someone other than a parent. Instead of trying to get children to distinguish between strangers and those known, be more specific. Role-play with children what they should do if a babysitter, neighbor, schoolteacher, cousin, friend, older child tries to involve them in sexual behavior.

2. Discuss as a family hypothetical situations children might face. Show and explain what children can do in each.

3. If *anyone* tries to touch children's genitals, children should yell and run away. They should also immediately tell someone about it. Remember that close relatives are responsible for a very high number of the cases of sexual molestation of children. (Johnson, 1982.)

Despite our efforts to teach them, many children will be hurt sexually. If a child is molested sexually, what is the best thing to do? First, we must be calm, loving, and reassuring to the child. We must take the child for a medical examination. This examination will reduce the likelihood of disease, and medical records may be needed as evidence if the police become involved. Then, because molestation can result in lasting harm, we should get professional help for the child. The goal is to help the child resolve the situation as rapidly as possible. We can go to the police, or to government social services. And while we are helping the child, we should, of course, inform officials of who did the molesting. Anyone who molests a child needs help and without help will usually repeat the molestation.

Sexual Language, Experimental Sexual Games, and Pornography

Older children are likely to try out other sexual behaviors, including sexual language, experimental sexual games, and pornography.

Usually sexual words are first used by children to talk about body parts and bathroom activities. When children use "toilet talk" in public, other children laugh, and this reaction may lead others to use the words to get attention. Moreover, the words violate social etiquette. Either of these is sufficient reason for us to expect children to regulate their feelings and their language in order to give themselves and others greater respect. Helping children regulate their language teaches them autonomy. When we require children to avoid some terms, we are asking them to regulate their behavior. We can compliment them, remind them, and impose some punishment to reinforce the behavior we would like them to use. If we also point out that their friends may not believe as we do about language, we can also prepare them for the time when they will make a choice between doing what others do and maintaining their own standards.

Knowing that some forms of language are not appropriate and that other forms are appropriate in some situations and not in others helps children learn to adapt. We can be clear about our desire to have children talk with us, tell us their experiences, and ask questions. In these conversations they can use explicit sexual terms. They also learn, while young, that there are some places and times when they are not to use some words. This way they will learn both the need to adapt their speech and the methods they can use to adapt their speech to situations and people.

At about six or seven years of age, many children participate in some sexual experimentation, such as running and chasing each other at school. First-grade children may tell of having ten girlfriends or boyfriends. They may even kiss on occasion. These are fairly normal and harmless games, and we can feel good that our children are having fun while learning about themselves and the rudiments of heterosexual communication.

But many childhood sexual games are not harmless. At sleepovers with friends or at unsupervised parties, for example, children have been known to fondle each other. For children over age six, these games are not the immature games of first-graders. They are genuinely sexual in nature. These are the early sexual experiences referred to later by many homosexual males and many child molesters, as well as by other troubled adults who were hurt by such experiments in childhood.

One young man, struggling with homosexuality, stated that his first sexual experience took place with some cousins when he was six years old. Whenever they camped or slept out, their activities included masturbation and oral stimulation. By the time he was eighteen, he had had numerous such experiences. As an adult he was confused about his sexual orientation because of these early experiences, and he was able to resolve his feelings only after a great struggle.

We can make it very clear that sexual activities are not to be a part of campouts or sleepovers. Nevertheless, because many of our children will experiment in some way or another anyway, we need to have a strategy for dealing with occasions when our children participate in such experiments and are hurt by them. If we have completed our first task, to talk calmly and reasonably about sex, our children will feel comfortable talking to us. When they do talk with us, we can reinforce that choice through praise and warm attention. "Thank you for talking with me" is easy to say even before we answer a question. Children hurt by some experience usually benefit from talking about it so that they can examine their feelings and rid themselves of any shame. If we are warm, inquiring, and accepting, they will feel reassured and will be more likely to accept our help in ensuring that such experiences do not happen again.

Many children are introduced to pornographic or explicit sexual material at a very young age. At any public elementary school, children as young as seven or eight have sexually explicit pictures or stories in their possession. Sexual scenes on television, in movies, and in magazines on newsstands are readily available to children. Although we may not yet have complete, scientifically documented proof that exposure to these materials is harmful or that it is harmful in any specific way, our own common sense warns us that it can harm our children, and most of us want to keep it away from children vulnerable to its influence. Certainly, there is no evidence that pornography is helpful to our children, so they deserve to be warned against it and given suggestions for ways to avoid it.

Three boys found some pornography under a bed at the home of one of the boys. Because both parents worked, the boys had time to look at the pictures and magazines. For several days the boys stopped after school to look at them. At first the pictures were exciting and interesting to all three, but after a while Ricky got tired of it and started withdrawing. The other boys became afraid that Ricky would tell on them and began to threaten him, first by saying they would not be his friend if he told and then by threatening to beat him up if he betrayed them. One evening, Ricky asked his dad, "Why would anyone want to have their pictures taken without their clothes on?"

Interested, of course, his father asked questions, and Ricky began to tell his experience, eventually spilling it all out in a torrent of words and feelings. After listening to Ricky talk, his dad thanked him for talking with him. Then they talked about what Ricky had seen and what he felt about it. They discussed possible reasons why the people in the pictures could think so little of themselves and others that they would be involved in something like that. Then his dad asked Ricky why he thought it was wrong to look at pornography. They wondered together if Ricky could learn from these kinds of things to think it was all right to be disrespectful of girls. His father suggested that the reason the other boys threatened him was that they felt guilty and afraid. The father told his son that looking at pornography was wrong because of how it would make him feel about himself and about other people. They planned what to do if someone ever wanted to show Ricky pictures like those again. Ricky agreed to tell his dad if that happened. They also agreed that his dad should talk to the parents of the other boys.

When we discover that a child is looking at pornography, we should confront the child with our knowledge of the situation as quickly as possible. If the child has pornographic materials in his or her possession, we should take the material away from the child, asking for an explanation of where it was obtained and how it was used. We can assume that further parent-child talks are needed to reinforce the behavior about pornography we want the child to use. No one benefits by avoiding the discussion.

Self-Consciousness, Social Skills, and the Double Standard

Puberty changes the outward appearance of everyone's body. Our children may be early, average, or late in going through it, but all become more self-conscious because of it. If girls develop early, they may be self-conscious about being different from other girls. They often feel less well-liked and are unhappy until their friends mature. If boys mature early, however, they are conscious of improved physical prowess and of having the interest and feelings of older boys they may admire. For them, early maturing is usually a positive experience rather than a negative one.

Self-consciousness among early teenagers creates vulnerability to social pressure, especially to the attention of the other sex. Natural sex drives, of course, motivate children to seek the attention of others. Being liked by others brings feelings of confidence, a remedy for self-consciousness. Thus, children in their early teens are strongly motivated to closely associate with each other. If sexual participation is offered or used to keep the closeness, many will participate.

Sharon, aged fourteen, spent excessive time with her boyfriend. He stopped by in the morning to walk with her to school, and they were together nearly every evening. One evening they went into Sharon's bedroom. Her mother had been afraid they were getting too close, but had not said anything about it. Realizing that something needed to be done, she walked in and found them undressed and petting. Their initial embarrassment was replaced by anger, and Sharon criticized her mother for "intruding." After a short conversation, the boy left.

When the mother called me the next day to ask for some ideas about dealing with this situation, I suggested that she ask Sharon if she wanted to be pregnant before she was fifteen, and that she keep asking her daughter this question until she received a yes or no answer. She first asked the question at about nine o'clock that evening. Sharon responded angrily, "Get off my back! It's none of your business!" The mother's first impulse was to give up, until she realized that Sharon had not answered yes or no. Then she asked again, and Sharon became even more angry. After being asked this question several times, Sharon left the house. Her mother was afraid, but after an hour or two Sharon returned. At first she was quiet, and then she said, "No, Mom, I don't want to be pregnant, but I am afraid I'll lose him." This statement led to a conversation about the real emotional issue. Mother and father talked together and with Sharon to find ways to help her through her feelings of loneliness and self-consciousness.

Social skills have much to do with sexual morality. There are ways children can meet and succeed in relationships with others without being involved in sexual activities. Helping children learn social etiquette, teaching them how to get acquainted with others, give compliments, tell jokes, and ask questions in order to carry on conversations will help improve their social confidence and make them less vulnerable to many forms of undesirable peer pressure.

Our social folklore for a long time perpetuated the idea that girls have a less intense sex drive than boys and should therefore be armed with defenses against sexually aggressive males, who would move as far sexually as girls would let them. This notion placed a false and unfair burden on girls to maintain sexual standards and at the same time allowed many boys to avoid sharing the responsibility for sexual conduct. Further, and much worse, many boys first learned about sex as something they *did to* girls, talking and thinking about "scoring" with girls, using the language of conquest and victory over an opponent. Unfortunately, a great many people still think that way. In fact, because the "sexual revolution" of the last twenty years has sought to equalize the situation, girls and women are often more sexually aggressive than they would have been in the past. But thinking of sex in terms of aggression, viewing another person as an object to be conquered or used, is immoral and underlies the immorality of sexual exploitation found in sex between immature children and in pornography.

Both boys and girls deserve the opportunity to develop personal standards of sexual morality according to which each feels autonomy and responsibility for self. Both boys and girls can learn to regulate sexual desire. Both can be taught to appreciate that sex at the wrong time is exploitation.

Sex, Commitment, and the Courtship Dance

Increased maturity should bring with it a greater awareness of other people and increased sensitivity to them. In

dating, increased knowledge intensifies genuine feelings
of liking and caring. It is quite natural and desirable that
these feelings include sexual feelings. If chastity is not their
standard, young people will measure their "commitment"
to each other purely by their strong feelings of attraction
to one another. This thinking leads to the idea that sexual
intercourse is a natural and reasonable extension of that
"commitment." To avoid the trail of broken hearts (not to
mention disease or unwanted pregnancy) that often results, we can teach children that strong sexual feeling may
be an important part of commitment, but it is not all of it.
Commitment also includes a willingness to care for the
welfare of another person. We can teach our children that
a true, lifelong commitment of this sort should be con-
summated in marriage. We can teach our children that
because sex is so important and so powerful, it deserves
to be reserved for the condition of highest or greatest commitment: marriage. Chastity, we would teach, is the best
preparation for sexual passion and commitment after marriage.

If children understand both morality and immorality,
and if they have been taught that chastity is the accepted
standard for them to follow, they will more willingly accept
the suggestions we make to help them understand and
interpret morally circumstances involving sex. Many of
these circumstances are well known to us because we have
experienced or observed them. We can, for instance, recognize the consequences of such situations as a boy and
girl who like each other spending too much time together
alone; or a child having friends who are sexually active
(many girls and boys begin to have sex because their friends
do); or a child's moods change from positive to negative,
and we think the mood change is related to dating; or a
child is regularly looking at pornography; or a boyfriend
or girlfriend of our child seems usually demanding or possessive. Knowing the potential consequences of these situations and others like them will help us prepare our chil-

dren to be moral. In addition, watching what children do after we have talked about these situations can give us some idea of how well they are maintaining their standards. Keeping the lines of communication open between us and our children is vital in helping our children maintain their standards of moral sexual behavior.

Ranae, aged fifteen, often had arguments with her parents about failure at school, boys she dated, and her frequent sullen withdrawal from the family. Because she spent excessive time with boys she dated, and because several boys came around asking for her, her parents thought she was sexually active. Whenever she went out, they quizzed her, forcing her to make promises about what she would and would not do. She usually left angry and upset. As Ranae reported it later, when a date was coming to an end and she was kissing a boy, she would at that moment blame her parents for her unhappiness and would sometimes lead the boy into sex just to spite her parents. Her story is like that of many teenagers. She was defensive, she was often negative and angry, and she was not able to talk very openly. She exhibited the characteristics of children who do immoral things.

There is another way an understanding of sexual behavior can prepare children for morality. According to one researcher, there are twenty-four steps after the first physical contact between two people and before the most passionate sexual embrace. Holding hands is step one of this "courtship dance." Step two is squeezing fingers, and step three is intertwining fingers. This sequence progresses to placing a hand inside of an arm, placing arms around shoulders, putting arms around waist, and so forth until the couple is fully intimate. Dating couples use the sequence as a natural part of physically reflecting their level of emotional intensity. They also use the sequence to measure whether a partner is "fast," "slow," or "easy." If someone moves through the sequence quickly, he or she will be considered fast. If someone takes a long time to move through the steps (or doesn't move at all beyond a certain point), he or she will be considered slow. If someone ignores the earlier steps and attempts or invites intimate touching at an early stage of the relationship, he or she will be considered easy. Children can understand the sexual intentions of others by learning to recognize rates of progression through this sequence. (Birdwhistle, 1970.)

We can teach our children to use their knowledge of this sequence to regulate the progression of sexual contact. Such preparation and knowledge can add to their sense of self-control. Aware of the sequence, our children might decide that they will be unwilling to move beyond a certain point (kissing, for example). That decision will help them prepare to make moral choices when they are faced with the intense emotions of a moral circumstance where someone can be hurt sexually.

CHAPTER 7

CHEMICAL ABUSE

Until relatively recently, the problems associated with the abuse of chemicals affected the lives of children primarily because of the behavior of adults. Children knew of alcoholism and drug addiction because they observed it or heard about it, perhaps in their families, or perhaps only on television or in passing conversations. Now, however, more and more children are themselves using alcohol and other drugs, some to the extent that their lives are wholly controlled by the addictive and destructive effects of these chemicals. Many adults who had never thought young people's use of alcohol and other drugs was a real problem are going to rehabilitation centers, embarrassed to need help for their children, and they are meeting their neighbors there. A great many of us are shocked and dismayed at how great a problem we have let these addicting substances become in the lives of our children.

The shock and dismay touched Kathy and Stan Roberts in a different way. Their daughter Tammi was tall, slender, smart, just entering the real beauty of womanhood. She was excited about the homecoming queen contest and was genuinely surprised when she won. Helping Tammi get ready for the dance, Kathy was as excited as her daughter. Tammi's date was a very fine boy, well-liked, responsible. When he picked her up for the dance, he talked with Kathy and Stan in the living room while they all waited for Tammi to take care of the few last details. At last she was ready, and they left, smiling, happy. It was the last time Kathy and Stan saw Tammi alive. As they were coming home

117

from the dance, Tammi and her date were hit by a car driven by a drunk eighteen-year-old boy and were instantly killed.

The overwhelming emptiness felt by these parents was shocking and sudden. Parents whose children are addicted to drugs and alcohol also know shock and overwhelming emptiness. But whereas Tammi and her friend died suddenly, addicted children die a slow, living death. The killer is easy to identify, but it isn't easy to stop. And parents of addicted children often feel as helpless and angry as the parents of children who are killed by drunk or drugged drivers. Obviously it would be much better for all of us if we could teach our children that drinking alcoholic beverages and taking drugs are matters of great moral concern. Those who use these substances are invariably hurt, and they hurt many others who are innocent but are victims still.

In our society, many people smoke, regularly use prescription drugs, and drink alcoholic beverages. Many are parents who do not want their children to be hurt or to hurt others. Unfortunately, however, this example by adults is one of the major causes in children of what is now frequently called "chemical abuse." With so many parents using chemicals to regulate, stimulate, and otherwise change emotional and physical states, it is plain to see why we, as a society, have not established a moral standard for using drugs and alcohol. Trafficking in these substances is extremely lucrative, and it has created a huge financial establishment. Sellers find creative ways, legal and illegal, to attract buyers. Public efforts to curtail the use of legal drugs (including alcohol and tobacco) are met with equal pressure not to interfere.

Public education programs and the efforts of law-enforcement agencies may be making some headway against the proliferation of dangerous substances in our society, but they are not enough to protect our children. Our children need our help now. They frequently face choices concerning alcohol and other drugs. It is up to us to teach them how to behave morally when faced with such situations.

We can all recognize the immorality in some acts involving drugs and alcohol. It is obviously immoral to sell drugs to young children or otherwise to influence them to use substances that will be harmful to them. But do we see the immorality in our using harmful substances and so introducing them to children who otherwise might never have been influenced to use them? We see the immorality in killing someone while driving drunk. But do we see the immorality of teaching children by our example that drinking is all right for us, even though it is not all right for others? People who know the harmful effects of certain substances but allow the use of these substances to harm their own lives and the lives of others are, in my opinion, acting irresponsibly in the face of moral issues.

Moral issues related to the use of chemicals harmful to the human body have become more complex as a result of the scientific discoveries of the past decade. For example, because of what we now know about the effects of "secondary" tobacco smoke on the health of people inhaling it (so-called passive smoking), smoking in a public place (or in a home with children) is no longer merely an issue of choice.

As they mature, children will have to reason, decide, and act in many moral circumstances, obvious and subtle, that will challenge their understanding of how chemical substances affect them and others. Some children will find themselves asked to buy, sell, or deliver illegal drugs. Many will know about the illegal acts of someone else and will have to choose either to "rat" or to remain silent and thereby become an accessory to a crime. Many more will be faced with less dramatic but equally challenging situations involving choices between doing what others do (in order to be liked and accepted) and resisting (which could result in social rejection and loneliness). Children will have to decide what to do and say when friends use dangerous substances or when friends offer the substances or apply pressure to use them. Children will have to decide what to do when they are unhappy and know that chemicals are available that can make them feel better. In all of these situations, children can be prepared to reason, make judgments, and act morally. Our effort to teach them may save them and us great expense and much emotional pain. It may also help them grow to adulthood with self-respect, healthy, and free from addictions.

The first step is to decide on a standard of moral conduct for ourselves. We teach our children by precept and example what that standard is. Then we help them understand clearly what will help and what will hurt in the many moral circumstances involving alcohol and other harmful drugs. We may need to teach them what the chemicals do to the human body and mind and how to "say no" when invited to use these substances. Then, because we can foresee the kinds of situations they will face, we teach them how to act to regulate their emotions and their behavior when decisions about alcohol and other drugs are most likely to be required.

A Moral Standard for Using Alcohol and Other Drugs

It does not require much evidence or logical thought to recognize that total abstinence, except for careful medicinal use, is the moral standard our national community should establish in regard to mind- and body-altering chemicals. Anything less than that standard is irrational and illogical. The chemicals in drugs, alcohol, and tobacco are substances damaging to the human body. For these substances to be tolerated, changes must take place in our bodies to accommodate them. To the extent that we require our bodies to make these accommodations, we develop a physical and/or mental dependency on the substance.

Individuals differ in their abilities to make these physical and psychological accommodations—in other words, individuals differ in their abilities to "tolerate" foreign chemicals in their bodies. For example, some people have very little ability to tolerate foreign chemicals; others have a great deal. Part of this variation in vulnerability is believed to be inherited. That is why alcoholism, or the predisposition to alcoholism, is often found in several generations of the same family. The variation in ability to tolerate chemicals presents problems to parents. Parents may not know how any particular child will be affected by any small or large dose of alcohol or drugs. "Social drinking" may be practiced by parents and "taught" to children, without the parents realizing that a child has a particular vulnerability to addiction in a way they themselves may not. Obviously, then, only total abstinence is enough protection.

The problems associated with the use of alcohol are compounded by social factors. In many areas, social and business opportunities are attached to drinking—if you go to parties and drink cocktails, you are likely to get ahead. For teenagers, status is often attached to drugs and drink— the more you can take, the more impressive you are. Thus, instead of helping us and our children avoid or even limit the harm of alcohol and other drugs, social requirements set the stage for pride in the variety and quantity of these substances we can use.

It is easy to see that we live in a society with a double standard: on the one hand we recognize the enormous cost in money, family unity, and human life created by alcohol and other drugs. On the other hand, we justify drinking and using certain drugs because of certain personal and social "advantages" that come from so doing. The problem is just like the one we saw with sexual morality. Instead of teaching and reinforcing a moral standard that would protect us and our children from harm, society accepts the reality of the harmful behavior and suggests only that we take steps to minimize the effects.

What society fails to do, however, need not prevent

us from establishing a moral standard and teaching it to our children. If we drink, we may have to stop in order to avoid the hypocrisy of trying to teach our children something we do not do ourselves. It is a sacrifice, perhaps, but a small one to make if it can prevent harm to the children we love. When more and more parents rid themselves of alcohol and other drugs and become actively involved in teaching their children to lead their lives without such substances, these individual family efforts will make a great contribution to improving the quality of life for everyone in our society.

Identifying the Consequences of Using Drugs

Maintaining the standard of abstinence requires active avoidance. It may be difficult at first to think of *active* and *avoid* together. But anything tempting has an allure that must be resisted. Children cannot be passive in response to invitations to use drugs, for example, because those selling or inviting often consider silence or passivity as agreement and will continue persuading. Actively avoiding something or someone is demonstrated by using the word *no*. When asked to use cocaine, for instance, one boy said, "No, I want to keep my brain healthy."

Active avoidance is best motivated by knowledge of the consequences. That is why we must teach children a clear description of what we believe to be right and wrong about alcohol and other drugs and then explore the consequences of abusing them. According to our definition of *morality* as helping someone and of *immorality* as hurting someone, we can say that taking into our body anything that hurts or damages it is wrong—immoral. By the same definitions, it is not wrong to use drugs as medicine, if they are used to help and are carefully regulated to prevent addiction. In every other case, though, the possibilities for harm make abstinence the moral standard.

A 1985 study of high school students in the United

States reported that between one in five and one in eight students have used drugs by the time they are seniors in high school. The use of some drugs, such as heroin, has dropped, but this positive indicator is offset by the fact that children start to use drugs at a younger age. There has also been a sharp increase in alcohol consumption by children in a variety of social and economic conditions. By the time they are eighteen years old, more than ninety percent of American teenagers have used alcohol. (Johnston et al., 1985.)

We might not be moved by these statistics if our own children are not at present using drugs or drinking. We should remember, however, that when children think of morality, one part of their concept of what is moral is their belief about what others are doing. If use of alcohol or other drugs is as pervasive as this research indicates, every child will come in contact with users and with direct or implied approval of chemical abuse.

Even young children can be taught about the unhappy consequences of alcohol and drug abuse. The concerned parents of one young family took their children to a meeting of Alcoholics Anonymous and listened to people talk about their struggles. They acquired some literature from the city-sponsored drug and alcohol counseling center that described the drugs most commonly used by children. The family read and discussed these brochures.

As a family, they collected newspaper articles and made a scrapbook of articles about accidents involving intoxicated drivers, drug-related crimes, or arrests and convictions of criminals. The children drew posters with slogans for not using any drugs. They attended a program sponsored by the Boy Scouts. Police officers showed them how drugs look, let the children smell them, and told what happens when they are used. Finally, the family visited a rehabilitation center and talked with a trained therapist about the effects of drugs and alcohol.

Another family activity might involve talking to physicians to learn what drugs and alcohol do to harm children and, by contrast, what good health practices do to help them. It also helps to teach children that using drugs or alcohol does not produce real popularity or bring close friends, which is what many children think it will do.

The physical harm caused by chemical abuse is sufficient reason to avoid it. But because drugs and alcohol are addictive, the consequences for using them extend beyond physical damage. I have lost count of the number of teenagers I have known who do not see any relationship between their use of drugs and alcohol and the difficulties they have with their parents or their inability to keep jobs or succeed in school. Almost from the first time children use drugs or drink alcohol, they have to stop doing something else they are doing. The greater their involvement with the harmful substances, the greater the amount of time, money, and energy it consumes, and the greater their decline in achievement, or even in their desire to achieve anything.

As bad as the loss of motivation to achieve may be, even worse is the pervading and enduring sense of inferiority or inadequacy that results from the loss of self-control that children experience as they become addicted to alcohol and other drugs. Abusers gradually lose control over everything. They try to achieve and cannot. They make promises they don't keep. They try to stop using the drugs or the drink and find they are unable to. They lose control over their emotions, and they are filled with anxieties, depression, and anger. Eventually, their entire life is virtually taken over and controlled by the harmful substance, the need for it, and the attempts to obtain it.

Occasionally, I have seen an eighteen- or nineteen-year-old who, having suffered the problems of drug or alcohol abuse for two or three years, has reached a point of emotional numbness and is grateful for it. The numbness seems better than the feelings of self-recrimination that preceded it. Usually, however, their loss of control creates such inferiority that children do not believe anyone could love them or care for them, and a desperate cynicism emerges. Then they find that the "friends" they acquired in the drug and drink scene are no longer interested in them.

Tommy (the name is fictional, of course) learned that truth the sad and hard way. He was a sophomore at a high school that had a deserved reputation for being cliquish. Although he had one or two friends from junior high, he felt alone when he entered the larger school. He tried a few times to meet others, but as the year progressed, he spent more and more time alone. In the spring he met some kids who introduced him to marijuana. Later, these "friends" asked him to a "party." He soon found that to these people, "partying" meant excessive drinking. Getting "smashed" was the goal. What had been decent grades for most of his sophomore year declined during his junior and senior years. Some last-minute extra credit and a summer class were required for him to graduate on time.

He continued to party. He spent nearly everything he earned on alcohol and drugs, and he occasionally stole money to support his habits. After one party he became ill. He had drunk thirty cans of beer, some wine coolers, and some vodka, although he couldn't recall how much. He vomited a sizable amount of blood. Out of fear he went to a doctor, who hospitalized him. While he was in the hospital no one went to see him, no one even called. It was then he learned about the shallowness of friendship based on alcohol, drugs, and parties.

Of course, children who do not use alcohol or other drugs still struggle with achievement problems and with inferiority, so we also need to discuss with them the consequences of actively avoiding chemical abuse. We need to teach our children about the rewards of a drug-free life so that they will have something positive to look forward to for their efforts in avoiding something that can be so tempting to them. Their primary reward may be their sense of control over life, which can be more easily maintained if alcohol and other drugs are never used. Along with the feeling of being in control of their lives comes an ability to find and feel what is happy and beautiful in life, including the true love and concern of others. Their creativity is waiting to be developed, creativity that can be diminished and distorted by drugs. People who keep their minds and bodies free from harmful substances can maintain the spark of life, a vibrant appreciation of life and its wonders that is the natural "high" non-abusers say they would rather have than the unnatural high created by drugs.

Learning How Drug Users Think and Feel

Knowing some of the reasons why children begin to abuse alcohol and other drugs will help us be more successful at preventing or eliminating some of the effects. Drug users generally start without knowing the effect drugs have on them. They may even be told that drugs cannot harm them. That assertion is rampant among those still trying to justify using drugs. Because this lie comes from friends, perhaps even many friends, it is often believed. This lie promotes denial, a psychological condition of ignoring reality, even in the face of direct personal experience. Part of this denial is maintaining that users "can quit any time." They may have heard stories about kids who have quit. Others deny the effects of the drugs they take by claiming that certain abilities are actually improved by the substances. While psychological and physical sensation caused by drugs can bring about a temporarily euphoric and confident state, that euphoria is certainly overshadowed by the much longer "down" period of reduced performance that follows.

Large numbers of children are led into drug and alcohol use because it is the fashion. The socially unacceptable part is getting caught using or using too much. When parents are confronted with that justification, a good response is to ask the children about valuing popularity more than self-respect.

In teaching our children to deal with others' "reasons" for using harmful chemicals, we also need to consider the role of moods or emotions in the problem. In the first place, psychological addiction to any chemical takes place because use of the chemical becomes associated with certain moods or emotional states. Many people drink alcohol or use a variety of over-the-counter and prescription drugs to combat pain, fear of pain, anxiety, shyness, depression, and loneliness. It is not surprising that drug abusers indicate that they are more likely to use drugs or alcohol when they are feeling lonely, depressed, unloved, or powerless. Some users, in addition, are thrill-seekers, "partying" to get a "buzz." Others have frequent bouts with self-pity and escape through altered states of mind produced by the chemical. Some, their immaturity exposed, feel anger toward an authority figure and mistakenly think they are thumbing their noses at parents, police, or school principals when they drink or take drugs.

When both the motives and the feelings of users are understood, we can formulate ideas about what we can do, even for very young children, to help them develop a personal standard of abstinence. We can help them develop a strong sense of autonomy, a sense of responsible self-control. We can guide them to the emotional competence that will enable them to maintain the positive emotional style that helps them resist temptations. An active orientation toward achievement will give our children stability, a sense of belonging, and opportunities for social recognition that inactivity does not provide. Further, their ability to talk openly with us about the moral implications of using drugs and about how to refuse them will help children control much of what happens when they are invited or persuaded to use harmful substances.

Because we know that nearly all children will one day face situations in which they must decide about the use of alcohol and other drugs, not one of us is exempt from teaching our children. And because children are now coming in contact with these substances very early in life, we must begin teaching when they are very young. We should concentrate on the development of moral traits and avoid the conditions—including our own use of alcohol and other drugs—that make children vulnerable. If we do that, we help prevent chemical abuse by eliminating some of its causes.

Avoiding the Dependency That Creates Vulnerability

Many children addicted to some chemical have family backgrounds, including a parental discipline style, that have reinforced a sense of dependency. Children are members of family system that may or may not reinforce health. By defining a family as a system, we mean to say that each person affects others and is affected by them. Such a view of the family precludes the singling out of a parent or child as the cause of a problem. In family systems, parents and children interact to create many personality traits. If we view dependency as a precondition for chemical abuse, we can see it as a problem jointly created by parents and children.

One girl I remember had a chronic illness, first diagnosed when she was five years old. Most members of her family also had some sort of continuing health problem, many of them somewhat exotic. Rachel was fifteen years old when I first met her. She had been referred to me because her illness had remitted, according to her physician's diagnosis, but many of her symptoms continued. The physician suspected that her problem had a psychological component.

I learned that her parents still drove her every day to the bus stop, a block from home. She fell ill frequently, often when she felt any stress. Such stress could come from homework, chores, or an accusation that she was "not really sick." She was the youngest child, and her parents spent considerable time helping her, taking care of her, and arguing with her. Together, they had created an addictive system of interaction in which both the girl and her parents were dependent on certain aspects of their relationship to one another. Since Rachel "had to" convalesce from her chronic illness, she was not able to make close friends. When she did go to school, she used the drugs or alcohol she was offered in order to feel that she belonged. It was not long before she became addicted. In her case, her addiction and the attempts to treat it became a continuation of the dependency relationship already formed with her parents. When I recommended that she enter a rehabilitation program, she said that it would "probably be a good idea, because I cannot stop myself, but I don't want to go because I don't know what I'll do if I give everything up." In other words, she didn't know how she would survive without the dependency she had known for so long.

Rachel's situation is not typical, but in other more subtle ways many of us create dependent children who sense a need for some type of "crutch." If we want to prevent our children's finding such a crutch in drugs or alcohol, we must help them avoid the need for a crutch. That usually requires that we find ways to teach and reinforce autonomy. To do that we can, right from the beginning of their lives, avoid doing for them what they can do for themselves. During their first year of life we encourage them to explore their surroundings (home) and to walk, run, and speak when they are ready. Then—again, when they are ready—we help them learn to eat, dress themselves, and tie their shoelaces by themselves.

Many opportunities exist for us to help our children acquire the sense of self-control and responsibility that characterizes autonomy. We can help them learn responsibility for their chores, their homework, and their mistakes. We need to be willing only to supervise, require decent and reasonable work, and help them talk about their feelings of responsibility for their own actions. Further, we can ask them to make decisions and carry them out, reporting to us when they have done so. Asking our children to choose between two times when they will do their chores or to choose chores from a list of alternatives will help them feel our respect for them and our trust in their ability to make responsible choices. Our seeing to it that they do what they have agreed to do at the time and in the way they have agreed will teach them the importance of completing tasks and resisting distractions while doing so.

But while we are being firm with our children in guiding them to accept responsibility, we should not be rigid and inflexible. Many children who use drugs and alcohol are members of families where parents exert excessive and harsh control. This style of exercising parental authority produces children who are as dependent as those of parents who are overindulgent. The dependence in this case, however, is not the submissive helplessness we often think of as dependency. It is, rather, a persistent anger focused on the parents that leaves children with little desire or even ability to do much for themselves.

Dependent attitudes can be created whenever the emotional relationship between us and our children is misused. Children who are overcontrolled or overindulged without our setting any limits on their behavior, children who are physically neglected or abused, children whose parents withdraw affection after mistakes or abuse them verbally— all are likely to develop dependent feelings. Children are made dependent from loneliness, from fear that they are not loved, and from anger due to mistreatment.

And besides all of that, as we saw in Rachel's case, children are made dependent from the results of their own manipulation of others. As all parents find out, children are capable of manipulating us to get what they want (and once they reach a certain age, what they want is usually money). If we allow them to manipulate us successfully, we will together create a system of overindulgence. If we excessively supply every want, for example, to avoid their emotional traps, our indulgence will make us partners in their dependency.

Three forms of manipulation are common in childhood. The first and most obvious is when a child complains or whines. If we think the complaining is unjustified, we can deal with this maneuver by insisting that our children learn to accept no for an answer and demonstrate that excessive complaining will result in future no's. The second form of manipulation is the "fairness" ploy. When children are not treated equally in families or treated the same as their friends, they may come to us with the complaint that we are unfair. If we feel guilty, we may give in and try to make the situation more "fair." If we do that, we can be assured that they will use this approach again. We can avoid falling into this guilt trap if we openly admit that we are not "fair" parents in the way they want us to be and, further, that we don't intend to be. Instead, we want to treat each child according to her or his needs, without having to treat everyone alike. After we admit that we are not "fair," our children will discover that they cannot manipulate us by inducing this form of guilt in us. (That is true, of course, only if we are not deserving of guilt.) And the third form of manipulation comes after parent-child conflict.

All of us have conflict with our children at some time or another. It usually hurts everyone involved. Afterwards, however, when we are all calming down, a child's compliant, humble, and soft responses may prompt us to "undo" what we caused with our anger. We might try to do away with our guilt for getting angry by giving the children what they asked for in the first place or give them something else "to make up." One father of a drug-dependent, twenty-year-old son described their repeated conflicts. The boy was not working, he was failing school, and his only interest was in partying. The father frequently got angry and lectured, yelled at, or threatened his son, telling him what he ought to be doing with his life. Then the anger would subside, and the father would be sorry. One evening, an hour or two after such an incident, the son went to his father, saying that he was going out. The father asked him if he needed money and gave him twenty dollars.

The solution to this problem is obvious. If we become aware of what we are doing, we can avoid assuaging our own guilt by giving too much. In the middle years of childhood and thereafter, our children can be cured of dependency and the effects of our indulgence if they are able to develop compassion, a willingness to be of service to others, and a good, old-fashioned responsibility for self. When we give chores to children and help them responsibly to complete them, they learn that doing work, and doing it well, is a matter of personal responsibility. Everyone benefits from the sense of mastery that results from accomplishment. When children achieve, they feel stronger and more in control of themselves and their lives.

We also help children overcome dependent feelings if we help them accept responsibility for their mistakes. When mistakes are made, children may blame others in an attempt to shift the responsibility from themselves. A sense of responsibility for self does not result from our arguing with them over who caused the mistake. It comes from a willingness on our part to see mistakes as a natural part of growing and then calmly to ask questions about who did what, or what happened and when, and keep asking and listening until the child accepts and understands his or her share of responsibility for what was done. If we are quick to anger and threaten, children will not learn to accept responsibility and might lie to avoid our wrath, compounding their denial of responsibility.

After receiving a low grade, one of my sons explained

that the teacher didn't like him. I was less concerned about the grade than that he did not seem to recognize his own role in achieving it. I asked him, "Who has the grade on his report card, you or the teacher?" "Me," he replied. "Then," I went on, "your choice seems to be what you will do to help yourself rather than letting your feelings about the teacher prevent you from doing the best you can." We talked about that for a long time until I felt he understood that he was more responsible for his grades than the teacher was. It took many other episodes like this one before he gained a complete understanding of his own responsibility for his grades.

Dependency is also minimized and autonomy enhanced when children are asked to serve others by giving of their time and energy. Service to others gives a sense of usefulness and competence. We need to help children sympathize with others by talking about situations where someone is in distress. We need to include children in family projects that help others. We can ask them before school if they know of anyone who needs help and afterward ask if they were able to help anyone. When children help us in our concern for neighbors, relatives, or friends in distress, they acquire compassion for others and an appreciation for their own importance in the world. Helping others also makes our children happy and content. Such positive emotions are so satisfying that they fill unmet emotional needs in our children and remove many causes for dependency.

Handling Relationships

Adolescence is the period in our children's lives when smoking and using alcohol and other drugs are most likely to begin. As they begin to separate from us and engage in activities with friends, they will find that drinking, smoking, and using drugs are prominent among the things teenagers do together. Children do not usually begin to smoke, drink, or do drugs completely on their own, and they will not usually use these substances when they are alone, unless they are addicted.

This means to us that to help our children be moral, we need to understand the social and emotional situations most likely to be associated with children's use of harmful substances. It is most important for us, in coming to this understanding, to be aware of the power of peer pressure in American society. Children in America form groups in order to gain confidence, confidence that serves them as they enter new situations at school, as they deal with members of the other sex, and as they go through the process of becoming independent from parents. As these groups form, however, they exert pressure on each individual to follow certain "rules" or practices in order to belong. Children may feel pressured to use new words as an indication that they "belong," or to wear certain types of clothing based on aspects of the fashion of the day. In some cases, the clothing must be very specific to the group: preppies, punkers, surfers, cowboys, and jocks each have a particular and very identifiable style. Each group also demands certain attitudes from its members, such as toughness for the athletes, cynicism for the intellectuals, anti-authoritarianism for the deviant, status consciousness for the rich (or would-be rich), or aloofness and indifference for the ones who feel rejected.

Compliance to the "rules" of these groups is maintained by the possibility of exclusion and ridicule. It is easy to see how children might sense pressure to conform. In most cases the pressure is real. And it is often intense. Consequently, when it becomes a group "rule" to drink, or to drink excessively, to smoke, or to use drugs, some children who would not do it on their own will do it with the group. If they have the thoughts and feelings that contribute to their being vulnerable to such influence, then they will be even more likely to engage in immoral behavior. We need to be alert to the likelihood of chemical abuse by our children when they (1) are involved with friends who use drugs and alcohol—even if our children claim they themselves are not, (2) have feelings of social inadequacy, (3) do not belong to a group and feel lonely, (4) are exposed to excessive peer pressure and are controlled by others, (5) have conflict with us that produces strain and frustration.

Our challenge is to help our children develop the ability to maintain their standard of morality concerning alcohol and other drugs, even when they are feeling pressure from others. We can do several things to help them.

One is to avoid withdrawing our emotional support from our children. When children do not follow family rules, or when they treat us unkindly or disrespectfully, it would be easy to withdraw our attention and affection. That withdrawal only increases their susceptibility to the influence of others. Emotional support does not mean that we give our children whatever they want. It is, rather, communication filled with affection, interest, concern, and warmth. Teenagers who are feeling great pressure to violate their moral standards need our emotional support in order to know they are safe and secure at home.

A second way to help our teenagers is simply to teach them to understand peer pressure and to notice its effects on them. High school health classes or social science classes are often useful in helping teach about peer pressure.

A third way to help is to review our family rules to see if adjustments can be made that would give our children more time for good activities they may want to participate in. Even small adjustments are noticed and usually appreciated.

The effects of peer pressure are moderated when children feel more secure with their family relationships. When communication is good and family members are close, children are less threatened by the effects of pressure they feel from others. Although most of us sense that to be true, we often fail to realize that children must be taught how to participate in relationships with others. For one thing, they start out in life quite egocentric and spend much of childhood concentrating on themselves. Developing the skill to relate successfully to the members of their own family helps increase children's confidence in relationship to others and increases their chances of being able to resolve successfully the conflicts that come from peer pressure.

Children dependent on chemicals of some kind often use the substances as a means of maintaining relationships with others. A close look, however, reveals that such relationships are shallow and are based on more immature feelings than are the relationships formed on the basis of social skills. For instance, many groups of teenagers exhibit what seems on the surface to be a genuine concern for one another. That concern, however, is narrow in its focus. Sometimes, relationships are based on who supplies the drug or drink, who makes people laugh the most, or some other similar and limited characteristic. The relationships among the members of the group are often one-sided, with one teenager exploiting another. Conflicts arise as they make attempts to "right" this "wrong." Side-taking and immature gossiping ("tearing people down") are characteristic of such conflicts, and the participants lack the mature social skills needed to talk over and resolve problems.

In an attempt to prevent this from happening to our own children, my wife and I ask them as they start junior high school whether they want a good relationship with us or a strict set of rules to follow. So far, each child has voted for the "good relationship." We have found, however, that they did not know what we meant by "good relationship," so we have needed to have several talks about it. In these talks we tell our children that a good relationship is made up of love, trust, and affection and that it means frequent communication about many different concerns. We are willing, we tell them, to say what we will do and we will do what we say. In return, they will tell us their plans and we will expect them to do as they say. We also explain to them that people in a good relationship do not retreat from disagreements in silence but try to work them out so that people on both sides are satisfied.

As the years have passed, we have spent much time talking with our children, trying to teach them how to participate in a "good relationship." We have discontinued almost all of our "flat" family rules. Instead, we ask each child to be responsible for herself or himself in such matters as cleaning rooms, coming in at night at a reasonable time, keeping us informed of plans or changes in plans. When they fail, we talk things over. Underlying their willingness to participate is the idea that this is the price they must pay to get along with us. In other words, by doing this, they will get more than they would if they didn't do it.

In these conversations we have been clear about what we believe our standards to be, and we have asked our children to say what they believed, too. We praise them by telling them that it is important to us that they sit and talk with us and that we like it very much. When they want to do something away from the family, we ask that they talk with us so that we know what they are doing. We also ask them to share family time with us. There have been times, of course, when confrontations have taken place and feelings have been hurt. We have misunderstood each other and have occasionally failed to keep promises. But the "good relationships" have survived all this, for the children have accepted our love and deserved our trust.

The purpose of family relationships that are emotionally fulfilling and informative is to give children security, to let them know that there is a place for them in the world. If we create and maintain bonds with our children that are characterized by warmth and open communication, in most instances our children will find peer groups that reflect what we want for them, or at least they will be able to make choices that reflect our standards and values whether others do or not.

Sometimes we are afraid that we do not know enough to help our children succeed in keeping their lives free from destructive substances. We should be reassured, however, to know that in most cases if we let our children know of our efforts to learn and our intent to love, they will be helped by a sense of our interest in them. Even if we make some mistakes in what we say or do, we can avoid making the mistake of letting our frustrations or anger come between us and our children. Children need as much emotional support during their teenage years as they did at any other time of life, and sometimes they need even more. Our love, affection, and involvement will make a difference to them. Even if they make errors of judgment that bring harm, they will probably recover more rapidly if they know we care.

CHAPTER 8

FRIENDSHIP: HELPING CHILDREN BE JUST AND FAIR

Children's friendships can mean pressure to violate personal standards of morality, but friendships can also help children develop morally. Most parents want their children to have friends and to be good friends to others, because good friends make us feel happy and secure. Friendships also provide conditions for learning, practicing, and demonstrating ideas about justice and equality. Friendship, in fact, is made up of the very skills that build success in many other areas of life.

Friendship is a special moral relationship of "concern, care, and sympathy." (Blum, 1980.) It includes a willingness to give that goes beyond what is given in other relationships. The caring within a friendship is built upon knowledge, trust, and intimacy. Good friendships exist when each friend identifies with the good of the other person. This type of friendship usually appears at later stages of development, only after children have learned a great deal about the morality of relationships. To enjoy mature friendships children must be able, for instance, to think of and about others as well as themselves; they must have a "moral orientation" toward what helps and what hurts others, and they must have a sense of responsibility about being fair and just. (Keller, 1984.) Friendships provide a great variety of situations in which someone can be helped or hurt. Friendship can involve the support one friend gives to another, loyalty in time of crisis or need, sacrifices made in the name of love, but friendship can also involve promises made and not kept, disloyalty found in malicious gossip, criticism, misjudgment, or choosing some friends while rejecting others. These situations and others like them present the moral circumstances of friendship, and they give our children opportunity to choose and then act to help or to hurt.

As a result, we teach our children to be good friends. Instead of letting all social opportunities occur by happenstance, we might want to involve ourselves, although not too much, at those times when children might benefit from our experience and help. Because satisfying friendships require justice and fairness, helping our children succeed in friendship will provide us a particularly good opportunity to teach our children to be just and fair, as all moral people are.

The Development of Friendship

To learn justice and fairness, children must acquire a social perspective, that is, a view of themselves in relationship to another person. Children develop this perspective to some degree as they grow, but certain aspects of it must be learned. At about age three, children have grown beyond the stage of watching others or enjoying the individualistic style of relating to others called "parallel play." Children now want a real involvement with other children. Some unspoken, perhaps inherited, motive raises anticipation and excitement when they have someone their own age to watch and be noticed by. These early attempts to form friendships are, of course, temporary moments, and children soon want to return to the familiarity of home. As they mature and the time with playmates increases, so does the demand for social and moral competence.

Competence in friendship is acquired much the same way morality is learned in other circumstances. Children imitate adult behavior. They practice the rules of games and discover rule-governed behavior. They find that they must understand several situations, make judgments, and adapt, and they learn which of their actions will help or hurt. As children grow, the situations involved in friendship increase in number and complexity. Selman and Selman (1979) studied the social perspective of a large number of children and identified the following stages in friendships as children matured:

Momentary playmateship, ages birth through three years. Children choose friends on the basis of some attractive toy or physical attribute. Friendships last as long as children are curious and stimulated.

*One-way assistance, ages four through six.*When children begin to understand the intentions of other children, they choose friends according to who intends to do what satisfies them. Friends are whoever will do what they themselves selfishly desire.

*Two-way, fairweather cooperation, ages seven through nine.*Children recognize that friendships require some give and take but in a way to satisfy self-interest. When the self-interest of one of the children cannot be met, the friendship ends.

Intimate, mutually shared relationship, ages ten through thirteen. Children form valued friendships. They are usually exclusive, with children often feeling possessive about them. Cliques of friends may form, excluding those not "in" the group. Emphasis is on loyalty to one another and mutual help-giving.

Autonomous and interdependent, ages fourteen through adult. Friendships have deep emotional commitment. Children can understand both dependence on others and the need for autonomy. Concepts such as trust and caring for another are relevant. These friendships may become lifelong.

Children's concept of friendship changes because of their increasing ability to understand more about people than their looks, their toys, or their popularity. Children eventually learn that friendships require an equal give-and-take, with accompanying emotional investment.

We can foster our children's progress along the path to mature friendships just as we help them mature in other ways. We can, for example, teach them to use conversation to talk out misunderstandings. That will help them understand how avoidance at moments of difficulty in relationships can leave them ignorant of what to do to help and to avoid hurting. We can teach them to ask questions and listen to what others say—skills that will serve them not only in friendship but in other situations where gaining information is important. We can practice these skills with our children, asking them questions, listening quietly to them, and summarizing what they have said to us. We can also teach them good conversation rules, such as "not interrupting" and "not ignoring."

We can also teach children the rituals of courtesy and respect. For example, we can teach them to give and to accept compliments and to avoid unpleasant mannerisms and moods. While these rituals change somewhat from generation to generation and from place to place, knowing them helps children feel confident when they begin to expand their social world and make friends.

Children display different and appropriate skills to participate fully in each level of friendship. Under ordinary circumstances, children will progress through these stages and gradually achieve a perspective that allows emotionally intimate friendships. During the years of this process, they will also make mistakes. Understanding how children learn to help and to hurt others will help us get a clearer idea of how to teach them to be moral and have successful friendships.

How Children Learn to Help or to Hurt in Friendships

An axiom of human relationships is that what others do to us, we will usually do to others. Children treated with consideration will usually treat others considerately, just as children who are treated hurtfully will usually treat others hurtfully. But factors other than mistreatment also contribute to our children's learning ineffective and hurtful ways of treating others. Some of these factors are children's own emotional style—calm or intense—their knowledge of social skills, how much and what kind of exposure they have to social situations, and, of course, the quality of parental example. Examples of how these conditions combine to shape children's moral and social behavior are readily found in developmental psychology. Some evidence shows that parents who fail to provide consistent and warm care influence children to become more anxious, resulting in misinterpretation and ineffective response (selfishness) with their friends. Even clearer evidence shows a connection between parental neglect when children are young and children's violent behavior toward others when they are older. A high proportion of people convicted of violent crimes, homicides, rapes, assaults, and battery have experienced prolonged neglect.

Children who are brought into contact with many people in their communities—neighbors, friends, storekeepers, at restaurants, in schools, in churches—show greater "social intelligence" than do children who do not have this contact. They can more readily adapt to a greater variety of people and situations. In contrast, children who are restricted in their contact with others tend to be more suspicious of others, more likely to fear making mistakes, and less aware of how to be helpful to other people.

Children inherit their temperament, or emotional style. Some aspects of the temperament appear at birth and remain throughout life. How easy or difficult it is for children to learn friendship skills can depend to some degree upon their temperament. Some children, for example, show from birth an intense response to their environment. At an early age these children display strong reactions to disappointments and to parental attempts to regulate their behavior. Their responses can be intense anger, temper, shyness, and anxiety. Later, many "intense" children exhibit exaggerated emotional responses, including dominating and controlling behavior or excessive submissiveness toward their friends. These responses lead to early failure in social relations. When children's first attempts at friendship produce failure, they often begin to worry more about being approved of than about learning appropriate friendship skills. The emotional goal of such a child is to please others.

We can imagine what can happen to children with inherited intense temperaments who are raised by parents who mistreat them, who exemplify poor social skills, and provide few positive social opportunities. Such children would be very likely to hurt themselves and others with whom they have close relationships.

Effective human interaction requires accurately recognizing another's emotions. To learn to do that, children need to learn to accurately perceive facial expressions, and to gauge correctly what different facial expressions mean, children must be able to maintain eye contact with others. When children either do not look at one another or misinterpret what they see, they are more likely to misunderstand one another.

One of life's great ironies is these misunderstandings. Almost always, feeling misunderstood makes people feel threatened or angry. Since misunderstanding may simply be "not knowing" and therefore as likely to be complimentary as derogatory, it is perhaps surprising that misunderstanding almost always hurts us or makes us feel uncomfortable. It is not surprising, in light of this human characteristic, that when children feel misunderstood, they typically compound the problem: instead of correcting the misunderstanding with more accurate information, they misjudge the person who is misjudging them, perpetuating the hurtful cycle.

So the ambiguity arising from misunderstanding makes

children feel threatened and angry. Because they are afraid of these feelings or because they are selfish, children may respond to such a situation by striking out. In early and middle childhood this aggression may appear as taking advantage of others by bullying, coercing, excluding, being unfair, fighting, and name calling. These immature social acts can form attitudes that lead in later childhood to such behavior as ridicule, discrimination, cliquishness, physical abuse, threats, and swearing.

So children learn to hurt others primarily because they are themselves mistreated, because their parents provide poor examples for them, and because they tend to misunderstand others and deal inadequately with being misunderstood by others. These negative learnings imply that it is possible for children to learn positive skills that will help them develop a sense of responsibility in relationships. We can, by precept and example, help them learn the morality of justice and fairness through their friendships.

The Meaning of Justice and Fairness

Justice and fairness, though almost synonymous, have different meanings when applied to social relationships. Justice is related to actions and the consequences the actions produce; justice requires that we accept the consequences for our actions in a responsible way. Moral acts produce moral consequences. Immoral acts produce immoral consequences. To be just, we must be concerned for the welfare of another person and be able to adjust to promote it. Further, to be fully just, we must be able to act with consideration even if another is unjust.

Fairness in relationships comes into play when all affected by a decision are invited to have a role in making the decision. In friendships, fairness is called upon when there is more than one person who wishes to participate in an activity or who wants to have a share in some object or commodity. For example, two or more children want to play the same game or eat the same candy. Fairness involves using a style of reasoning that considers everyone to be of equal importance to everyone else. Fairness, therefore, means giving to others to help them rather than withholding from them to hurt them; it means that we regard others as being deserving of receiving equally to what we receive.

Since children learn their basic attitudes about justice and fairness from us, we need, once again, to think about our own standards before attempting to teach a standard to our children. To do that, we can ask ourselves, Do I respect friendships and maintain them? Do I make and keep promises? Do I acknowledge responsibility for my actions or do I blame others for what happens to me? Do I tell the truth? How do I usually respond when I feel that someone has mistreated me? Do I retreat? Do I seek revenge? Or do I wait for the sting to go away, overlook the pain, and try to talk calmly about the problem in order to resolve it? How do I respond to people in different positions (prominent and powerful versus lacking in social status)? Am I able to meet a variety of people and feel comfortable? Do I sometimes feel superior or sometimes feel inferior?

If we think carefully about our answers to these questions, it should become obvious to us that it is possible for children to learn a great deal about justice and fairness from us. If our own views are warped, we will undoubtedly find that our children have warped views as well. Most of us have a strong sense of fairness in some situations but not in others. That is why it is useful to evaluate ourselves. It is important to accept the idea that being unique, or different from others, does not make us better or worse than anyone else. To teach elitism, we need only believe that others are less deserving than we are of such things as respect, consideration, and the blessings of life. Our arrogance and ignorance soon transfer to our children. By the same token, if we believe that others are more deserving than we are of respect, consideration, and other blessings of life, we teach our children that they too are less deserving than others. By squelching their aspirations and degrading them, we teach them to accept less than they deserve because they believe themselves to be less. What we believe as we compare ourselves to others will be our children's first lesson about fairness—and perhaps the one that lasts.

Teaching Children to Be Fair

Johnny Barton was six years old. He was playing with his friend Sam. Johnny asked his mother for a couple of apples, but Mrs. Barton had only one apple. The boys were undecided about what to do, until Johnny said, "We'll share." Mrs. Barton put the apple and a knife on the cutting board; both boys moved close. Mrs. Barton said, "One of you can cut the apple, and the other can choose first." That proposal seemed fair to the boys, and they were satisfied.

Mrs. Barton was helping these boys develop a sense of fairness. Fairness to her meant that both boys should be treated equally. So that they could learn to understand fairness in that same way, both boys were required to think about the other, and they were given a strategy according to which they could make things fair between them.

The Frandsens asked their eight-year-old daughter, Heather, to go to bed. She was playing with her dollhouse and did not want to go. She dawdled until her mother became exasperated. In response to her mother, Heather yelled, "It's not fair. Why do I have to go to bed before Ellen?" Ellen had complained to her mother a few days earlier that she was not being fair when Heather had received a new blouse and Ellen had not.

Their mother talked with both of them. "In a way, you're right," she said. "We are not treating you both in exactly the same way. So I suppose you could say we are not being fair to you. But your father and I don't intend to be that kind of 'fair.' " Her comment surprised the girls who, like most children, used the "unfair" argument to get more for themselves. Mother continued, "We treat each of you differently because you are different people and have different needs. If we try to help you get what you need, even if what you get is not the same all of the time, we think that you will be happier."

These examples illustrate how children can learn two aspects of fairness: one is based on equal shares and on using a strategy to achieve equality; the other is individualized and based on what each person knows about the other. It was fair for Heather to get a blouse when Ellen didn't. Fairness, in this case, was based on the mother's knowing that Heather needed a blouse and that Ellen didn't.

When children begin to form friendships, they usually learn the equality part of fairness first. It is simpler and easier to understand. At first, friendships last only as long as the reciprocity lasts. So our first task is to help our children resolve their tendency to selfishness so that they can both give and receive. Generally, the desire to play with friends is great enough to motivate children to learn equal sharing if we show them how to share and keep them from playing unless they do it. Praise and positive reinforcement will strengthen their ability. We can help children learn fairness by getting some special "sharing toys" and showing them how to share before a friend comes to play. Other fairness strategies children must learn for happy friendships include choosing sides for a game, making sure the sides are "even," taking the side of a smaller person against someone older or bigger, and crying "unfair" if someone is treated unfairly.

Since the strategies that children devise to promote equality are usually based on one of two general notions, we will help our children if we teach them these notions early. The first is that every person must get something; no one can be excluded. The second is that other people have feelings similar to our own, and so we will all benefit from taking turns. Children accept both notions if they are praised for being able to let another go first or get something they do not. We also teach our children that in certain situations a child needs to go to a third party for help. This person, usually a parent, can arbitrate differences by finding out what each child wants and by making suggestions.

Teaching fairness or equality is conceptual as well as practical. That is, we can teach ideas about it, as well as help children understand what they actually do. The following are some problems that can be used for practice in thinking about fairness:

1. Two brothers share a bedroom. There are two beds and one chest of drawers, the floor is carpeted, and there is a fairly long table with room enough for two work spaces. There is a bookcase that has shelves for books and for one brother's model airplanes. Their parents want the room kept clean, and cleaned especially well on Saturdays. How can they divide the work fairly?

2. Heather and Kathy wanted to rollerskate but could find only one pair of skates. How can they both have fun and do it fairly?

3. Billy and Tommy went fishing. Tommy brought some worms but no fish eggs, and Billy brought fish eggs but no worms. What do you think the boys should do to make things even? Why?

4. Mary, Susan, and Michelle went for a walk. They climbed far up a hill and wandered away from the trail by following a squirrel. When they started down the hill, anxious to get home, they ran into some bushes with thorns on them. Michelle and Susan had long pants on, but Mary was wearing shorts. What should the girls do to be fair? Should they go through the bushes and take the shortest route, or walk around the bushes, which would take longer?

As children mature, the way they think about one another changes. At first, they may know people by their
toys or other possessions—"Susy has a new doll." Then
they know other children by a physical characteristic, such
as height or hair color, or by where they live. That stage
is followed by knowing other children by how they act in
public—"Johnny is funny at school, and Lucy is shy." Just
before puberty, children begin to know others by understanding their individual personality traits—"Mary is kind,
and Jack is smart."

Knowing how children's social perceptions change and
develop, we can devise a way to teach strategies that promote the second notion of fairness, the idea that other
people have feelings similar to our own. These strategies
will help our children look for ways to help each individual
as help is needed.

Because younger children notice what is external, they
think about other children first of all in terms of what they
possess, then by physical characteristics, and then by the
way they act in public. With children basing their judgments on these kinds of observations, it is difficult to help
them learn to be fair on the basis of someone's need.
"Need" implies something about internal conditions that
younger children usually do not understand unless we
teach them to understand. That means that we must help
our children learn to see when people need something;
we must point out other people's needs.

Most people need recognition, need to belong, need
to be cared for. Particular needs often depend on particular
situations. We can help our children see and understand
many of these situations. In addition, we can ask our children to put themselves in the place of others and imagine
what these people "need." Finally, we can ask them to
evaluate their own needs in comparison with the needs of
others and to decide whose need in a given situation is
greater.

Mrs. Merriwether divided her sixth-grade class into

two groups. Each group was to write and present a short patriotic play. Some time each day was devoted to this activity until the plays were ready. All the children worked hard, and some good ideas emerged and were blended into a script calling for actors and actresses, producers, and directors. On the day that the children were chosen to play the parts, Jennifer, a friendly and outgoing girl, was absent.

The following day, when the time came for the children to practice, Mrs. Merriwether remembered that Jennifer had not been given a part. But before Mrs. Merriwether could correct the situation, Jennifer discovered she had been left out and immediately slumped into her chair, head down, fighting back the tears. Mrs. Merriweather invited all the children to sit in a large circle at the front of the classroom. She presented the problem to the entire class and asked them for a solution. At first, some of the children were flippant, but others quickly pointed out that anyone would be hurt if they were left out. The mood of the group changed, and they began searching for a solution. "Well," a boy said, "it is her fault for not being here." Another student suggested that maybe somebody with a part would give it up and let Jennifer have it. "Then someone else would be left out," was the reply. They sat in silence while they thought.

"It can't be just anything," one boy said finally. "What would Jennifer like to do?" Jennifer was silent. "I know!" a girl exclaimed. "Jennifer could be the narrator for both plays." Although the idea was new, it seemed just right because it fit Jennifer and it gave her something to do. Jennifer happily agreed.

This example illustrates both types of fairness. The children were concerned that everyone be treated equally. More than that, however, they searched for something that matched Jennifer's need. Equally impressive is the way the teacher helped the children learn fairness by considering one another's feelings.

We can do the same for our own children by helping

them understand what people need in a given situation and then integrate that information with what can be done to be fair or helpful. "What is that person like?" we might ask. Or we could point out what we notice: "She seems very shy." After making the evaluation or helping the child make it, we then suggest what can be done to help: "So we won't make her pin the tail on the donkey; let's ask her to be 'it' when we play the song game." In this way we teach children to think about the traits of others and to create fairness by doing what can be done to satisfy the needs of that individual.

Helping Children to Be Just

Children's relationships get them into many situations involving unkind or inconsiderate actions. Every parent has calmed hurt feelings created by mistreatment, or chided and scolded a child who has been unjust to another. Because there is a sequence involved—one child's actions are followed by the responses of another—we think of the actions as being the cause of the response. When we ask, "Who started it?" we are trying to find out who acted first and "caused" the problem. The trouble is that in a situation like this, each child sees his or her own behavior as a response to something the other has said or done, so each will think the other caused the problem and is at fault.

To teach children to be just in their friendships, then, we must teach them to understand and to say how their actions affect their friend, to withstand a friend's unjust treatment without seeking revenge, and to talk with a friend about a problem as a way to find a solution without giving further offense. When children understand and can say how they affect others, they are able to accept responsibility for what they do. When children can resist the urge to get revenge for being mistreated, they exhibit a sense of justice because they do not wish to inflict on someone else the same hurt they have experienced. When children learn to talk about ways to solve problems, they are being just because they are seeking a shared solution. To teach children these three parts of justice, we can tell them what they must learn. Then we can help them apply what they know when an opportunity arises.

Applying Skills to Learn Justice

We can teach our children to understand how they affect their friends. When children are meeting someone new, we can say, "What do people like about you?"

When there is a misunderstanding, we can say, "How do you cheer up your friends or make them sad?"

During conversations about our children's friends, we can say, "Let's talk about what you did to your friend. If your friends feel happy around you, they will like you. Do your friends feel happy around you?"

We can teach our children not to seek revenge if they are treated unjustly. If one of their friends says something mean, we can ask our children, "What do you think would make someone act that way?"

If a friend ignores or excludes our children, we can ask, "What can you do other than what your friend did?"

If a friend hits our child, we can ask, "Can you make other friends so you don't have to rely on just one or two?"

If our children are ridiculed or embarrassed in public by friends, we can say, "Some people do things without realizing they hurt. I wonder if your friends did that?"

If friends play a trick or a practical joke and our child misinterprets it, we can say, "Make up your mind you will not do what your friend has done to you."

We can teach our children to talk to solve a problem. When a friend says hurtful things, we can help our children practice saying, "Do you know it hurts me when you say . . . ?"

When a friend neglects to ask for our children's opinion and tries to control them, we can help our children practice saying, "I want to make up my own mind. Please don't decide for me."

When a friend manipulates our children to get food, a toy, or some money, we can help our children practice saying, "I don't like it when you try to get me to ask my parents for things. Please ask them yourself."

When friends ask your children for more than they give, we can help our children practice saying, "I think we had better talk about this."

When a friend ignores what is important to our children, we can help our children practice saying, "I can tell that you don't know it is important to me because you don't notice. I want you to let me tell you how important it is to me."

When our children make a mistake and hurt someone, we can help our children practice saying, "I have not been a good friend to you, and I am sorry. I want to talk about it."

Friendships provide social stimulation, enjoyment, and new opportunities to learn. Children need to be encouraged to make and keep several friends so that they will be helped to grow. While participating in friendships, children will discover that the ideas and actions that produce close friends are the same as those involved in the morality of fairness and justice. By teaching children to be just and fair, we not only help them have good friendships but also help them be moral toward all people. Our families, our schools, our communities, our country, our world all need more people who know how to be good friends.

CHAPTER 9

MONEY AND PROPERTY

The task of teaching children morality about money and property has been made more complex by trends in our society that have moved us away from the collective sense of responsibility we once felt as a nation. The antiwar movement, the civil rights movement, the women's movement, and other such movements had in common a belief that true freedom is best expressed in individual rights. Nevertheless, in our headlong race to right long-standing wrongs and increase everyone's freedom to exercise their individual rights, we may have failed to consider carefully enough the proven idea that increased freedom brings increased responsibility. One result of this failure is that many of our young people possess a strong sense of individual freedom but lack an understanding of the corresponding individual responsibilities.

Consider the age-old conflict between striving for material wealth and working to develop intellectual qualities and personality traits that uplift and inspire others. Individual freedom without responsibility to others can become a selfish materialism in which people are the means and achieving possessions is the goal. Anyone who has this view of life can easily concentrate on making money and acquiring possessions. For such a person, devotion to principles, companionship with family members, teaching their children, service to others, are all expendable in the single-minded pursuit of money.

Every culture has values related to property, and as parents we try to teach these values to our children. Be-

155

cause most people in the United States believe in the sanc-
tity of private property and the rights of ownership, issues
about property are viewed as moral issues. As with other
moral issues, we may have strong feelings about what we
think is the right or the wrong way to regard property.
Yet we are not all agreed about what that right way is or
even on the specific roles money and property should play
in our lives. We have our own styles of managing money
and of caring for or not caring for the property of others.
We see these values emerging in the lives of children as
they grow. Some children appear to care relatively little
about possessions, and others think possessions are extremely important.

The pursuit of possessions has brought us both help
and harm. It has resulted in jobs, security, compassionate
giving, and other things that make life satisfying, but the
desire for possessions, when unrestrained by moral judgment and moral conduct, has resulted in graft and cor-
ruption, theft, violent robbery, treason, and murder. For
example, we hear frequently about varieties of scams that
have been used to bilk millions of dollars from unsus-
pecting investors. The victims of these crimes are often
easily hoodwinked because their own greed leads them
into believing wild promises about easy ways to increase
material wealth. To help our children protect themselves
from becoming involved in such dealings, we must begin
very early to teach them a clear and definite morality about
material possessions.

In our culture property and money play such a large
role in our lives and relationships with one another that
no one is free from contact with money and property or
from dealings with other people about them. Recently, I
read a newspaper account about some people who were
seeking help from the local government to force a neighbor
to improve the appearance of her house and yard. Her
failure to keep her lawn mowed and her house painted
led to lower property values in the neighborhood. The

neighbors were upset and felt justified in their feelings. As a result, the woman was compelled by the city commission to take care of the problems that led to the complaints. We have only to become aware of such attitudes to see that they are all around us. At any business luncheon, for instance, conversations can be overheard about the acquisition and use of property, about who owns which house or building, and, if we listen carefully, we see that a person's social status, at least in part, is determined by income or property. For many of us, such attitudes are woven so thoroughly and so deeply through the fabric of our thoughts that we accept their place without feeling their true significance. To help teach our children what they need to know, we need to be conscious that money and property play an important role in many moral circumstances because of the help or hurt that results from the decisions made about them.

Moral Circumstances for Using Money and Property

To be prepared to reason, to decide, and to act morally where money and property are concerned, our children need to know something about the way people think about money, about how money affects people, and about how people relate to one another when money or property is involved. I remember a time when my own father taught these principles to me. We were shopping together, and he advised me to watch a salesman closely while he was talking to see if he was being honest. "People won't look at you," Dad said, "when they are about to tell a lie." He also warned me never to let someone push me into buying something before I felt ready: unscrupulous people use false deadlines and play on our fears to motivate us to buy. My dad also taught me to make comparisons when I shop, in order to get the best bargain. He taught me that in any business deal I should make sure that both people feel satisfied about it. "Even if you are within your rights," he would say, "it's a bad deal if one person is unhappy about it." In this way, my father informed me of his views of people and their relationships to money and property.

As we teach our views to our own children, we carefully point out examples of selfishness, greed, and dishonesty. Every town newspaper is full of examples: money and property will forever attract people who think of schemes that hurt others. We also want to help our children learn generosity, kindness, sharing. The fairness and justice we have helped them learn in their relationships with family and friends will help them deal morally with many other people. If we point out to them the fair and the just (or the unfair and the unjust) dealings of others, they will learn to understand the intentions of others and improve their awareness of potential consequences in moral circumstances involving money and property.

We can also help children be aware of their feelings when they want something new. Quite frequently children hurt each other over toys and other possessions. These experiences give us many opportunities to help children understand the feelings associated with moral judgment. If children's desires for "things" are greater than their concern for others, they can learn to adapt and be more considerate of other people. Once a neighbor boy offered several large "steelies" to one of my sons. These were highly prized during spring marble season. In exchange he wanted an old radio he had seen in our home. My son was so interested in getting the steelies that he grabbed the radio and was about to leave to conclude the deal when I asked him if he knew who the radio belonged to. "Aw, Dad," he said, "it's old and no good. No one wants it anyway." I pointed out that his desire to get what he wanted was clouding his thinking a bit and that he needed to make certain that trading the radio was a right thing to do. At first he resisted thinking about his feelings, but as we talked more, he admitted what he felt. He took the time to talk with all family members to see if anyone objected to his trading away the radio. As he left at last to make the deal, I passed on the "make sure both people are happy" idea I'd learned from my father, and my son worked out a fair agreement with his friend.

Helping children think about their feelings and intentions and the feelings and intentions of others prepares them to act morally. Now they need to have a full and clear understanding about a moral standard, and they will be ready for the moral circumstances involving choices about money and property.

A Moral Standard for Using Money and Property

Because we live in a property-oriented society, it makes sense for us to teach our children to use property and live with it in a moral way. In other words, where property is concerned, our children must learn to choose properly between greed or generosity, sharing or selfishness, and must have a balanced attitude about the relative worth of people and things. Greedy people collect property simply for the purpose of ownership, even if others are hurt in the process. Selfish people deprive others of property when it would be possible for others to benefit in a share. Those who steal (thieves and robbers) take what belongs to another. We recognize that *greed, selfishness,* and *stealing* are terms describing behavior about property that hurts people and is therefore immoral conduct. *Generosity, sharing,* and *having respect for others* are terms describing behavior about property that helps people and is therefore moral conduct.

To make our own attitudes clear, we can ask ourselves questions such as these: Is it moral to use money and property to help people? Is it moral to hurt people to get property? Is it moral to use property to exploit or control people? Do we have a responsibility to care for our property so others are not hurt? These questions raise concerns that most of us face whenever we deal with property in relationship to people. When our dealings in this relationship are honest, we are said to have integrity. If we have this integrity ourselves, we will be more successful in teaching it to our children. They will need integrity when they confront their own questions about property and people.

George Murdock came to school as a new student. He was in the third grade and had just moved into town. He looked at the other boys and girls playing. They seemed to be having fun. He went over to join in, but no one invited him to be on a team. He waited for a while and then went into the classroom. During lunch he went to a store across the street and bought some candy bars. One of the kids noticed the candy bars and said hello. George offered him one of the candy bars. The boy stayed and played during the rest of the lunch period.

The next day George brought more money to school. He met his new friend and showed him the money. During lunch the two went to the store and bought some more candy. This time George gave some of it to two or three other boys. They all played together for the rest of lunch recess. The next day George did not have any money. One of the boys said, "Where is the candy, George?" Because he did not have any, the boys ran off and left him. The next day George had some money. The boys sent him to the store for the candy while they played. When he came back and shared, they played with him. Every day after that George brought some money.

During a parent-teacher conference Mrs. Murdock confided in the teacher that George had been stealing money at home. Had the teacher noticed anything at school? The teacher had happened to see George bring candy to the boys and then knew why George was stealing the money.

Many of us witnessed such experiences in childhood. Our children may be like George or one of his playmates. Yet many of us think nothing of giving things to people so that they will like us. What was wrong with George's actions? What could we teach George to do instead of what he did? To teach a moral standard to our children, it will help if we begin by recognizing that money and property are mediums of exchange that symbolize one person's attitudes toward another. Generosity with money, for example, shows compassion for others. Fairness with money symbolizes respect for other people, and honesty about money signifies a belief that people and their needs are as important as money and property.

We trade, bargain, buy and sell, give and receive, share or withhold. The morality of property we should establish for ourselves and our children is that as we participate in these transactions, we act according to our belief that property is of less value than people. A real estate agent I know demonstrated this morality. He had tried to sell a particular house for several months. Business was slow and he was in a tight spot himself, which put him under a great deal of stress. A young couple saw the house, liked it, and made an offer. They had a small down payment, and their banker was willing to make a loan, so the deal could have been concluded. But after the agent found out about their work plans, plans for their family, and anticipated future income, he realized that the amount of money they had offered was really more than they could pay, and he tried to talk them out of making the purchase. He told them, "I can't in good conscience sell you this house without telling you that I very strongly believe that the price you have offered will be far too heavy for you to pay." He then explained his reasons in detail. He valued people and their welfare more than money or possessions.

In an example that is unfortunately somewhat more typical, we may encounter the car salesman who, when we explain what we can afford to spend, ignores this information in his attempt to sell us a car. This action indicates an insincere and possibly dishonorable person. As our children grow, we can help them refine their ability to converse in ways that will enable them to learn about others and express themselves until they are able to make a transaction a gain for everybody.

Money and Property as Social Exchange

A standard of morality is learned in teaching moments accumulated over a period of years until the decisions made according to it are automatic. If we want our children to make automatic "right" decisions about money and property, we will have to help them establish in themselves a "right" standard.

In the following example, Burton (1984) describes how a moral standard for property can become automatic. His daughter Ursula, aged one-and-a-half, came home from Halloween trick-or-treating and tried to take some candy from her sister's sack and place it in her own sack. The sister yelled, "No, Ursie, that's mine!" Her father explained that she should put only her own candy in her sack. A few days later the older sisters found some of their candy in Ursie's bag. "That's stealing," one said. This time Ursula's mother explained to her about not taking someone else's things. The next day a similar event took place, and her mother explained again. A day later her father saw Ursula in Maria's room. She looked up and said, "No, this is Maria's, not Ursula's."

Several months later Ursula took a plastic toy from the store and had to return it to the manager and say she was sorry. One day when she was in first grade, Ursula came home with someone else's pencil. Her parents explained again about temptations and honesty, and they asked her how she would feel if someone took something of hers. Seven years later, Ursula found a wallet in Yellowstone Park. She began frantically to gather bills that were blowing in the wind. She found the address and mailed wallet and money to the owner. When asked if she was tempted to keep the money, she replied, "No, that would be stealing."

This account shows that morality is cumulative and

eventually becomes automatic, so that when faced with a decision, children do not deliberate painfully but simply react according to what their experience has taught them.

Many such decisions are automatic, and we need to be consistent over the years as children grow so that they will be able to identify and follow a clear standard of morality about property. There are certain situations, arising more often when people are older, in which moral judgments are not automatic and in fact require us to thoughtfully deliberate in order to make the moral choice. On the simplest level pertaining to money and property, however, very young children can start along the path to automatic right decisions by learning not to take something that belongs to someone else. If this principle is reinforced many times in their early years, then a later temptation to steal will be met with a firm decision to refrain from doing so.

Helping children learn an automatic moral response about property is not the only thing we can do very early. It is possible to teach very young children to have empathy for others. At age two or three they can be helped to understand how other children think and feel in many circumstances—when other children do not have something to play with, for example, or when one child will not willingly share. Very young children can feel the happiness that comes from giving something to someone else, and they can learn the social skills attendant to giving and receiving graciously.

One important thing we can teach children to do is to talk with us about their ideas about money and possessions. Little children will have toys they love and others they don't like so much. One set of parents gathered their children in the living room once a week to play games and teach little "life" lessons. On one occasion they had each child bring out a favorite toy. The parents asked each child in turn to explain why the toy was the favorite.Then they asked their children, "Do you think other children have favorite toys, too?" "What should we do about the children who have no toys?" "What happens if we share our toys with one another?" The children were able to talk quite openly about feeling sad if someone didn't have toys and feeling happy if toys were shared.

The children in this family were learning to talk about property and their feelings about it. They were learning that possessions are involved with friends and family relationships. If their parents continue to provide them with experiences like these, the children will grow up able to use conversations about property to help them make moral decisions and to prevent others from exploiting them. They will be able to test the sincerity and integrity of others by expressing their own feelings about property and money and then watching how others respond.

Careful Management: Generosity and Sharing

Careful management of property carries with it attitudes of respect that are related to generosity and other virtues. During middle childhood, children can be taught careful management of their possessions. Managing their possessions requires that they learn to regulate themselves—as an aspect of autonomy. We do not often think about how generosity, integrity, cooperation, and sharing can come from learning to be careful about our own possessions. Certainly many children who are not good managers are able to give to others. True generosity, however, is a gift by someone who knows the true value of the gift. It is not just an attempt to please someone. When children have something that is "theirs" and learn to manage it well, they gain feelings about property based on an earned understanding of worth. Children who do not own anything or who fail to care for what they own often cannot determine the real value of things and therefore cannot know as well about cooperation and integrity.

Most of us, for example, try to get our children to keep their rooms clean or to perform chores thoroughly. The

most common method to teach these skills is to ask our
children, sometimes repeatedly, to keep their room clean
or to perform chores thoroughly and then to get angry
when they fail to do what we ask. But those of us caught
in this pattern need to try some other approach because
our frustration with nagging is as great as our children's.

Another approach is to show them what we want them
to do, tell them we expect it done before a certain time,
and then leave them to it, perhaps promising a reward
(paying them) when it is done. This approach can work,
but it can get expensive. So just how do we get our children
to care enough about something they own, have a share
in, or have responsibility for, so that they will consistently
demonstrate this care? We need to begin by recognizing
that ownership is as much responsibility as it is privilege.
Children tend to think only about the privilege or pleasure
ownership creates, especially if they are given most of what
they have. For children to be careful managers, they might
need to earn a possession, or some part of the cost of it,
through actual effort. We can also ask them to demonstrate
the ability to care for something very well before they get
something else. For example, children must take good care
of an old bike before getting a new one is possible.

Careful management is more than doing chores: it is
also discovering what will prolong the usefulness of something. Some people are careful because they are niggardly
and selfish, but others are good managers because of a
respect for the property that is cared for. If we want children to know what to do as careful managers, we must
think about how to prolong the usefulness of some object
and teach this routine to our children. What do we do to
prolong the usefulness of a car, a vacuum, a bedspread,
a mixer, or a lawnmower? If we know, do we teach our
children?

Careful management also teaches morality about
money. Many adults do not know a standard for using
money morally, and they show it when they spend more

than they have or earn, spend for foolish reasons, cheat to get more money, or even steal money from others. If we do not want our children to engage in any of these immoral behaviors, we can use middle childhood and early adolescence to teach them the moral uses of money. The principles are straightforward, and we can teach them if we have the will to be consistent and follow through with what we begin. Here are three principles for us to consider:

1. Money that is earned by effort is usually spent more wisely than money received as allowance. When children work and are paid for their work, they see a relationship between an amount of effort and an amount of money.

2. All uses of money involve choices. Whenever children are going to spend money, discuss the choice with them and if possible place the responsibility for the choice on them. (If they are going to make a very unwise decision, however, we should exercise our right to decide for them.) Once the money is spent, we can help the children evaluate how they spent it by asking, "What was wise, and what was not?"

3. If they have money to spend, we can require that children spend less than they have. Regardless of the amount they save, children who save will exert more control over what they spend. Maturity means being able to carry money without spending it all. Regulating behavior is the key to financial maturity.

The Consequences of the Moral Use of Property

One positive consequence of the moral use of property is the idea that "someone else's gain is my gain." It is felt as peace of mind and satisfaction. To know this consequence, children will have to understand that their own gain must not exploit others; they must understand empathy. When our children have successes in sharing with someone or receiving from someone, we can point out and reinforce the feelings these experiences bring. When they

have unhappy experiences, such as someone's refusing to
share with them, we can help them understand the sources
of their unhappiness (someone else's selfishness, perhaps
compounded by their own unreasonable demands). Developing an ability to feel content with someone else's gain
is basic to morality in circumstances involving people and
property.

The competition was keen for junior high cheerleader,
and all the girls felt the pressure of it. Two of the girls who
were competing, though they were not close friends, occasionally walked home together from the bus stop. As
they were talking one day after school, Judy confided to
Karla that she did not think her chances were very good.
"Why?" questioned Karla. "Well, I am not as good as the
rest," came the answer. "That's not true," Karla protested.
"You dance and move as well as anybody." There was a
long moment of silence. Then Judy confided that she
thought her clothes were not as nice as the other girls'
clothes. She was especially worried about the outfit she
would wear while trying out in front of the studentbody.
Karla offered to let Judy wear her sweater and skirt if they
did not have to try out at the same time. She also offered
to help her work on a routine for tryouts. She went home
and talked about this proposal with her mother, who gave
suggestions.

The next day at school arrangements were made so
that the girls would try out at different times. Karla's
mother kept track of the situation, continuing to talk with
her daughter and help her think about what might happen
in this moral circumstance. With her mother's help, Karla
thought about the possibilities: both of them could win a
position, both of them could fail, one of them could win,
and the other could fail. The hardest possibility for Karla
to think about, of course, was the possibility of Judy's
winning and her losing. "What would you do if that happened?" Karla's mother asked. "You know that you really
want to win yourself." Karla thought about it.

A few days later, it happened. Judy became a cheerleader, and Karla did not. They both cried, though of
course not for the same reason, and both tried to be gracious. Having been taught well, Karla went to games to
support Judy. The two girls became close friends.

The moral use of property means that in our transactions with others we find a way for both parties to benefit
or to receive equal value for what they give. Sometimes,
as Karla learned, it will require great effort to regulate our
own emotions in order to share in the pleasure or the
excitement of the gain of another.

In our families we have obvious opportunities to teach
our children that principle. Children ask for something
from us, often without thought for anything other than
the pleasure of getting it. We can help them expand their
moral understanding if we ask what they will do with what
they get and tell them what happens to us as a result of
our giving it to them. This might mean, for example, that
when our children want us to give them money, they
should be prepared to tell us how they think getting the
money will affect them and also to tell us how it will affect
us to give it to them. If we fail to ask them to think of
these consequences, children can become so concerned
with their own desires that they do not understand what
fulfilling their desires can cost someone else. Many children ask for and receive money and only later find out, if
they ever find out at all, about their parents' sacrifices to
give them what they wanted. For many children, the work
their parents do to bring home the money is invisible.
Because they have little awareness of the work parents do
to earn the money, though, the children will be concerned
only with getting what they want, unless we teach them
otherwise.

We neglect to teach our children about this relationship
between our work and the money we have available to
give them for several reasons. We may not want our children to know about us and so might refrain from telling

them much. Or it might not be much of a sacrifice just to give them what they want. But we can help our children develop the sensitivity they should have if we occasionally take the time to ask them to tell us about their needs and invite them to listen to our situation. When we see them involved in some transaction, we can help them ask the questions and judiciously offer the information that enables both parties to work out a fair arrangement. Being able to participate in these kinds of conversations will help our children make good judgments about what is fair in moral circumstances involving money and property.

We can begin teaching this fairness very early. Little children can be asked to tell why they want a certain toy when they are fighting over it with someone else. If children fight simply to prevent someone else's having something, they can be faced with a choice either of talking to work out something agreeable to both or of having the toy removed so that neither can play with it. Later, as children learn to share and bargain, we can encourage them to think about both people in the transaction. If we are worried about our children's being exploited by others, we can help them understand cooperation. Generosity and cooperation are reciprocal behaviors, which means that if one person gives to or cooperates with another, the other feels the need or senses an obligation to give or cooperate in return. Our children need to be prepared to give, even if they will not be given to. (If that situation happens very frequently, though, we should look into the matter.)

One father prepared a small garden plot for his daughter. He spent enough time with her to explain about planting, weeding, watering, and even told of the enjoyment the fresh produce would bring. He showed her how to make the rows and plant seeds, and then he left her to do the rest of the work. He showed interest by asking whether or not the plants had come up. As the plants grew, he showed her about weeding and left her alone to finish. He evaluated her work with her and showed her how to improve. More than this, he took her to other people's gardens and pointed out the difference between the gardens of someone who took care and someone who was indifferent. They talked about the two kinds of gardens, and he explained to her that he wanted her to grow a garden that would be like the gardens of the people who took care. He did not tell her how much weeding or watering she had to do to achieve that goal. He left that for her to discover. He occasionally went with her to check her garden but did not do much to help her unless she asked him to. He talked about what she was doing, though, and pointed to both the good and the less-than-good, hoping to avoid discouraging her.

The first year her garden was not especially good, but she still liked doing some of the gardening. The next spring she told her father what she intended to plant and talked of what she had learned about the plants she had grown last summer. He complimented her, helped her prepare the soil, but left her to do most of the work. This summer the garden was better because she cared for it better. They both took time to compare her garden with those nearby until she could see that her care was as good as that of the other people. She was excited that she had some vegetables to give to the neighbors and insisted that she be the one to do the giving. Each year thereafter she planted a garden again, and her father came occasionally to see her work. He complimented her often.

It is not always as easy to teach sharing as it was for this father to teach his daughter. Many of us struggle in frustration to get our children to do their duties and care for their possessions. And children often have difficulty learning to share genuinely. We learn that the whole process takes much longer than we would like it to. If we are having trouble, we might want to think about whether or not we have helped our children truly feel that what we are asking them to do or take care of is theirs alone. The solution might be to provide them an opportunity for discovering that they are on their own when it comes to caring for something. If we assign a task and then leave them to it, going and returning as they work, evaluating their work, and praising more than criticizing, we will help them learn to be careful and begin to discover generosity and sharing.

Stealing and Vandalism

Money and property can present different problems for teenage children, depending on their circumstances. Money might represent status among their friends because of cars, clothes, and social opportunity. Many who are well-to-do have comfortable lives and use money liberally to obtain whatever they want. Those with less money have to find ways to get more of it in order to have many opportunities. Though their situations differ, both the well-to-do and the less-well-off have problems and potential.

The wealth of some children enriches their opportunities in life, but it can also stimulate attitudes of superiority or indifference to others, which are antecedents of immoral behavior. Well-to-do parents often do not limit the money they give their children and then discover that their children have not developed a sense of value about money or have not learned to be helpful and considerate people. Children who have no ready supply of money recognize the need to find jobs. While most of us tend to think that is laudable, it too can bring problems. For one thing, working can interfere with achievement in school. Work, money, and the things money can buy, can easily become more important than anything else. Some surveys indicate that many high school students work nearly forty hours a week to buy cars and clothes and suffer a corresponding reduction in friendships and academic experiences. It is clear that the moral value of money for teenagers must include balance between possessions and development in other areas of life.

When attention to money and possessions is not balanced with concern for people and moral values, the results can be very harmful. Stealing is the name we have for acquiring property in violation of moral standards. People steal because their desire to have something is greater than their motivation to be moral. Sometimes what the person wants is not only the object stolen. In many instances of shoplifting, for example, children steal both to get what they don't have and to get the thrill that stealing gives them.

A teenaged girl named Tina brought home several new items of clothing. When her mother asked about them, Tina said the clothes were borrowed from her friends. Having no reason to doubt her daughter, Tina's mother accepted her answer. But more clothes appeared, and some still had price tags on them. These facts made the mother suspicious, and she confronted Tina. Finally, Tina confessed. She told of stealing from stores at least two hundred times.

Had she been caught by the police, Tina would have had to go through the juvenile court system, which required some restitution and imposed punishment—the idea being, of course, that consequences of this type keep children from misbehaving again. Too often restitution and punishment do not work, however, as parents with children in this situation learn. Why? Because the child is not required to cross the bridge from immorality to morality. That bridge is crossed when a child carefully examines the purposes or intentions in the immoral behavior, clearly describes what feelings were involved in the actions, and admits that the actions were wrong.

In Tina's case, because she had not been caught by the police, her parents were faced with the choice of turning her in or of trying to resolve the problem themselves. For a variety of reasons, they could not bring themselves to call the police, but Tina would not talk to them about what she had done or her reasons for doing it. Nor could she talk about her feelings at the time she was stealing. When they tried to suggest the feelings she would have if she had integrity and refused to steal, she was quite flippant. She also showed little remorse. After several attempts to talk with her, they brought her to my office and explained the situation.

At first, she was as unwilling to talk with me as she was with her parents. Eventually, however, she was able to talk about experimenting with stealing and told how she found it to be exciting. Besides, she said, she was able to get new clothes. In the interview, she talked about her parents. Her feelings were not fully happy. She felt very much controlled by her mother and described her as a "nag" and "overprotective." Gradually, after imagining herself in a store owner's situation, she was able to think about feeling guilty and was able to describe what she might feel if she did not steal. In the course of our conversations she decided that she should take as much of the clothing back as she could to the store she had taken it from. To do this she was to find which lines of clothing were sold by each store and then return the corresponding items to the manager. When the clothes had already been worn, she and her parents worked out a plan for her to earn money to repay the store.

I then asked Tina to go with her father to a store, pick up an article of clothing, and then put it down. She agreed to do this at least ten times on four or five different occasions. Then her parents purchased for her a new outfit of shoes, pants, blouse, and coat. She was asked to write down how she would care for these items in the best way possible. When she balked, she was, in kindness, given the choice of learning how to be a "good manager" or being reported to the police for stealing. She decided to learn how to care for her clothes by washing, ironing, folding, and hanging them in the closet, and cleaning her shoes weekly. After doing that for two months, she was able to talk about what stealing was doing to her. There was no recurrence of her stealing after that.

Vandalism is another form of behavior that indicates inadequate understanding of the moral value of property. Vandalism is the destruction of property as an expression of hostility to others. It may be done by thoughtless people as an isolated act, but most often it is done by those who are angry and have not yet accepted moral values about property.

Three teenaged boys broke into a new elementary school. They damaged many chalkboards, drew obscene pictures in many classrooms, urinated on the carpets, and left small bottles of urine on a few teachers' desks. After an investigation, they were caught. Two were brothers who lived in a home where conflict was the most constant event in the family. Others in the family had broken the law. The third was a boy who reported that he felt friendless and isolated. On the surface of it, there seemed to be no adequate explanation for their destructive acts. A deeper understanding, however, revealed that because they could not openly express their anger toward the abusive authority in their lives and because they could not express their frustration and anger at being lonely, they made a gesture of defiance in the dark of the night, thinking no one would know and there would be no reprisals. Their actions were exactly suited to attracting the attention of the people in our sleepy and conservative community. Their gesture seemed to say, "We'll make you notice us." While their behavior was extreme and improper, what they did fit their feelings.

They were required to pay for the damage they created. They were required, with their parents, to clean a local baseball park. They had to participate in family counseling to talk through what they were feeling. Their situation was not as serious as many I have seen, but their behavior can teach us what even the most angry people are attempting to communicate through their destructiveness.

If our children destroy property simply to destroy it, or to express their anger or their frustration at being lonely, the first step in teaching a moral standard is to stop the destruction. That is accomplished by identifying who did it and by confronting them with their acts. Imposing a consequence that requires careful management also helps. For most, that will correct the problem. For others, intensive work to change their feelings will be required so that they no longer use destruction of property to symbolize their distress. Sending children to jail is often necessary when their underlying feelings cannot be resolved and they are not able to acquire a standard of respect for law and property.

Fads and Fashion

Nearly every teenager takes part in the fads and fashions of music, clothes, and other social customs. To keep up, a teen must know the names of popular songs, groups of singers and instrumentalists, and the "in" brands of clothes, and he or she must own some of the right recordings and clothes and be able to afford the dates and other experiences that bring prestige. It is easy to see the dilemma for many teens. Money will buy belongings. Having money or knowing the most popular fads will help them belong and avoid isolation, the most feared social condition. Of course, the most fashionable clothing, tapes, and dates cost more than the "ordinary" ones. So our children bring their dilemmas over fads and fashions to us in the form of requests for money. Now we have to decide. Do we buy the newest and latest name brand shoes so that they can feel good socially, or do we spend less and risk their social disappointment?

If we do not have the money to spend, then there is no question about what we will do. If we have enough to buy what our children want, we might do it. Whatever we do, though, if we do it without teaching them something about morality, we will have lost a great opportunity to instill in them the moral standard about money. They must

learn that people, including themselves, are more important and more interesting than money. If children rely on
the fads to bring popularity, they will find instead shallow
and temporary friendships. We can help them see that
having money or not having it is not the main problem.
Adolescence is a very good time for children to focus on
friendliness, warmth of personality, sense of humor, courtesy, and consideration as the chief means by which a
lasting popularity is achieved. That is not an easy lesson
to learn, and many conversations and decisions will be
required to help children truly internalize it.

Danny Thompson is fourteen. He is good looking. He
has brown eyes, brown hair, and a clear complexion, but
he is small for his age. He will be in ninth grade this coming
school year. His parents sought family counseling because
they had found him sneaking out at night and had discovered that he had stolen a few things, but, worse, he
had made several strange decisions. He had gone on a
church-sponsored campout in the mountains. In spite of
clear instructions from leaders of the group about what he
could or could not take, he had hidden some cans of food
and large amounts of candy in his pack. That was unusual
because he ordinarily did not like candy very much. He
also took some clothing that was not allowed. Another
time, he dismantled a good clock in order to take out one
part. He suddenly became a "hot" fan of a rock group,
and when he went to the barber he returned with a "buzz"
on one side and a colored streak on the other. When his
parents objected to these things, he became secretive and
sullen. He began to spend more time in his room alone.

When I first talked with him, he was very reluctant to
say anything to me. But when his parents left the room
he began to talk about feeling stupid for having to see a
psychologist. I asked about those feelings, and he told me
his friends would tease him. I took that statement as a clue
and began to ask more about his "friends." They were
larger than he. They had money. They had haircuts like

his, and they wore "neat" clothes. After a while, he seemed more relaxed as we talked about some of his unusual decisions. He was embarrassed as he talked about his mother's clock and about the church camping trip. When I asked him for his reasons, he paused a moment, and then with more intensity told of how he had to do "special" or "terrific" things or he would lose his friends. We talked about that feeling at some length. We examined every possible reason for his thinking that his friends would not like him for himself and would like him only if he did these "neat" things. Then one day he said brightly, "You know, I am tired of doing things that these guys want. I don't care if they leave me. If I am not good enough for them, I will just be a 'no pal' for awhile." Together, we talked about just how bad that was, and he decided that he could survive it.

Money, carefully managed and used to demonstrate that people are more important than things, is a blessing. Money without these standards often hurts people. If we remember that learning a morality of money and property is cumulative, we will use each teaching moment along the way to teach young children to share and be generous, to be good managers, and then to make decisions according to this standard.

Because children learn moral behavior gradually as they mature, the chances are good that they will make mistakes along the way. In adolescence, children are especially vulnerable to money and property and are likely to make many mistakes. These mistakes may give us an opportunity to teach them a more constructive and moral way to act if we remember that the bridge from incorrect behavior to correct behavior is a careful examination of intentions, of feelings and the basis for judgment, and of the consequences of actions.

Therefore, although it is wise to be somewhat tolerant while children experiment and learn about personal standards, it is also wise to tell them we know about their deviant behavior. For example, if we discover some pornographic material under the bed, we can immediately let our child know we know about it, and if our standards reject its use, we can persist until the child gets rid of it. If we are surprised to learn that a child is using drugs, we can quickly let the child know we know and become involved in a constructive plan to stop it.

What if we know about a lie? What about a speeding ticket, or cheating at school, or malicious gossip about someone? In most cases, when our children know we know, they will think of ways to correct the behavior. Or, if they do not correct it—some children are beyond our ability to influence—they will at least have our standards reinforced in their minds.

When children have deviated from a community standard as part of their private experimentation, a change in their lives usually must involve telling some "authority" (someone who represents the standard) about it. That may take the form of an apology, a confession in a religious setting, or some other obvious attempt to assume responsibility by making restitution. Once children have done these things, they will have realigned their personal standards with those of their community.

One thing seems clear. It is the *practice* of correct or moral behavior that brings about true moral character. It is not merely ceasing immoral behavior or making a restitution that does it. Moral character is formed when children see examples and then *act* according to these examples themselves. Sometimes that must be done repeatedly. By encouraging them to live morally all through their childhood, we can expect with greater reliability that the character traits our children develop will be those of people who can balance the pursuit of things with ample concern for other people and their needs.

CHAPTER 10

AUTHORITY

Of the many things children learn in families and take with them throughout life, perhaps nothing is learned more thoroughly than ideas about authority. Authority, the use of power to influence and control, exists in every family, usually in a variety of ways. Parents, of course, exert authority over children. Older children use authority over younger ones. Authority is part of any relationship when work is required, when rules exist for games and family activities, and when children are required to share and cooperate. Since there are so few areas of family life where some application of authority is not present, it is easy to understand why children come to sense authority everywhere in other activities and relationships outside the family.

We have seen that any situation involving drugs, money, or sex is a moral circumstance. That is also true of any situation in which authority is exercised: there is always a possibility in these situations for someone to be helped or hurt. Our children will face these circumstances both when someone has authority over them and when they are exercising authority over others. It is our task to help our children learn to meet these situations in a helpful, moral way.

Standards for the Moral Use of Authority

In a democratic society such as ours, the proper and beneficial application of authority is a matter of considerable public interest. A quick glance at any newspaper or magazine will demonstrate the emphasis we give to situations involving the application of authority. Many of these situations are crimes that result from breaking or abusing the law. Others are abusive applications of authority in business or family life. Still others involve the use of power to help or sustain someone.

In all of these descriptions we can find implied, if not directly stated, a consensus of opinion in our culture about the proper exercise of authority: authority is moral when it promotes the welfare of those who are affected by it, when it is applied with the intention or actual consequence of helping people. Authority is immoral when it is exercised to control others and hurt them by simply maintaining power over them or when it requires those affected to perform immoral acts.

The Role of Parental Authority

As we have seen before, it is one thing to define a standard and quite another to teach it. Perhaps that is somewhat surprising in the case of authority, because experience with authority is such a fundamental part of our lives. At first it would seem that we should have many clear and firm notions about how to teach our children to use and respond to authority. After all, there are few of us who could not clearly describe the way our parents exercised authority, whether they were "strict" or "lenient," for instance, "harsh" or "gentle," or perhaps "consistent" or "inconsistent." Impressions about our parents and their authority over us create our first ideas about our own application of authority. But these ideas are usually not enough to determine exactly how we teach our children. What does determine whether we teach our children to use authority in a moral way is our own strong sense of morality when it comes to authority over our own children. If we start with the commitment to use authority only to benefit or help our children, never to hurt them, then we are on the right track. If we occasionally make mistakes, such as expressing too much anger because of our frustration or weariness, we will compensate for them by the times when we use authority correctly and by the understanding our children have of our intentions to help them. If, however, we are ambiguous about our style of authority or if we often use authority in a way that hurts our children, then we are immoral ourselves. Our actions, which our children observe over a long period, determine whether or not our children come to understand and live the moral standard for authority.

As children, we may not have been permitted to discuss openly with our parents how and why they used their authority over us. Now that we are parents, we are frequently so caught up by the need to regulate our own children that we may respond out of habits learned years earlier. Many of us promised ourselves that when we became parents, we would not do the wrong things our parents did. We then find, to our dismay, that when we are faced with similar situations, we do those very things. By the same token, many of us would like to be able to do the right things our parents did, but we find that our circumstances are different enough to make that difficult. Obviously, relying on our instincts where authority is concerned will not guarantee that we behave in the ways that we want to behave ourselves and that we want to teach our children.

When we carefully examine our ideas about parental authority, it becomes plain that traditions about family authority are readily passed from one generation to another. Remember the man who said, "Yes, I hit my kids. My dad hit me, and I turned out all right. Of course," he added, "I take my rings off before I hit them so I don't mark them." Another man had grown up so frightened of authority that he would not let himself get emotionally close to anyone. His parents had used authority inconsistently and often harshly. He exerted authority over his own children only when his wife pushed him to it, and then it was often excessive. Although he knew something was wrong about what he was doing and wished he could do something else, he was unaware that his aloofness and his abrupt, intense responses were the same actions he openly blamed his father for using with him.

Many others of us, fortunately, had parents who exercised authority in more beneficial ways. Of course, it is possible for people who were treated well as children to mistreat their own children. And it is also possible for children mistreated by the authority of their parents to learn as adults how to apply parental authority in a more moral way. Whether or not we have been blessed with a healthy tradition to follow, we can develop a better style of using authority by becoming aware of how authority was applied during our childhood so that we will better understand what we are likely to do with our own children.

Parental Authority Styles

One widely known description of parental authority involves combinations of control, affection, and anxiety, which form eight types of parental authority. (Becker, 1964.) These eight types are as follows:

Neglecting. Parents use little authority and show little affection and anxiety. Consequently, their children are often delinquent, aggressive, and uncontrolled.

Rigid controlling. Parents use high control with limited affection and low anxiety. Consequently, their children may be shy, socially withdrawn, anxious, and self-punishing.

Democratic. Parents use high affection with limited control and little anxiety. They are warm and supportive of children, and family rules are set by the parents and the children together. Consequently, the children tend to be socially outgoing and may sometimes be viewed as nonconforming. They also tend to find achievement self-rewarding.

Organized effective. Parents exert high control with high affection but little anxiety. Consequently, their children usually have strong consciences, are compliant, and have high standards of excellence. They respect people in authority over them.

Anxious neurotic. Parents use low control and low affection and are very anxious about other people. They often feel they are unable to cope with children. Consequently, their children are also highly anxious, often perform antisocial acts, and may excessively punish others.

Authoritarian. Parents use high control and show much affection but are very anxious. Consequently, their children are often shy but do develop warmth. They often abuse authority over others.

Overindulgent. Parents use little authority but show considerable affection and anxiety. They fear they will frustrate their children's development by rules. Consequently, their children are often independent and manipulative, and they usually have poor consciences. They lack compliance and are aggressive and mischievous.

Overprotective. Parents are very controlling, use considerable affection, and are highly anxious. Their lives are centered on their children. They control by manipulation and by withdrawing their love. Consequently, their children may be compliant and dependent. They develop strong consciences based on guilt because of parents' withdrawal of love.

Considerable research supports the correspondence Becker shows between certain types of parental authority and deviant behavior in children and between the types of parental authority and children who develop strong consciences about right and wrong. When parents fail to organize a family government or are highly inconsistent in showing affection or enforcing rules—when they are negligent, rigid, overanxious, harsh, overindulgent, or overprotective—their children are likely to be confused about the moral use of authority. They will probably develop self-serving attitudes leading to disobedience and have poorly developed consciences.

In contrast, when parents organize a family government that involves children in making rules and when parents are consistent in enforcing the rules and in showing affection, their children are likely to understand the moral use of authority. They will probably develop strong consciences and respond appropriately to authority.

Parental authority is moral when it is not excessive and when it is imposed with affection and little anxiety. Such parental authority uses a few rules clearly defined and firmly enforced, with abundant conversation to explain obedience and disobedience. As children grow older, if they are given greater participation in forming the rules, they will likely accept and comply with parental authority.

How Children Learn about Law and Order

Many police departments now have a public relations program called "Officer Friendly." Representatives present programs at public schools about police activities, hoping that children will develop positive attitudes about police officers and the work they do. These programs were begun in the 1970s after the country went through a period of civil disobedience that was aimed at abuses of authority by many enforcement agencies. As might be expected, much of the disobedience was also abusive and dangerous. Many were shocked to discover the extent of negative attitudes about the police. Those involved in law enforcement learned from this experience that they had not done enough to inform the public about what they did.

Behavioral scientists became involved in finding ways to increase our understanding of the roots of this problem. Some assumed this national frustration was mostly on account of the Vietnam war and the divided loyalties it created. Others looked for family or social causes for the hostility toward the police that many college students displayed. Kenneth Keniston (1965), for example, wrote about youth who were alienated. Their sense of belonging to a community was upset because of economic problems, family conflict, pursuit of intellectualism without the pursuit of supporting values, and participation in rapid and uprooting societal change. Keniston proposed that these conditions led to attitudes that left many young people uncommitted to our system of laws and government: they had developed a pessimism about America.

Keniston at first assumed that youth were troubled primarily because of conditions existing in schools and in government. Further investigation, however, revealed that the attitudes of young people were virtually identical to attitudes expressed by their parents. Keniston was able, therefore, to find a strong relationship between parental attitudes about laws, police, society, and community.

Another noted behavioral and social scientist, Nevitt Sanford (1965), wrote about similar questions, describing how individuals are influenced by events or conditions in society, including the family. Like Keniston, he too found a strong relationship between parents' sense of community (the standards of the community) and four types of criminals, who by definition are examples of the failure of effective moral, social, and family conditioning. His descriptions give us some insight into what we might do to help our children learn a positive sense of law and order.

Presocial criminals are immature and suggestive individuals who are influenced by any group they are with because they have undeveloped abilities to abide the rules and laws of society. The lack of a cohesive family unit where children sense belonging and responsibility to help other family members makes children more vulnerable to the influence of others who do help them feel that they belong. Children gain a sense of cohesion, or belonging, from shared family experiences, including love and affec-

tion, similar work and play experiences, conversations,
sympathy for one another, and respect for parental authority.

Antisocial criminals are individuals who usually have
had conflict with abusive authority and learn to attack it
by disobeying laws and rules. Most antisocial criminals
have had experience with abusive parental authority,
which leaves lasting impressions on children's notions
about law and order. Antisocial criminals often feel justified in breaking a law because they believe that those in
authority are abusive or dishonest. Occasionally, children
reared by abusive parents even believe they are gaining a
measure of revenge or are helping someone by breaking
a law.

Asocial criminals are individuals who have limited
knowledge of laws and organize all their activities toward
satisfying themselves. They may want to be the "big guy"
who displays money and power and indulges in sensual
activities purely to seek gratification. The asocial person is
ignorant of family rules or the need to obey them. Parents'
inconsistency or neglect has much to do with the formation
of asocial attitudes. If we want children to be law abiding,
we must treat our pronouncements with respect ourselves
and ask or insist that our children do likewise. One mother
I know told her child not to eat cookies before lunch. When
the child ran past the room where she was visiting with a
friend, she excused herself to her friend, found the child,
removed the cookie, and reminded him that she meant
what she said. No further punishment or consequence was
necessary. By consistently following through on her "parental requests," she not only showed respect for herself
but also taught her son to respect her and her authority.

Impulsive-addicted criminals are individuals who know
the laws and occasionally respect authority but sometimes
give in to impulses they cannot regulate or control.

Such individuals failed to learn how to regulate their
emotions. They have a good knowledge of the rules or

laws and most of the time are obedient to them. Under certain emotional conditions, however, they cannot control an emotional impulse and at that moment they are disobedient. Our task as parents is to help our children regulate the excessive displays of emotions that appear destructive or are deviant to a family or social rule. We can do this as part of routine family life by insisting that children take "time out" and leave the situation, placing them on a chair, and insisting they stay there until they are calm. We can show in our own behavior examples of emotional control, praise their improved ability to exert control, and teach an overall impression that exercising self-control is the mark of a more mature person.

In summary, children's attitudes about law and order are learned first in families. As parents we have a real and significant role in helping children know the laws or rules and developing a positive attitude about being obedient to them. If we respect proper authority ourselves and teach our children to cooperate with us in forming family laws that benefit all family members, then we can expect our children to learn similar attitudes and skills.

Teaching Children What to Do When Authority Is Used Immorally

We work hard trying to teach our children to be obedient, so it may seem strange to teach them that there may be a time when they need to be disobedient in order to be moral. During their lives, their chances are good that they will have experiences with people who use authority immorally. Sometimes, to be moral, we are responsible to disobey authority that is being used immorally and in some cases to end the authority of those who use it wrongly.

Remember Milgram's famous study in which individuals were told that a laboratory supervisor would take "full responsibility" for whatever happened. Then, looking authoritative in white lab coats and acting the part, these "supervisors" asked the subjects of the experiment to increase the voltage of the shocks even to the point of giving what they thought to be a lethal amount to the person who was the confederate of the supervisor. In this research, if people wished to stop, they were told (1) "It is absolutely essential that you continue," (2) "You have no other choice," and (3) "The lab supervisor will be entirely responsible." Milgram and his associates demonstrated that many individuals would administer what they thought were lethal shocks (in other words, do an immoral thing) if certain conditions were created.

Kohlberg (1983) wanted to learn why some of the individuals in Milgram's study obeyed and why others disobeyed the instructions of the supervisor. He found that people were more likely to disobey this immoral authority when they had a highly developed sense of how their actions affected others. These people understood a "universal principle" of morality that human life is more important than obedience to authority.

London (1980) gives us additional information about people who are willing to disobey immoral authority. He interviewed people who disobeyed the Nazi authorities and helped many Jews escape. London described these individuals as having a very strong attachment to at least one parent. As children they had been forewarned that they might have to make some difficult decisions in the future but always to make the right one. He quoted one man as saying, "My mother said to me when we were small, 'regardless of what you do with your life, be honest. When it comes the day you have to make a decision, make the right one. It could be a hard one. But even the hard ones should be the right ones.' "

We can apply what others have found in order to help our own children know when to disobey authority used immorally. Schulman and Mekler (1985) proposed that parents avoid telling their children, "You should always obey the authorities." Such flat, fixed rules can prevent children from developing the flexibility necessary to respond morally to requests by people in authority over them. It is better for parents to teach their children that each person will be responsible for his or her actions, regardless of who is in authority. Coincidentally, there is a strong connection between having a sense of personal responsibility and being willing to help others.

Next, these writers suggest, we should help our children develop confidence in making their own decisions. Parents who use anger and threats to control children and parents who always make children's decisions are less likely to rear children who have confidence in their own decisions. In contrast, parents can build confidence by asking children to voice an opinion about some matter, accepting their answer without criticism, and asking them to justify their decision or opinion by explaining why they think as they do. Occasionally, we could ask our children questions about the consequences of different choices in order to help them clarify what they think. If we question them with great love and warmth, our children will come to feel that they can make choices without threat to themselves. Parental warmth is very significant.

Many parents have difficulty with their children because they tell them too much of the time what to do, and they often react harshly when children are allowed to choose and then make a mistake. One mother, starting when her children were young, told them, "I will tell you what to do, and you do it!" A man tried to keep a close relationship with his children by never letting them disagree with him or his wife. Ironically, of course, he created more conflict than if he had allowed for disagreement and discussion. Another man asked his children why they had done what was done. After hearing their answer, he replied, "That was stupid. I'll do the thinking around here." Another said that he could not express his feelings very well, so when difficult issues came up between him and a daughter, he pointedly and heatedly stated his opinion about what she should do. Then he withdrew from the conversation, telling her, "I can't make up your mind for you." Of course he hoped that his raised voice would convince her to make the decision he favored. Events in her life proved that she often had difficulty making even the simplest decisions, and many decisions she made were not good for her. It would have been better for everyone had the parents seen decisions as the result of interchange, which may take time but which helps children identify what they themselves think and also learn their parents' opinions.

The more confident children are in themselves, the more likely they will rely on their own judgment when it is time for them to make moral decisions. It is helpful for parents to see children's decisions as part of an ongoing conversation in which we participate with them. We can ask questions, we can ask to make suggestions, we can even point out mistakes in their thinking. After we do all that, we can ask them to state what they have decided in order to make clear both the decision and the decider. In many cases when they themselves have chosen, and chosen well, we can encourage them to do what they have decided.

If they make mistakes, the mistakes need to be understood and talked about rather than only condemned. We can ask children to evaluate their own decisions. We can ask them to find the mistakes, and we can warmly approve of their thinking and encourage them to improve.

Lastly, Schulman and Mekler suggest that parents help children evaluate things on their own. We can teach children to define words they hear by asking, "What does that person mean when he says ——?" Or, while watching a news program on television, for example, we might ask them to evaluate a criminal's statements, a politician's speech, or a schoolteacher's language to help them identify signs of people who can be trusted or mistrusted. Further, we need to help our children ask questions about the statements or behavior of others. Moral authority is usually asserted in the bright light of public opinion and can stand questions. Immoral authority usually is secretive, and those using it often will avoid questioning from others.

We can help our children evaluate the intentions of others by teaching them to ask questions. Asking questions will also help children identify arguments or objections about what those in authority might try to do. We can also help our children evaluate by teaching them that nearly all plans have advantages and disadvantages. Being able to determine both the arguments for and the arguments against something will permit children to make a more reasoned and more moral response.

Helping Children Learn to Use Authority

Responding to authority is only half the authority relationship. Applying authority is the other half. Our children need help also in learning how to use authority in a moral way. They exercise authority during play, at school and other organized activities, with friends, and in other relationships in family and at work.

The moral standard for authority is control or power used to benefit people. Children learn this standard bit by bit. Authority comes into play when children choose games they play, share toys, decide where to play, and so on. Young children, for example, often use decision games to select who is "it." One familiar decision game involves two individuals alternating their hands on a baseball bat with the one getting the top spot being the one to choose. Another is "one potato, two potato," and so forth. These games or rituals help children use authority with a sense of fairness.

As children grow, however, they will be in situations where someone takes, is elected, or is given positions of authority over others. They may become class president, or den leader, or club officer, or patrol leader. In these

official positions they must make decisions that affect others, and, to be moral, they need to do so in ways that will
help and not hurt. That requires that they know some ideas
about people and what people need, what helps others,
and how to organize to bring helpful things into reality.

A group of Scouts met to select their activities for the
next month. Some wanted to go camping in the nearby
mountains, others wanted to go swimming, and some
wanted to visit a new planetarium. The group could do
some of the activities, but they could not do all of them
and still carry out the other parts of their program. The
thirteen-year-old senior patrol leader, faced with the conflicting proposals, asked the adult leader what to do. The
adviser suggested a vote to see what the majority wanted
to do. Most wanted to go camping. A couple of boys looked
discouraged by the vote, however, and the adviser realized
that they did not have camping equipment. He suggested
to the senior patrol leader that he hold a meeting with the
other patrol leaders during the next week to work out the
details. During that leadership meeting, the Scoutmaster
told about the two boys without camping equipment and
presented the problem to the youth leaders. They discussed how to help the two boys find some equipment.
By borrowing a sleeping bag from one boy who had two
and by using some equipment owned by the troop, they
were able to solve that problem. The Scoutmaster, however, raised others. He asked, "How are you going to get
the food organized, the transportation arranged, and a
schedule of activities drawn up?" He suggested that the
leaders divide up the assignments by asking instead of
telling and that they set a time when the assignments
should be completed.

This Scoutmaster understood how to help the Scout
learn to apply authority in a moral way. He helped the
boys get information from those whom the decision would
affect. He helped the leaders be sensitive to others' needs,
and he gave them a method to involve others so everyone

could participate. These same principles can be made a part of families, especially when we are preparing to make a big decision that will affect our children. A family meeting, or council, can be called. We can ask children for their opinions, select an option, and involve each child in the preparations. If we use this process repeatedly, our children will learn this method of applying authority in a helpful, moral way.

Bossy and Clinging Children

Young children have ways to express their feelings about authority. Two of the most common are bossing and clinging.

Bossy children exert control by verbally regulating other children and occasionally their parents. The emotional root of bossy behavior is fear of being controlled. When this fear is accompanied by the example of a controlling older sibling or parent, bossiness is an obvious result. When children between three and seven years of age begin their quest for friendships, they often select friends who will do what they ask. In the case of a bossy child, finding someone to boss around is the primary way they participate in social exchanges.

One six-year-old girl I know of is an excellent example of a bossy child. She told her five-year-old neighbor what to say to her parents, when to speak, how to walk, how to dress, and what the rules were of the games they played, and she required that the five-year-old girl join certain "clubs." Her parents became acquainted with the true nature of this friendship when the five-year-old came home and announced she was a member of the "nasty" club. Their interest piqued, they learned that the six-year-old would not play with the five-year-old unless she agreed to join. The idea of the club seemed innocent enough until the father overheard the friend state that she would be the leader and his daughter would be the follower. The bossiness was so overwhelming in that game that the parents decided to intervene and prevent the two girls from spending much unsupervised time together. Later the parents found that to be in the club, each child had to take down his or her pants in front of the other children. Obviously the parents were happy they had acted earlier.

Bossy children are anxious. They require the response of someone else to feel significant. In the bossy child's early years, bossiness is a form of immoral authority because the bossy child's goal is to find self-gratification (security) rather than to help someone else. This situation deserves attention so that neither the bossy children nor the bossed children are hurt.

A possible solution to bossiness can be to require children to learn methods of cooperation: sharing some plaything or toy, doing small child tasks such as cleaning a bedroom or washing dishes, taking turns in a game, sharing communication by both talking and listening, and taking turns being the leader and the follower.

In some instances bossy children may not learn from cooperating with others and will need to be told directly about bossy behavior and the need to change it. Such a conversation is best held alone with the child in a calm, not an agitated, state. Otherwise, such criticism risks increasing the child's anxiety. Parents can help the bossy child by using speech that is not bossy, such as questions and requests. These can be practiced at meals and at other times until the children have learned them thoroughly.

Clinging children are also anxious, but they manifest their feelings by excessive physical contact and demands on parental time and attention. Clinging is often accompanied by whining and complaining. Often to avoid the guilt or annoyance of these emotional manipulations, parents become unwitting partners in maintaining the clinging behavior. Sometimes we push clinging children away from us because we feel oppressed by their behavior, and we try to anticipate their demands so they won't whine or complain. Children pass through periods of fear and will usually grow out of exaggerated dependence. In such instances, we can make the clinging worse by our own pushing and anticipating behaviors.

When the clinging persists, however, that is an indication that we are too powerful, too volatile in our behavior, or unjust in our discipline. If our evaluation finds these conditions existing in our children, we can understand why they want to stay in our presence for fear we will reject them or leave them unprotected or unprovided for.

Perhaps the best solution for clinging is to recognize that children's fears can be overcome by helping them achieve more on their own. That will require that we examine ourselves and eliminate our own frustration and anger so that they will not be too frightened by us. We can then ensure that we give them enough affection and warmth. Then we can begin to help them gradually move away from us.

At first we insist that clinging children stay close by us, even grasp our legs for thirty minutes each day. This attachment needs to be just as exaggerated as their demands for our attention. Whether you move across the room or to another room or just stand still, require the children to stand close by and touch your leg. Clinging children will soon tire of this and move away. That is exactly what we want. Repeat this procedure a few times, and eventually children will be glad for time alone.

This method works fairly well because clinging children are moving away from us rather than we from them by pushing them away or trying to escape them.

Giving clinging children little projects to do will keep them occupied and involved. One mother of a clinging two-year-old kept some beads and bottles handy so that when her child decided to leave her, he could find these toys and spend time with a familiar activity. Soon he was playing with other toys rather than spending so much time with his mother.

Bratty and Bullying Children

As children grow older, difficulty with authority changes from clinging and bossiness to the rude and insolent behavior we know as bratty and the overaggressive behavior of bullying. Since these behaviors indicate an inappropriate or undeveloped understanding of authority, they too require change to ensure that children better adapt to situations when authority is applied. If we are certain that our use of authority is clearly moral—that it is used to help and not to hurt—then we can fairly, and without hypocrisy, correct our children's behavior.

Bratty children are usually quite talkative, having participated in numerous verbal exchanges with parents. These conversations usually take place when parents tell children to do something the children do not want to do. Their reluctance to obey is shown in their attempt to distract parents by disagreeing and arguing. Such disagreement can become habitual and may be accompanied by rudeness in an attempt to avoid an active, compliant response to the parent's request. When we see rudeness and try to reason with the children, they simply become more adept at countering our explanations, eventually developing a large vocabulary for explanations, reasons for not obeying, and insinuations that we do not have the "right" to tell them what to do. As they grow older, they find additional ways to "show us" that we cannot control them. They often pick out the very things we try to get them to do just to refrain from doing them. If we require combed hair, theirs is messy. If we want them to act appropriately in social situations, they break social rules. If we want chores done, they mess, dawdle, distract, and only comply if forced.

Usually the best way to correct bratty behavior is to recognize that lengthy explanations from us and dialogue with them is not effective except to obtain compliance in the immediate instance. Begin by asking bratty children only twice, and then take steps to begin their movement toward compliance. With younger children, after asking twice, we can take their hand, leading them to the place where they are to perform the task we have asked them to perform. While the task is being done, parents can engage in distracting conversation of their own, telling wild stories or unusual tales so the children have no parental words to react to with words of their own. Sometimes pointing to the work, leaving, and then returning often at brief intervals to inspect is all that will be needed for a younger child to learn that bratty language will not prevent them from having to comply.

If children are very practiced and advanced in their brattiness, more extreme measures may be required, measures that do not involve conversation or traditional forms of punishment. If we attempt to talk with children who are rude and insolent, they will see it as an opportunity to retort and reply, continuing the behavior we want to get rid of. If we use ordinary forms of punishment, bratty children see the punishment as unfair and often seek revenge without having learned to adapt and adjust to authority.

One successful way to impose control that does not involve conversation or a traditional form of punishment is to give the bratty children authority in some task that requires them to be a supervisor and get someone else to perform. School or some other public setting is usually better for this measure than home is. Siblings usually dislike having another supervise them; however, if more than one child is involved, this authority can be given to a different child each week or some other time period. Most bratty children sense that having authority places them in a more powerful position and will willingly accept the authority first. Quite often they learn more trust from having authority and learn to comply more willingly when they have to apply authority to others.

This approach worked well with eleven-year-old Sue,

who was mistrustful and argumentative with her mother. Sue was assigned to work with two children at school. These children, younger than Sue, had mild behavior problems in the classroom and often did not complete their assignments. In cooperation with a teacher and school counselor, Sue was placed in charge of the two children for an hour of tutorial work each week and was expected to consult with the teacher for help. She was told she would get a reward when the two children made progress each week.

At first, she was very kind to the children, and they, hoping to impress her, worked effectively. Everyone was pleased. Then the two "students" became tired of the routine and started to balk. Sue became frustrated and asked the teacher for some help. This experience helped her mature, and she became more respectful to her mother.

If this strategy does not work, sometimes another, equally direct and effective, will. Billy was eight years old, very bratty and disrespectful, the oldest of three children who lived with their single mother. She worked full-time outside the home and was often tired. As is the case for many of us, she had tried to get Billy to perform by talking, explaining, pleading, and yelling. He was immune to all these techniques. He spent most of his time arguing, insulting, and refusing to perform. A few fights had taken place, and both mother and son had hit each other. She was afraid of him and disliked him. He was afraid of her and disliked her.

Because the mother was quite large and physically strong, I suggested to her that she make a sandwich and pour a glass of milk, and then grab Billy and sit on him for forty-five minutes while she ate her lunch. She could sit on him without hurting him by exerting enough weight to demonstrate that she could physically control him.

He, of course, would struggle, but she was to sit on him until the time elapsed. If he had to go to the bathroom, she was to make him beg and only let him up if he promised to return. She was to do this for two or three consecutive days. When she left my office she had renewed hope, a lighter step, a firm glint in her eye, and confidence in her ability to cope.

The next time I saw Billy, his hair was combed and he sat quietly without interrupting. When I asked him if he had made his bed, he nodded assent. Then I asked him what would happen if he did not make it. In very respectful tones, he said with some awe and trepidation, nodding toward his mother, "She will sit on me." Eventually she did not have to sit on him. Along the way he learned such other benefits from complying with authority as warmth and appreciation from his sister and brother.

Like bratty behavior, bullying is also an inappropriate form of responding to authority. It usually stems from unjust or abusive authority having been imposed on children. Children feel very insecure as a result. Bullying is their attempt to increase their self-worth at the expense of a smaller or weaker child. Bullies are often not fully aware of what they are doing, thinking that the force and pressure they apply is "deserved."

We need to be prepared for two cases: first, when our children are the bully and, second, when our children are bullied by someone else.

When our children are the bully, we begin by examining the type of parental authority we ourselves apply and adjust it if necessary to make certain it is not unjust or abusive. We may be abusive if we frequently yell, hit, push, or shove while disciplining our children. We may be unjust if our punishments—spanking, grounding, and so on—are excessive, do not fit the misbehavior of the child, or are imposed without explanation. If abusive parents are unable to change their own behavior, they need to find someone to help them—perhaps a neighbor, a schoolteacher, a minister, or a professional counselor could help. Abusive behavior is destructive and should be changed.

Then parents need to help bullying children feel more secure. The best way to help them is to teach them empathy and concern for others. That can be done by teaching such positive verbal skills as giving compliments, asking attentive questions, and sharing. If we do these things too, they will soon learn that bullying is not as much fun as getting along with others and helping them.

Jacob was a ten-year-old bully. He was large for his age and could be found intimidating other children during recess and after school. He was a difficult child to control at home. One day, after some effort to help him talk freely, his counselor learned that Jacob's father kicked him when he didn't do what he was told. His mother yelled and made him do extra work if he disobeyed or argued with her. During a conference with his parents, they agreed to use other methods of discipline, such as restricting privileges, which Jacob could avoid by practicing doing correctly what he had earlier failed to do. For example, if he fought with his brother, he could be restricted or he could avoid the restriction by playing together with his brother and doing some friendship things. Further, for every problem that arose, Jacob's parents agreed to use conversation as their first attempt to find a solution. That meant that Jacob and one of his parents would sit and discuss what happened and then Jacob would be asked to decide what he would do to improve. He would not be permitted to do anything or go anywhere until he made a choice. The parents also worked with the school counselor to find ways of getting Jacob to help other children. Two weeks later, the bullying had disappeared.

When our children are being bullied, we need other techniques. We should instruct our children to tell us when anyone bullies them. Then, knowing about the situation, we can see if our children contribute to the problem by talking back to or taunting the bully. Next, we can explain that the bully actually needs help and enlist our children's help in finding ways to help the bullying child find more social and emotional support. Taking a child to school and discussing the situation with a schoolteacher, for example, are good ways to let children see that we are attempting to help the bullying child, who is insecure and in need.

If these or similar attempts to help do not work, then it is advisable to inform someone who can help the bully's parents. Usually, unless we believe the parents are constructive in their approach to teaching their children, it does not help to go directly to the parents of the bully. They may already feel great pressure and after learning about the misbehavior of their child, they may apply even more unjust and abusive discipline to the bully. It is best, therefore, to begin the process by talking with someone who can help the parents. A schoolteacher or school counselor is such a person.

One man had tried all these measures and found that his child continued to be bullied. The bullying took place when the children were waiting for the school bus at the beginning and at the end of the school day. He decided to be there at both times, and sometimes he took cookies with him. He gave the cookies to the bully to distribute to the other children and complimented him whenever it was appropriate. After a while he gained this boy's confidence. He talked with the boy about the feelings of the children he bullied and asked if he wouldn't rather be liked than feared. At first the boy denied he had done anything wrong, but this man kindly and warmly continued. After seeing he would not receive harsh treatment, the boy continued to talk and learned to help rather than to try to control or hurt other children.

Rebellious and Overconforming Children

Two improper responses to authority appear during adolescence in the form of rebellion and overconforming. Rebellion is quite well known to many who see their children use chemicals, break laws, and ignore and attack family rules. Overconformity is less well known but appears often enough to be of concern.

Overconformity exists when children drift along without apparent purpose. They may get into trouble because they follow other more aggressive peers. They spend a considerable time in such passive activities as watching television. We are concerned about this behavior because our children seem unproductive, weak, and vulnerable. They are vulnerable, of course, but they often are not weak. Overconforming is a calculated response to parental authority that children believe to be dishonest, hypocritical, or overcontrolling. When children seem excessively compliant, it is usually a message of resentment shown without the risks of open frustration.

Overconformity is immoral because the children exercise no will or initiative and therefore sense little responsibility for what they do. They merely place themselves in situations or are pulled into them and then go along with excessive compliance. Such children express neither opinions, desires, nor preferences. "It's all right with me," their actions say. "Whatever you say." On the surface such agreement might seem pleasant. But these same children must be prodded, pushed, reminded, and retold in order to get them to actually do what they have earlier "agreed" to do.

Overconformity is often difficult to change because it is safe, requires little risk, prevents parents from being harsh (until we can't stand it any longer), and it works. That is, it works as a form of retaliation. When it seems necessary to help children out of overconformity, we may try to encourage or coerce them, give them more freedom, ignore them, wait them out, lecture to them about being "weak," and then find that none of these tactics work.

We must approach the problem of overconformity without focusing direct attention on the overconforming behavior of the children. If we do give attention to it, we may actually reinforce what we don't want. If we tell children they comply too much and that we want them to change, they will agree to change and conform to our new request—which, of course, is a continuation of the old problem. Instead, we can use the cause of the problem of overconforming to help solve it.

The best solution is a form of paradox and confusion— we do something different from what we say. This solution requires a little acting, but if it is done with warmth and concern, it will not hurt. The goal is to get children to act on their own to make their own way in life. Several forms of inconsistency may be used. We can make two contradictory requests of them and then act as if we are unaware that we have done so. If and when they point out the contradiction, disagree at first, ask for explanation, and then make an adjustment without pointing out that they have acted responsibly. Sometimes we can say one thing— "I want you to work in the yard today"—and later tell them to do something else. Overcompliant children like to point out our inconsistencies. To invite continued conversation, we can mildly disagree and get them to add proof. Finally, when "cornered," we admit our mistake, but we do not point out that the children are doing something responsible.

Because overcompliant children like to notice our faults, we can announce to them that we think we are the possessors of an obvious trait—for example, hardworking, generous, happy—then act in ways that contradict the trait we have said we have. This intentional hypocrisy invites overconforming children to step out of their passivity in order to correct our hypocrisy.

We can ask them what they would "like to do," which most often will receive the answer, "I don't know" or "I don't care." Then we can act as if we do know exactly what they want and appear as if we are going to supply it. Usually overconforming children will respond to our actions by telling us what they really do want. When we make exaggerated assumptions with overconforming children, they quickly act and become responsible in order to correct our opinion.

Occasionally, overconforming children do things that are deviant and do them with their friends. Their excessive compliance allows them to feel that they are not as responsible for what happened as the others are. At such times it is often difficult to avoid lecturing when we attempt to tell them what will happen if they get into trouble. It is wise, however, to reduce "telling." They will learn about consequences only if they actually experience them. If they break the law—usually they commit misdemeanors at first—then let the law run its full course. If they break a rule at school and receive some punishment, it is usually best to allow the school authorities to fulfill completely the terms of any consequences.

Overconformity may require some professional help to change. It is wise to recognize it as a problem that will not go away by itself and may have scarring effects on the moral development of children. To resolve overconformity, children must feel an improved sense of security and be able to talk about their anger and their disrespect for parents. Then children can be helped to appreciate the need to have a greater sense of personal responsibility.

Rebellion, like overconformity, is a complex and complicated problem. It is often an attempt by children to communicate that they angrily reject parental authority because we use it too much or use it too little. We accelerate our efforts to control our children because we think they need it, but then we discover that they accelerate their attempts to avoid control by doing the very things we wish they would not. In some cases, parents are joint creators of their children's rebellious behavior. Most often, however, rebellion stems from family conflict when children have friends who encourage them to deviate or rebel against family rules. To help children develop a moral response to authority, we need to fully understand how to prevent the family conflict that promotes rebelliousness.

Parental authority associated with rebellion is harsh and abusive, inconsistent because parents vary excessive power with overindulgence, or uncertain because parents disagree and children cannot discover what family rule to follow.

Authority can be made reasonable, consistent, and united when parents express warmth to children and use conversations to solve problems, plan activities, and correct mistakes. Parents can read books to get new ideas about child discipline and seek professional help in attempting to regulate children who are erratic or explosive. Further, use of authority can be adapted as children mature. Some parents find these suggestions easy to apply because they experienced them as children. Others find showing warm affection and "talking" with children very difficult. There is, however, a fairly direct and effective way for motivated parents to develop the ingredients of parental authority and prevent rebellion.

It begins by recognizing the relationship that exists between us and our children. This relationship is filled with feelings for one another because we are important to our children and they are important to us. Except for the very hardened and indifferent, this relationship grows naturally through the many shared moments of family life from a child's birth onward throughout our lives. Children are affected by us and we are by them.

As children grow, we prevent rebellion by adapting our relationship with them. In their early years, we impose authority in the form of consistent expectations, consequences, and some family rules. As the children mature and we talk with them and teach them, our imposition of authority needs to be adapted so that they are required to make choices themselves and participate responsibly in a pleasant and positive relationship with us.

Mark and Janice developed a parental approach based on these ideas. When each of their children reached puberty, the parents held a private conversation with them in which the parents asked, "Would you rather have a lot of rules or have a good relationship with us?" Even without being able to articulate what a good relationship with parents might mean, they chose that option because, like most children, they were tired of school, family, and social rules. Most children do not usually realize that parents are tired of rules also because we have to enforce them or make decisions about them. Parents, too, prefer a good relationship.

Mark and Janice Thompson told their children that a good relationship involves *communication* to keep the people in the relationship informed and making decisions together; *trust*, which is created and maintained by people saying what they will do and then doing what they say; *affection and respect,* which the people in the relationship show to one another; and *time* they spend together. The rules of the relationship, the children were told, are a little more difficult to learn than the rules they had lived by previously, but in a good relationship they will have more freedom and so will the parents.

From this point, the parents assumed the children must learn how to be participants in such a relationship, and they used family events to teach them. For instance, when children asked to go somewhere or do something, they heard, "Well, let's sit down and talk it over together and decide what to do." During these conversations the parents asked the children what they thought and then shared their own thoughts, too. Through questions, they learned what the children planned to do, when they planned to be home, who they were going with, and how they were getting from one place to another. A decision was made together. Sometimes, of course, children could not do what they wanted. Then the parents stated their opinion, gave reasons for it, and maintained it. In a good parent-child relationship, parents and children are not equal. As parents we are still responsible to use our wisdom, and sometimes we must regulate what the children do.

Jenny Thompson was old enough to drive and had taken the car to a high school basketball game. She told her parents she would be home by 10:30 P.M. She called at that time and told her parents that her plans had changed. She was at her friend's house and "having a lot of fun." She wanted to stay longer. Earlier Jenny and her parents had agreed that if anyone changed plans, to promote trust that person should tell the others as soon as possible.

Mr. Thompson asked what time Jenny would be home. Since it was Friday, she said, "Twelve o'clock." He suggested, "Twelve-thirty," but she insisted, and so he agreed. When she was not home by the time they had agreed upon, he went to get her. He was in the garage getting into their second car when Jenny drove in. Seeing him there and assuming he was angry, she said, "I guess I won't be able to drive for a while, huh?"

"I don't know why not," he replied. "You are a good driver."

"Then why are you out here?" she wondered.

He reminded her about the relationship. "I was coming to get you. You made a promise to me. Our relationship is based on trust, and I just wanted to see if you cared about it."

Jenny said that she did. They talked for a minute and then each went to bed. The next week, Jenny asked to use the car again. Her dad asked her about her plans. They were similar to the ones of the previous week. He then inquired, "When will you be home?"

"Twelve o'clock," Jenny answered. Rethinking, she quickly adjusted and said, "Twelve-fifteen."

"That would be all right with me," he answered.

When 12:15 A.M. came, Jenny was in the house. Her parents thanked her for being someone they could trust.

All this may seem somewhat impractical until we appreciate that the Thompsons were very serious about teaching their children to participate in this relationship and using it as a means of exerting control. They understand that control goes both ways, and children have control, too. Such two-way control prevents children from feeling mistreated and ignored because they can get many of the things they want by consulting with their parents rather than by rebelling against them or manipulating them.

The key to their success was that the Thompsons told of their own feelings in a very personal way and asked their children to do the same. There was a genuine attempt by both parents and children to understand and be understood and to show warmth and affection. The information collected from these personal conversations was often used in making decisions together.

The day Johnny was cut from the basketball team during tryouts, he came home discouraged and angry at the coach. He would not talk with anyone at first, but later he told his parents about it. The next day, Mr. Thompson left work, picked up his son from school, and took him to lunch. They talked about the situation. The father had a chance to give support and show his concern and love, and Johnny didn't go out and get drunk to show his displeasure or do something to gain revenge. They handled his disappointment together.

The Thompsons were successful in teaching their children to participate in this relationship, even though it took several years to make it work smoothly. We can see the advantages for the children's future as well as seeing why the children would not want to rebel from this form of parental authority. Further, this method did exert control and allowed both parents and children to influence each other.

Having a good relationship with our children requires us as parents to satisfy its conditions, too. Obviously it takes conscious work and patience for us to show our children that we want them to have this sort of relationship with us and enjoy it. It is unfortunate that we often do not show this commitment until our children have made it impossible to ignore them and what they do by performing rebellious acts. Then we must pay for counseling, pay for damages, and pay emotionally by watching them do destructive things. It is wiser—and easier—for us to prevent rebellion in the first place by paying attention, giving warmth, learning to participate in conversations, expressing our feelings in words, and learning to trust and be trusted. But no matter what stage of development our children are in, we can start now to improve our communication with them, build mutual trust, express our affection and respect for them, and spend more time doing things together.

CHAPTER 11

WORK: AT HOME, AT SCHOOL, OR IN THE MARKETPLACE

When we use our physical strength or mental faculties to achieve a certain objective or result, we call what we are doing *work*. Experiences with work present moral circumstances to our children, and children learn their first ideas about work at home.

Attitudes toward work and work-related behaviors are first learned when families divide the labor that must be done in order to survive and succeed as a family. Such family activities as cleaning the house, doing the laundry, preparing food, cleaning up after meals, and doing yard work all present opportunities for parents to expect children to contribute to the common effort and to assign work to them so they do contribute. Experiences at school are a very natural extension of such experiences in the family because children are required to do work there, too, and, perhaps for the first time in their lives, their work is judged by someone outside the family. When children later enter the work force as adolescents or adults, many of the attitudes and working skills they first learned at home and in school are applied in the marketplace to jobs and careers.

As children grow up, work helps them develop concepts about responsibility and dependability. Work gives them opportunities to tell the truth and give honest effort or to cheat and lie. It leads to their developing a standard of excellence that will motivate them to a high level of performance, or it leads them to an attitude of just "getting by," by apologizing and giving excuses to look acceptable to others. Children may learn to work independently, starting and finishing work by themselves, or they may always require some supervision to work effectively at all. Some may concentrate on the result of their efforts and disregard other aspects of their work such as co-workers, friends, family, and enjoyment of the work itself. They may even hurt others in order to achieve a valued goal. Others may be so distractable that they fail to develop constructive plans and so produce little in their lives.

I was very impressed when I heard somewhere that three characteristics of a mature person are being able to start and finish work without being supervised, being able to carry money without spending it, and being able to withstand an injustice without seeking revenge. I have mentioned these characteristics to many others, and they too have seemed impressed. Once I asked someone what impressed him about these ideas, assuming that he would be most interested in the third, as I was. I was surprised that he focused on the first. That one, he said, gave him the most difficulty with his children.

It gives employers much difficulty, too. American retailers, for example, estimate that 20 percent of potential profits are stolen from them by their own employees. Time management consultants have found that many individuals working in offices near several co-workers actually work effectively only six hours of each eight-hour workday. The rest of the time is spent on breaks, social conversations, and other distractions. It has been estimated that employee absence, much of it for invalid reasons, costs business and industry thirty billion dollars a year. (Johns, 1987.)

Students' behavior in schools indicates similar attitudes. Most students in high school confess to cheating by using crib sheets for exams, handing in papers written by others, copying one another's homework assignments, and feigning illness to gain more time.

If we assume that children first learn work habits and

attitudes at home, then what we teach them about being responsible, dependable, and moral in their work will have a lasting effect on them. Such habits and attitudes will in large part influence the quality of their work at school and on the job.

A Standard for Work

Most of us could easily identify the community standard for work. Much in our national character is related to initiative, hard work, productivity, individualism, dependability, inventiveness, and creativity. As a result, most Americans believe it is good to be hardworking and responsible, to complete work without supervision from others, and to give honest, dependable effort and time in return for wages received. We also recognize the immorality of not giving honest effort, of wasting time, of embezzling or other forms of stealing from employers, or of hurting others in order to advance ourselves.

As parents we can set a standard of work for our children that includes *independence*, so that children can see the results of their own efforts; *thoroughness* in doing work well and completely; *dependability*, which includes a sense of duty to perform work; and *responsibility*, which suggests that work is a reflection or an extension of the person who does it and that work itself can be enjoyable and satisfying.

Current social conditions can make teaching this standard somewhat difficult. Affluence and complexity of work can make it difficult for children who are forming work habits to see the importance of the work they do and to see connections between what they do, how they do it, and the results they achieve. I was reared on a farm, and I learned at a very early age that the work I did was important to my family. It was work that needed to be done, and if I did not do it, someone else had to. If I had been assigned something, it was obvious to me and to my parents whether I did it or not, and how well I did it was obvious, too. Very few children nowadays have a chance to see connections this direct between work and "important" results. Large classes in school and complex business institutions tend to hide individual efforts. When people believe that others will not notice what they do or when they think that what they do has little importance, they can have difficulty learning a moral standard for their work.

Then, too, parents are somehow extra busy these days. We may be single parents working long hours to provide for children and then coming home tired and having to face cooking and cleaning. Even if there are two parents, it is likely that both have jobs outside the home. To teach our children effectively and to make certain they follow through with their assignments, we have to communicate with one another in the midst of busy schedules. If one or both parents get caught up in other demands, children may be left to their own devices, which usually do not include doing "work." Even if one parent does not have an outside job, the rounds of carpools, children's activities and lessons, civic duties, church and volunteer responsibilities, and the like also press upon us, and we may hope that someone else in church or school is compensating for what we are not teaching our children about work. Nevertheless, taking enough time consistently to teach and reinforce moral standards will prevent our needing to spend even more time later to correct immoral behavior that results from what our children do not know. Examples of immoral standards about work abound in our society, and our children will be hurt by them and will hurt others by following them if we do not prepare them to do otherwise.

Since much of our own work probably takes place away from the observations of our children, they might not be able to learn morality in work merely from our example, even if we live by a high moral standard on the job. We must find ways, then, to share cooperative experiences with our children so that they can learn honest effort, responsibility, and dependability in a setting where they

can see what we do, show us what they do, and learn that
what we all contribute is important to our family.

Anyone who knows a person who can work but refuses
to, or a person who has grandiose plans for getting rich
quick, also knows a spouse, children, and possibly many
others who suffer from such a person's behavior. In one
instance I know of, two businessmen made unreasonable
promises to shareholders who were persuaded to take second mortgages on their homes in order to reap promised
rewards of high interest. The deceit of these two businessmen combined with the investors' hopes of quick financial gain cost these investors millions of dollars. Six
hundred fifty families were affected. Many lost their
homes, uprooting their families and forcing them to adapt
to a much different standard of living.

Situations such as this one are dramatic evidence of
the need for renewed effort in teaching the basic value of
honest, responsible, and dependable work that will help
and not hurt others. That standard of performance takes
time to teach, but the result is certainly worth the effort.

Work and School

School probably provides the first opportunity most
children have to work for someone outside the family. At
school, children have "jobs" to do and are "paid" (in recognition, awards, grades) for their efforts. They have to
report on time and stay till "closing"; they have "breaks"
(recess, lunch, class breaks) and vacations. Because school
is such an obvious preparation for later work not only in
content but also in structure, we can reasonably expect
that children whose performance in school is dishonest
and irresponsible will carry the same lack of personal standards into their paying jobs.

And these paying jobs can come quite early. There is
a growing trend for teenagers to combine paying jobs and
school. This attempt brings them to choices that can them-

selves become moral issues. Teenagers who have cars, for example, often must choose between spending time studying and spending time working to pay for car expenses. Other children work to have money for clothes, dates, tape players, and so on. All of these children are making decisions that illustrate their values about the importance of learning relative to the importance of possessions.

A disturbing trend in students' values is that instead of university study being seen as the way to improve one's mind and character, to acquire knowledge about ideas, people, technology, and the world, schoolwork seems to be seen by the average college student as the way to get things, to acquire attractive and impressive possessions. The goal for many students, then, is not to "know" but to "get"—good grades and a good job afterwards. If such students have little appreciation for the value of honest learning in order to be well informed and well educated, it is easy to see how they can rationalize cheating and lying as a legitimate means of achieving grades and graduation. What kinds of behavior can we expect from such people later in their jobs or careers?

Responsible and Dependable Work

Although some children seem naturally to value and appreciate their own accomplishments, such attitudes are not universal. Many children will just as naturally think it is all right to be lazy or to spend all of their time playing.

I don't know what I would have valued "naturally." Life on my father's farm was mostly work, and that is what I learned. Growing up, I assumed that everyone else had to get up early and often work late. During my first year at college I learned otherwise. Many slept in until late morning or early afternoon, missing classes and assignments. This, they said, was because they were up late the night before. Their statements surprised me because I had learned that farm work must be done whether one stays up late or gets to bed early: animals must be fed and crops and fields must be tended. To fit in with my roommate, I tried to sleep late sometimes, but I was never able to sleep much past eight o'clock, and I had to work hard to sleep until then. I just "naturally" woke up at 6:00 or 6:30 A.M., as I always had. When they found out this fact, some of my friends in the dormitory began to avoid me.

Children can learn early that work is a regular part of life and, in my opinion, they are better off for knowing that. Because work and achievement are significant building blocks of self-esteem and self-confidence, we can include work in our moral training of children by giving them chores, especially those that require them to care for themselves. Cleaning bedrooms, helping to prepare meals, and helping to keep their clothing organized are appropriate chores. Whether or not children comply with our requests to perform their chores depends on our doing several things:

Make the work significant and important. We need to show our children how their efforts will help others and will help them feel good about themselves.

Show the children how to do the assignment successfully. We often only have time to tell children what to do, and we fail to teach them a standard of how to do it well. We can best help them to do something well by showing them in small specific steps how to do it—for example, making their beds one sheet and one blanket at a time—until the final result is achieved.

Use incentives or positive reinforcement and avoid excessive criticism. Children often enjoy earning rewards for what they do. We can begin teaching a new task to children by associating a reward with it. Children will keep their rooms clean in order to earn a family activity such as a picnic, a movie, or an outing. These incentives can be gradually removed as work efforts become habits.

Put undesired work before desired privilege. Bedmaking,

homework, or dishwashing can precede reading for pleasure or watching television.

*Avoid distracting arguments from children by being calm and
knowing how to get compliance.* If we ask children to do
something and then they argue and demand reasons, we
should either walk away or state encouragement: "You
may think you can't do this, but I know you can," or "I
know that you might be unhappy now, but you will feel
better when you are busy." In extreme cases of refusal to
perform, children may need to spend time sitting on a
chair because they "cannot control themselves" and perform their tasks. They can get off their chair when we think
they are ready to comply.

Build a worker's identity in children. We tell our children
about their ability to get things done, and we tell others,
too. We help children understand that achievement is a
highly valuable part of what they think about themselves.

There are, of course, many other techniques that may
be tried in order to get children to work. Most succeed at
least some of the time as long as they do not involve abusive
anger and harsh punishments, which might get children
to work but will not teach them moral work behavior.

Independent Work and Task Completion

We can teach children to work responsibly on their
own and to finish tasks without supervision. We can begin
teaching this concept when they are very young. At age
two or three years, most children begin to want to do things
for themselves and push us away in order to dress themselves, tie their own shoelaces, and the like. We can encourage and promote those actions. Some children, however, seem to like having us do things for them and will
make concerted efforts to bring it about. For these children,
we might do a few things as a cooperative gesture, but if
they want more and more from us and a pattern of asking

develops, we should begin to make our help cost them something.

One young child wanted her mother to dress her for school every day and refused to get ready on time unless her mother helped her. The mother dressed the child but created some discomfort by putting the child in an uncomfortable position in order to dress her and by dressing her incorrectly—buttoning things improperly, putting pants on backwards, and so on. After a few days, the child stopped asking for help. Because the mother could not be relied on to dress her the way she wanted to be dressed, the child had to learn to rely on herself.

Too often, children will train us by working only when we are near and attentive to them. In that way they can prolong our contact with them, which they value. If we reinforce them in this behavior, we should not be surprised to find that they might only work when the schoolteacher stands by them or gives them individual attention. These children are not self-starters. They need help in learning to work independently, and we need to learn how to give them this help.

Independence in work means being able to start and finish without excessive supervision. We are interested in teaching them independence because we want better performance from our children and less hassle getting it. In addition, helping children to start and finish work independently is the primary means of teaching them responsibility and dependability, two other parts of our moral standard for work.

Two techniques effectively teach independent work habits: "leave and return" and "unexpected reinforcement." "Leave and return" is easy. After starting children on some task, we tell them we are leaving and will return in a few moments to see how they are doing. We leave the room, usually for a few seconds, and then return. If they are working, we praise them and hug them and look at what they are doing. Then we repeat the procedure.

We gradually lengthen the time between leaving and re-turning and vary it so that children cannot accurately pre-dict when we will return. Always we show interest in their work. If they are not working when we return, we simply direct their attention to what needs to be done without criticizing them for dawdling or being lazy and leave again. Doing this when children are young will help them learn to work by themselves.

Unexpected reinforcement is a little different. When children are working, and only then, we interrupt them at their work and reward them unexpectedly. One parent starts her daughter at piano practice. She leaves for a few minutes and then waits until she hears her child playing. Then she returns with some reward, perhaps a small piece of candy, a loving embrace, a compliment. These unex-pected rewards encourage children to continue working; if they are not working, they receive no reward. Persistence will come to have pleasant associations for a child, and eventually the rewards will be less important.

Children also benefit by learning that responsibility often means finishing what they start. Some tasks, how-ever, are not worth finishing, and children will need help in knowing which are and which are not. Some of us tell children they must always finish what they start, so they feel pressure and guilt if they quit. The father of a Little League baseball player tried at first to make his son finish the season when he announced he wanted to quit. But after listening to the boy tell about the coach yelling, swear-ing, and shoving the boys, the father went to a practice to see for himself. What he saw helped convince him that his son would be better off away from the situation.

Instead of requiring that children finish everything they start, we teach them to make responsible choices about when to continue a task and when to quit. We can help them take the following things into account: What are the expectations for a task? Are they clearly explained? What promises were made at the time the task was begun? What are the consequences for the children and other people involved if the children finish? if they stop? By helping children answer these questions, we can teach them to make good choices about completing tasks or quitting before they have finished.

Competition and Cooperation

Most of us grew up with the idea that we would have to compete—for grades in school, for positions on athletic teams, for the jobs or careers we want. We read motivational stories about people who successfully competed in business, had the "winning edge," and won. We temper this emphasis on competition by emphasizing "teamwork," so that the pressure of competition stays within useful limits. Children are asked, for example, to be good "team members" on their athletic teams and in learning groups in school. The same team effort will be required later in the work place.

Competition and cooperation are thus mixed in a curious way. In some situations we are expected to compete as individuals—in playing golf, for instance, and for grades in school. In other situations we cooperate as a small group to compete with other groups. There are also times when we cooperate individually with others to achieve together, as in a school project or when several people help a neighbor in need.

As a result of these experiences and others like them, most children learn both competitiveness and cooperation. A problem arises when some children learn excessive competitiveness, so that every task is begun with the idea that there will be one winner, and the one with the best performance will be it. Many parents unwittingly contribute to this mindset in their children. For example, because parents understand the importance of grades in the competition for scholarships and admission into the best colleges, they may put great pressure on their children for high performance. Schools can add to this pressure by grouping children according to achievement levels and making children aware of status difference based on performance ("turtle" and "bluebird" reading groups, for instance). Schools may also publicly rank students, which further emphasizes competition and adds pressure. If competition is excessive or is expected in many different situations, children may come to feel that their worth as human beings is related to winning, and they may fail to recognize the kinds of performance that will build lasting self-esteem.

Such children have a sense of rightness based on winning and in some cases are willing to cheat themselves and others to attain that goal. These individuals may compete even when cooperation is called for. They may ignore the idea that if they always compete and win, then others will always lose. They may suffer from a lack of friends and social success. They fail to understand how to combine individual performance with consideration for other people.

Competition thus becomes a way of life for some and may affect close or emotionally intimate relationships. Overzealous competitors will, for instance, act as if there are limited amounts of love and warmth and will compete for these because they want to be the ones to get them. They are surprised when their competitive approach produces suspicion and resistance with the result that they receive less love and warmth than they would otherwise have received. Such competitive people live with excessive amounts of performance anxiety and look to find life's rewards from the thrill of beating someone else.

Competition among children has been justified by the assertion that it seems to motivate them to higher performance and is effective at teaching individual responsibility. Alfie Kohn (1987), however, has suggested that the facts do not support this assumption. According to Kohn, competition is a less effective motivator than enjoyment of a

task and an internal standard of performance that children
are trying to reach. Children will perform better, Kohn
says, if they believe that their performance will help others
and that others depend on them to do well. These cooperative efforts increase self-esteem and build better social
relationships.

One objection to cooperative efforts is that group accomplishment often depends on the efforts of a few hardworking individuals while others sit back, give less, and
benefit from the work and efforts of others. When children
are expected to work together or cooperate to clean rooms,
wash dishes, and solve school problems, some will do less
than others but expect the same reward. For that reason,
parents, schoolteachers, and employers tend to be somewhat afraid of cooperation. If parents and teachers accept
a moral standard of work, however, and are dedicated to
teaching it to children, they will be able to help children
learn that taking unfair advantage of the work of others is
not cooperation. It is possible to use even those situations
that are unavoidably competitive to teach the kind of responsibility and dependability that cooperation demands.
One form of that is "good sportsmanship." When they are
faced with problems at school or work, people who know
how to function only in a competitive mode often assume
that they must work everything out alone. They fail to see
other people as potential helpers, and they fail to understand how one's own happiness and self-esteem can be
built by helping others achieve.

There is some evidence that failure to cooperate results
in lower performance both at school and later at work.
Kohn (1987) describes how learning situations that require
children to cooperate result in higher performance as well
as increased self-worth and better social skills. Researchers
studying the effectiveness of cooperation in Japanese work
organizations reach the same conclusions: cooperation results in a high level of worker satisfaction and productivity.
The key both in school and at work seems to be learning

how to cooperate in order to develop a real sense of making a contribution and a desire to act responsibly so that others will be helped rather than hurt.

It should be obvious to us as parents that we are preparing our children to act morally when we teach them that they have a significant contribution to make to other family members and must act responsibly in making that contribution. Both schools and workplaces are moving toward increased cooperation as the means of improving students' and workers' performance. We are seeing increasing emphasis on including in the individual preparation of students and employees the skills to cooperate with others in learning and producing.

We have many opportunities to teach children cooperation. A warm and loving family life depends upon our taking advantage of these opportunities. Members of families that do cooperate have a sense of belonging, an appreciation of individual importance, and a strength not found in the families who exclusively emphasize competition. The following suggestions will help parents teach children to cooperate:

Every individual is important and has something to give everyone else. When parents take time to talk with children about the abilities of all family members—at mealtime, for example—it is possible to help family members identify what each one contributes to the family. In my family, Jeremy brings us a happy sense of humor, Jennifer contributes sensitivity, Jon gives determination to whatever he attempts, and Ashley brings warmth and fun. Dad and Mom provide love and security. We also tell our children that each one can give what the others give, too, so no one is held back or limited. We often have a short program on Monday nights called family home evening. We organize these evenings so that every person contributes something. One leads us in a song. Another offers a short prayer. Someone is assigned to teach us a short "saying" that we all repeat. These sayings are usually motivating and teach a sound idea—for example, "A smile is a curved line that sets things straight." Another person demonstrates a "good manners" technique—for example, a boy standing to show respect when a woman enters the room. Someone presents a short lesson or a game to play, and someone else chooses and prepares refreshments. Everyone has a part in the program. We hope each one learns that he or she makes an important contribution.

Cooperative work. Children can be assigned chores that require each of them to do some part in order to complete the whole project. One family, for example, requires that children help with the evening dishes: one sets the table, one clears the table and sweeps the floor, another rinses the dishes and then washes them or puts them into the dishwasher, and another cleans the pots and pans and puts them away. Together they all share in completing a task that would be more difficult if only one person did it. Each one depends on someone else, and each one makes a contribution.

Cooperative planning. Shared family time is something that each family member can make a contribution to. Parents can begin some activities by discussing what each person, including the parents, would like to do for a short trip, a long vacation, or just one evening. (The conversation itself shows cooperation as much as doing whatever activity is chosen.) Then, after a decision is made, all can be asked to do part of the work. A picnic, for example, can involve some in preparing the car, some in buying the food, some in fixing it, and some in organizing games. After a few practice sessions like this one, children readily accept the morality of cooperation.

Noncompetitive motivation. We should not use competition to motivate children. Trying to get children to do routine things is often a hassle that some of us tire of, and we may use competition to motivate them. Getting two children to race to see who can be first to brush their teeth or get their pajamas on works to get the teeth brushed or the pajamas on. The children will run to avoid losing; however, there is always a loser. If competition between children is used to motivate them, we can expect them to argue, be less cooperative, and separate themselves from one another because of the tension they feel. It is generally better to motivate in ways that permit everyone to win, with a race against the clock, for instance, instead of against one another. We can also tell children to achieve one thing (brushing teeth), so that they can participate in the next thing (reading a bedtime story.)

If we apply these other "cooperative strategies," we will generally find that children begin to work better alone, as well as together. They will have a sense of cooperativeness, enabling them to go to school and feel like they belong.

When we do not teach cooperative strategies, our children may develop characteristics like Ronnie Hamilton's. One day his second-grade teacher asked all the children to divide into groups of five. She gave each group a strip of butcher paper and asked them to draw five turkeys. She told the children that each member of the group was to draw a part of every turkey. The children talked among themselves and decided who would draw the head, the body, tail feathers, legs and feet, and who would add color. Most groups decided to take turns so that each child could draw his or her part of each turkey. Everyone knew how to cooperate except Ronnie. He insisted that he draw his own turkey. All of it. The other four children in his group were frustrated at first, but eventually they let him do what he wanted—they could not do otherwise—and they went to work on the other four turkeys. Ronnie worked alone while the others talked with each other about what each was doing.

When they were asked to show the drawings to the other students, Ronnie made a big point of telling which was his turkey. Although he was accepted by some of the children, it was possible to feel tension and discomfort for

him with those in his group. When it was time for recess,
he stayed behind the others, almost as if he knew he did
not quite belong.

When Children Don't Complete What They Start

As parents know, most young children can easily be
distracted. When they are preschool age, their being distracted is more acceptable than it is when they reach the
age of being asked to perform school tasks or family chores.
Then we want them to be able to give attention to the task
until it is completed.

Behavioral scientists have noticed that from birth children differ in the amount of sustained attention they are
able to give something. This ability is called "selective attention," meaning that children can focus on one thing
while disregarding others. As the human brain develops
and becomes more effective, selective attention usually
increases. Some children, however, remain distractable
and cannot easily finish what they start. In more extreme
cases, these children may be diagnosed by a doctor or
school psychologist as having Attention Deficit Disorder
(ADD) or as hyperactive.

Whether their condition is extreme or not, children who
cannot work to finish what they start are not only frus-
trating to us and disadvantaged when asked to perform,
but they are also somewhat more susceptible to temptations that lead to immoral behavior. If children can forget
to finish a school assignment or family chore, they can
forget they have a moral standard of some kind when
confronted with a pleasurable distraction. In the interest
of promoting morality, it is important for us to help children acquire the ability to finish what they start or at least
to reduce their distractibility.

Parents can use some specific techniques to increase
children's task-completion skills. First, we can emphasize
the importance of finishing by making certain that children

know what the finished product of their work looks like. We can, for instance, show them what a clean room looks like, what a completed homework assignment is. Then we can reinforce children when they complete their work. "Work until you finish," we might say, or "Finish what you start." Praise and affection are usually enough reinforcement, but more tangible rewards, such as books to read or toys to play with, are also helpful.

Second, we need to recognize that children can learn selective attention by developing some related cognitive skills. These include vigilance, or paying attention to the details of a task. Teaching vigilance simply requires that we ask children to notice what they will need to complete work. We can, for example, give children milestones to notice when they are one-fourth completed, one-half completed, three-fourths completed, and completed. We can also help them identify the tools that are required to complete their work. School work requires pencil, books, papers, crayons, and the like. Chores at home require specific steps, which might be written in a list to begin with.

Third, children can be punished for being distracted by having to rehearse doing it right. Sam's mom used this approach. One day when Sam did not complete a chore that he was asked to do, his mother talked with him about the importance of finishing what he started and then asked him to perform some simple sorting tasks (paper clips from safety pins). After he had demonstrated that he could complete that task, he was asked to return to his original chore and to work until he finished.

Fourth, self-commands are useful. When showing children how to do something, we can request that they whisper instructions to themselves. "Make your bed; pick up the clothes and put them in the hamper; vacuum the floor; put toys away." When children whisper these commands over and over, they become self-commands that can influence behavior when we are not around to supervise.

When Children Cheat

As children grow they are faced with many more performance opportunities. These necessarily involve supervision by parents, teachers, and, later on, employers. Sometimes children mistakenly learn that the approval of others is more important than what they are to learn or the work they are asked to do. In cases when children have not been responsible, they may dishonestly try to gain approval by cheating. The two most common forms of cheating are lying to give an acceptable excuse and claiming someone else's work as one's own.

We can help children learn a standard of performance that precludes cheating and lying by following some simple procedures. One is to have the children evaluate their own performance, explaining what was good or not so good about it. That will help them acquire the notion that they must be concerned about their own actions as much as they are about the opinions of other people. Children between the ages of six and twelve can easily learn to examine their own work and tell how they feel about it. We might ask them to tell us what they have done well, what they did not do so well, how they feel when they do something well, and how they feel when they do less well.

Another procedure is to help children predict what level of achievement they think they can obtain by their efforts. Instead of telling them what we think they can do, we can ask them to tell us what *they* think they can do. That helps them understand that they are to live up to a standard they set themselves. Then, after they have evaluated what they have done, we can ask them to make a prediction on another task.

For example, when they are working math problems, we might ask, "How long do you think this will take you?" "How many problems do you think you will get correct?" "Do you like to make your work neat?"

After they have finished the task, we can ask them how

their performance matches their predictions. In some cases we may need to show a standard of performance and let children know we want them to admire it.

The times when children are caught cheating are useful times for us to emphasize our opposition to it. Researchers have attempted to investigate why some children cheat and why others do not when they are given the same opportunity. Children who did not cheat reported that they knew cheating was wrong, that their parents would disapprove, and that they would feel guilty if they did it. That tells us that we should spell out for our children exactly what cheating is and be very clear about its being wrong. We can also tell our children, as often as it is useful, about our happiness when they act honestly and about our disappointment when they cheat.

Finally, we can tell stories about children or adults who were honest and did not cheat when they could have. Usually these stories abound in schools and work. One of our family's favorite stories is about a schoolteacher who gathered test papers, took them home overnight, and corrected them without marking the grade of the papers. The next class period, he gave the children their papers back and read the correct answers, asking them to mark and grade their own papers. He then called for the grades to be given orally by each student. Only one student reported the same grade as the teacher had given her when grading the papers himself the night before. The teacher named this student publicly and praised her. He talked with the other students about honesty, telling them he would give them another chance to be honest.

When Children Lack Initiative and Self-Confidence

Certain technological products, such as television, videocassette recorders, and video games, have a passive role in helping our children learn. This training in passivity has a telling effect on some children. Researchers in California found that as television watching time increased, children's grades went down, in both elementary school and high school. One teacher explained it this way: "We are pitching knowledge to children, much the same way we used to, but there are fewer who want to catch it, let alone get involved enough to go after it."

Lack of initiative and low self-confidence are related to immorality. Often, when children have a passive approach to learning or work, they are motivated more by the thrills of sensory experiences than by the satisfaction that comes from earned achievement. Because real, lasting satisfaction cannot be found in the thrill of sensory experiences, children keep trying to repeat and increase the sensations. They may try violent (gory, terrifying) movies, fast vehicles, drugs, alcohol, sex, and any other excitement that presents itself.

If we want to promote morality in our children, we need to promote initiative and self-confidence in our children by encouraging and expecting activity instead of passivity.

Jean Piaget's well-known work on cognitive development (1952) suggests what parents can do. First, of course, we must be willing to restrict the amount of time children spend in passive roles. If we are willing to help our children be active in their approach to life, we should help them explore and be curious about the good things they find in the world. Then we should praise them abundantly for their efforts to learn, and we must eliminate almost all criticism. (Many parents still mistakenly think that criticism is an effective means of motivating children.) Initiative comes from doing, and being encouraged leads to stronger beliefs that more can be done. Cultivating children's initiative usually requires much more praise and other positive reinforcement than most parents are used to giving.

If we are positive enough, our children can learn initiative and self-confidence through the opportunities provided in our homes by family, by friends and relatives, and by necessity when they find that life is unhappy when they do nothing.

Many adolescents benefit by working in groups and feeling a part of something everyone accomplishes. They may also require opportunities to work side-by-side with us until they feel enough support to try on their own. We can help this process by organizing genuine success experiences. I have a friend, for example, who has for years hired teenaged boys who have little initiative. At first they do not show up for work on time and do not do much. After finding that others are expecting them to do their share, they often try to quit. At that point he interviews them and tells them, "You are not going to be fired. The only way you will leave this place is if you choose that yourself. We will work with you. Work with us and learn." Given this opportunity and this confrontation, many of the boys he has hired have turned their lives from indolence to responsible, active work.

Occasionally, more extreme measures must be taken. Some parents send their passive children to such work settings as ranches and camps. There children learn to work because they have to. After these experiences many return to school and normal life more excited to try. In the western United States, many children participate in "Outward Bound" or survival programs. The organization and planning of these programs are interesting. From them we can get some ideas about what to do with our children. Groups or teams are formed, and several activities are required. Some of these, such as rappelling down a cliff or building or walking a rope bridge, involve real risks. The children go through "confidence building" experiences together—getting acquainted with each other and building trust between them by taking one another on walks blindfolded—before they move on to other, more "real" challenges. In some cases, every member of a team has to perform in order for everyone to get a reward. If any one fails, all fail. These programs involve rather drastic and forced cooperation, but if children have developed an intractable passivity and show very limited initiative, such activities can help.

CHAPTER 12

SELF-DESTRUCTIVENESS

According to our definition of morality, it is immoral for people to hurt themselves. Some people are surprised by this part of the definition, having considered immoral only those acts that involve one person hurting others. Stealing, for example, is thought of as immoral because the thief hurts other people by depriving them of their property. But by our definition, self-inflicted harm must certainly be considered as immoral as anything that hurts other people. If our children are self-destructive—that is, if they willfully inflict hurt on themselves—we need to take steps to help them learn a moral standard that will prevent their hurting themselves, just as we help them learn to help and not to hurt others.

Even though we might nod in sad acknowledgment when we hear of someone's eating disorder or attempt at suicide, we may be less likely to intervene than we are if we hear of one person physically hurting another. In a certain sense that reaction may be useful, because self-destructive children are more deserving of sympathy and support than of condemnation. But increasing numbers of children are turning to self-destructive behavior, harming not only themselves but also the people who love them and the society that suffers from the loss of what they could have been. Our indifference to the self-destructive behavior of others may be as immoral as the self-destructive acts themselves.

Such self-destructive behavior as excessive fear of failure, anorexia, bulimia, compulsive overeating, alcoholism,

drug addiction, anxiety, inferiority, and suicide are problems difficult to solve. I believe that the unity, even the
survival, of our human communities is affected by these
problems as much as, and perhaps more than, by any other
immoral act. And even though public consensus has not
yet decreed that self-destructive acts are deserving of concerted energies and concern, parents of children whose
lives are damaged, perhaps even ended, by acts of self-
destruction certainly feel the urgency for more attention
to this problem.

In our attention to individual freedom, we tend to explain how people can be free to have different, equally
acceptable values by asserting that what someone does is
"all right" (not immoral) if it "doesn't hurt anyone else."
Although that can sometimes be true, it often keeps those
who use it as an excuse for their own behavior from appreciating how their acts do affect others. In fact, there is
very little that any one person does that does not affect
someone else.

The differences of opinion in the matter of individual
rights and the collective rights of others have played an
important role in American life. But these differences are
not an obstacle to a universal morality. The individual
differences among us will show in how we participate
morally in certain situations. There is more than one way
to be helpful (moral) in any situation, and we need not
judge everyone alike or expect everyone to behave in exactly the same way. It is not necessary, for example, that
we all share the same religious beliefs in order for us all
to recognize that when someone hurts himself or herself,
others are hurt, too.

We can't do anything to help a child who has starved
herself to death; we should have helped her before she
became anorexic. We can't bring back a boy who has died
from drug overdose; we ought to have helped prevent his
drug addiction. By the time it appears, self-destructive

behavior represents a conclusion, not an idea in the form-
ative stages.

Self-destructive acts mean that children have made
judgments about themselves and have concluded that
hurting themselves is the "best" thing they can do in light
of their thoughts about themselves and others.

If we have never met a self-destructive child, we might
be unable to imagine why anyone would decide to hurt
himself. Experienced observers know that children who
make this immoral choice have had many struggles and
may have been so hurt themselves that they have lost their
threads of relatedness with others and have turned inward.
Convinced that they are not cared for, that they do not
belong, or that their life is a mistake, their self-destructiveness is a statement of ultimate despair. Children in this
state are unaware that they have the power or the right to
make choices for themselves and would not admit that
they do what they do because of choices they have made.

I remember an account of a college student plucked
from a bridge in Minneapolis, Minnesota. He was there
thinking about jumping into the Mississippi River far be-
low. The police took him to a counselor who expressed
great concern at the boy's indifference to his own life. "No
one cares," was the reply when he was asked why he was
going to take his life. "I do," the counselor replied. "No,
you don't," came the denial. The counselor wisely and
calmly said, "Notice my hands. See how they are shaking."
The boy looked and was willing to believe this obvious
indication of caring when he disbelieved the counselor's
words. For a few moments, at least, he was willing to
believe that some other person cared, and so he, too, would
care a little.

As we know—or can guess, if we didn't already
know—it is children's actual experience that gives rise to
their conclusions of pessimism about themselves and be-
wilderment about their worth. For such children, life may
be one angry round after another. When their decisions

lead to self-destructive acts, the way back to happiness, if they ever find it, may be long and arduous. It would be far better for these children to have been kept from reaching those conclusions in the first place. Certainly, that is what we will want for our own children.

Our efforts to help children actively maintain self-respect are made more difficult when our children are hurt by others. These hurtful experiences, which we call by the general name of abuse, are increasingly part of many children's lives. Children are hurt by relatives or friends. They might be hurt by our mistakes. They might be delicate and turn away when confronted with what they fear. Even if we prepare them well, we will not always be able to prevent our children's being hurt by others. But if we do prepare them, it is more likely that a harmful experience will not leave a permanent impression that leads to self-destructiveness.

To help our children be moral, then, we need to prepare them both to develop and maintain positive relationships so that they will have an enduring sense of self-respect and to learn to recover when they are hurt by others or by themselves.

Morality and Self-Respect

Self-respect is an attitude, in fact, the moral standard to which our efforts in preventing self-destruction should be aimed. Self-respect is not an attitude of arrogance or superiority. It is a sense of personal power, an appreciation that one's thoughts and acts have a place in the world equal with those of any other. It is an awareness of one's talents and flaws, strengths and weaknesses. Its close companion is humility. Someone who has self-respect seldom needs to prove it by demonstrating it to others. Those with self-respect have their own ideas about personal success and are more interested in fulfilling personal goals than in seeking the approval of others.

The six characteristics of a moral person are the characteristics of a person with self-respect. We remember that those characteristics are autonomy (a sense of self-control and a sense of responsibility for one's acts), empathy for others and willingness to help, acceptance instead of prejudice, a positive emotional style, the ability to converse with others, and an active orientation towards achievement. Children without self-respect are those who feel vulnerable with no sense of self-control, who are defensive and fearful, negative, prejudicial, passive, and isolated from others. If we want our children to have self-respect, a good approach is to help them develop the six traits of moral people.

Self-respect depends on self-awareness. To have self-respect, children must have a great deal of information about themselves. Children without self-respect seem to be aware only of their weaknesses and problems. They are less aware and less appreciative of what there is to love about themselves. In addition, the social mingle of one with another sometimes makes it difficult for individual children to know what part they play or have played in any group event. If we allow our children always to attribute both blame and success to others, then we are missing an opportunity to help them be aware of their own contribution to what goes on around them. If we let them always assume a sense of total responsibility, even when it is not fully deserved, they will come to feel arrogant about successes and overwhelmed about failures.

A Little League football coach I know begins each season by showing all the players how each one is important to the success of the team. "Every play is designed to make a touchdown," he says, "but only if everyone does his job." He describes what a player at each position does to help everyone else. Then he describes how it is not possible to make a touchdown every time because the players on the other team will force some of us into mistakes. "That is why," he explains, "each of you will need to learn your

own position and how to help one another." His efforts
to form a successful team are based on the idea that each
player has to feel self-respect based on his importance to
the other players. He successfully produces self-respect in
another way as well. He tells the boys that each will make
several mistakes during the course of the year, but all will
not make mistakes at the same time. No one, he says, has
the right to be critical of another's mistakes. Further, since
mistakes are going to be made, he convinces his players
that a mistake is not a failure and that the proper response
is simply to get back into the flow of the game as quickly
as possible and not spend much time worrying. The boys
who play on his team learn as much about life and self-
respect as they do about football.

The ties of feeling and attitude that bind us to others
are worth thinking about. There are many who maintain
that individuals have no connection to others and are free
to live in pursuit of purely personal aims. But to teach
morality and self-respect, we need to create a feeling in
our children that they are important parts of families,
schools, congregations, teams, towns, and countries. A
sense of self-respect depends in part on feelings of relatedness, on a sense of obligation and significance to others.
Paradoxically, if children feel no tie or responsibility to
others, they can, through excessive blame, criticism, and
threat, assume too much burden for others and live impaired lives because of guilt when they forget to think about
how their actions reflect on others. No one has self-respect
who carries an inordinate burden of guilt and obligation.

Balance is the key. Freedom from the pressure of inappropriate obligations to others must be balanced with
an appropriate sense of concern for others in order for a
child to develop self-respect and true moral character. We
can help children develop both healthy concern for self
and healthy concern for others, though each requires different experiences.

Concern for others is called altruism and is expressed

in what is sometimes called *prosocial behavior*. Altruism motivates people to do something to help another without thought of a reward. Children learn this by following someone's example and by actually doing service to be helpful. Sub-for-Santa programs at Christmas or giving to neighbors in need are examples of prosocial behavior that arises from altruism. When we lead children into serving others, we help them develop empathy and a sense of caring.

Concern for self is similar to autonomy. It requires that children identify their own goals, thoughts, feelings, and motivations and feel a sense of responsibility for the consequences they bring into their own lives. Healthy concern for self does not mean selfishness or superiority; rather, it means separateness, individuality. Fully developed, individuality means that a person can express thoughts and feelings, clearly separating them from what others think or do.

In conversations with our children, we can help them balance these two aspects of a healthy personality. We point out to them, for instance, the need to have concern for others, and we talk with them about the need to achieve personal goals. "Be concerned about her and take care of her," we might say to a son as he leaves on a date. Next day we might say, "You need to work hard at school so that you can achieve your goals, even if your friends don't." Over and over we reinforce this balance in our conversation and by our example, so that our children's sense of morality will be manifest both in their respect and concern for others and in their respect and concern for themselves.

When Children Have Been Hurt by Others

Children are easily exploited by others. They do not have sufficient power to prevent it. They cannot overwhelm someone older or stronger, nor can they leave an exploitive situation and successfully fend for themselves.

They are often made vulnerable by the belief that they must submit or be rejected. In some cases, submission is brought about by threats. In one recent incident of sexual abuse involving a case in my professional practice, the abused children were made to watch a live cat being disemboweled in front of them. The abusers threatened the children by saying that the same thing would happen to them or their parents if they ever told what had been done to them.

It is not surprising that after being abused, children may be unwilling to accept help because the threats they have heard make them afraid of everyone. There is often a real risk that children who are hurt and threatened by others will not find hope again, at least not enough to try to overcome what was done to them. In some cases, they simply do not believe in anyone anymore. Our first challenge with children hurt by others will always be to find a way to give them hope and to bring faith back into their lives.

An increasing number of us, I believe, are going to be faced with the necessity of helping children when they have been hurt, and sometimes hurt severely. They may be children in our neighborhood, or perhaps friends of our own children. In most cases, these children will have been hurt by uncaring, insensitive people, and they will need caring sensitive people to help them. As we begin to help them, we must be willing to be steadfast and patient. Injured children may resist us at first, watching and waiting. It is not uncommon for this suspicion to continue for months without lessening. But a child's hope may depend on our willingness to show patient caring.

Patience is not always calm, however. After I had worked with one girl for a long time to show her that I cared and that others cared, she still failed to believe. One day when I thought my feelings of concern had been amply demonstrated, I took a risk. When she accused me of not caring for her, I jumped to my feet and stormed around my office, indignantly reminding her of the times when she had seen evidence of my caring for her. I hotly explained that her refusal to believe was one of the most selfish and immature things I had ever seen and that it was time for her to grow up and get off the track she was on. I told her of my genuine feelings, and I reached out and grasped her hand. "I cannot help you, if you will not receive my help." I told her it was time to try trust. She became angry at me, accusing me of being a "crummy and stupid psychologist" who couldn't understand her. She began to shake and then to cry. Since I was standing, she stood, walked into my arms and soaked the sleeve of my suit with her tears. The change she made after that was not sudden or dramatic. But in the ensuing days there was more trust.

After instilling in an injured child some hope or belief in our concern, we can proceed to help the child talk and reason about what has happened. We can focus on the following:

What actually took place, as the child remembers it?

What part does the child feel responsible for?

How were people (everyone involved) affected by the experience?

What feelings emerged then and are now felt about the experience? (It is useful to ask in detail and talk at great length about them.)

How can a new trust (not the old) and new concern be developed for others?

As part of these conversations, we will probably need to help change what the child feels. Helping a child change feelings of fear and anger and resentment into feelings of forgiveness, for example, is useful because the change frees the child from entangling feelings toward the abusers. Sometimes we will find that we ourselves have more difficulty forgiving than the child does. But helping a child use faith in our love, and faith in God, by first thinking about forgiving and then finding some way to show it, will help a great deal in the process of healing. Children who are hurt by others generally feel a great sense of shame, a sense of worthlessness, guilt (which is fear of the disapproval of others), powerlessness (which is a sense of vulnerability to someone's control), anger at themselves and other people, and fear-depression from the loss of trust in others and overriding suspicion of them. These emotions are often difficult to change, but when children are able to change them, it is because they have been understood. Children can be motivated to change their feelings by realizing that they have been hurt and that they do not want the abuser to cripple them permanently.

Children who have been hurt by others often hurt in return. One of the most difficult things to help hurt children see is that they can overcome their own pain by helping others. After learning that their nine-year-old daughter had been sexually molested by a neighbor and frightened by threats of awful things if she told, the parents first reacted with hostility to the teenaged boy. They instigated a campaign to have the boy and his family move from the neighborhood. The boy's parents went to them. After they met and talked, their feelings changed, and they stopped the hostility and began to help their daughter. They involved their entire family. They bought a new puppy, gave it to the daughter and asked her to care for it. They asked all the children to participate in "family hugs" and other demonstrations of love for one another. Over a period of time they were able to talk with their daughter about what had happened and her feelings about it.

They went even further and found ways to give service to others. The mother cooked food and had the children take it to neighbors. The family put on a party for several children. They sought professional help and learned how to help their daughter be assertive (to express verbally what she thought and preferred, rather than allowing others to exert excessive control). When the daughter tried to avoid playing with friends, the parents had to be stern in their requirement that she play a reasonable amount of time. Gradually, she overcame some of the shame she felt. For these parents, their initial shock and anger was followed by compassion, and this change greatly benefited their injured daughter.

Those of us who have not been required to face a situation like this may yet have to. And if we do, we will face a moral circumstance. If we have learned our lessons well, we will be able to choose to help, perhaps even help those who have harmed us.

Stress, Childhood Depression, and Self-Mutilation

Early childhood, from birth to age six, is a time when children are governed by impressions, emotions, impulses, and images, which they often cannot think consciously about and which they will not remember in detail. Many child psychologists have suggested that children's experience during this time is recorded without any narrative to go along with it. Therefore, children may not be able to speak about these feelings or remember them after a few years. Once recorded, however, the early feelings and impressions often have lasting effects. Many adults, consciously unaware of their early experiences, have problems that seem at first to be without explanation. But it is now quite firmly established that many anxieties and such problems as eating disorders may be tied to emotions about early abusive experiences. These findings should indicate to us that our children will not be able to tell us in words but will show us if they have feelings that limit their self-respect.

Some early warning signs help us know something is wrong even if there has been no abuse. When we are committed to teaching morality, these symptoms signal that we must correct something or a lack of self-respect will make our teaching task more difficult. Usually, the earliest signs of disorder will be the signs of stress. For children under the age of six or seven, stress is most commonly displayed by depressed emotional states, shown by both overactive and subdued behavior, excessive teasing, difficulties with eating and sleeping, irritability, and self-mutilation, usually in the form of picking small sores on the face, legs, and arms.

When any of these signs appear, we know that children are feeling enough stress to create doubt about their worth. To help in this situation, we might first look for tensions at home, such as family conflict, parental anger, or problems between siblings. In some cases, we might uncover the fact that the child showing the symptoms of stress has been neglected or abused in some way. Children showing these signs of stress are often the ones most susceptible to disturbance by the pressure of family troubles. At early ages, recurring illnesses such as allergies, asthma, and headaches may be symptoms of such susceptibility. Such children will benefit greatly when family problems are resolved. It is important to remember that these symptoms are not a normal part of childhood unless they appear rarely and quickly disappear. If they appear often or do not go away, we can be reasonably certain that something is wrong. If we cannot reduce the conflict or tension ourselves, we would be wise to seek professional help.

When I first met her, Beth was seven years old, freckle-faced, of average height, with a sunny, pleasant disposition. She had small sores on her nose and cheeks. Some of them were freshly made, open, with no scabs; others were older and had begun healing. She readily admitted that she had picked them. Her mother told me of times when Beth sat for an hour or more and pulled the lining from old couch cushions and quilts through very small holes. Further questioning yielded more information. Beth's mother reported that Beth was often quiet, spending two or three hours alone every day. Occasionally, though, she would be "hyper" and in such an elevated mood that she was difficult to calm. During these periods she would get angry, tease, yell, and have to be placed alone or put on a chair before she would calm down.

I asked her mother other questions about the family. There were several family problems, including marital conflict, problems with older teenaged children, and the threat of the father's losing his job. I asked about the possibility of sexual molestation, because the symptoms Beth showed are often related to this problem. The mother reported that Beth had no older brothers, relatives, or neighbors who had been spending any time with her. "What about times when you are away from home, or when she sleeps over with friends?" I asked. Beth's mother ruled out these possibilities. She also indicated that she had no reason to suspect the father. Later I talked to both parents and found them to be extremely intense with each other. Their comments were sharp and often critical and accusing. I inquired about the warmth and affection expressed in the home, about family games, enjoyable vacations, and so forth. Both parents said that there was very little of that.

We made a plan to decrease the family tension by increasing family fun. Both parents were willing to alter their schedules to create time for some enjoyable activities. Beth's mother cut Beth's fingernails, and we worked out a reinforcement program to help get rid of the sores. Because Beth liked gummy bears, her mother put some in a jar. Every time Beth picked at a sore, her mother took a gummy bear out of the jar. At the end of the day, Beth could have the bears that were left. In three weeks, most of the sores had disappeared. Beth picked no other sores for nearly three months. Then her father lost his job, marital tension increased, and Beth returned with sores on her face and two or three on her legs. They did not disappear until we were able again to reduce the stress she felt from her family.

Thinking that Beth's family situation was very unstable, I proposed to her parents that we involve her in

some achievement activities. They arranged for some summer classes in sculpture and arts and crafts. In addition,
they enrolled her in a swimming class. At home they made
her daily chores simple and specific. Together we planned
a system of rewards for all her accomplishments. As time
passed she seemed to grow stronger emotionally as she
concentrated on the things she was doing. It was apparent
that the focus on achieving had distracted her from some
of the family problems.

In this case, it is fairly easy to see how achievement,
greater autonomy, and positive experiences reduced the
stress she felt, alleviated her depression, and helped her
feel more positive. During our last conference she bounced
in, gave me a "high five," and chattered about what she
was doing. Self-respect had returned.

Obesity and Isolation

Such symptoms of self-destructiveness as stress and
depression that appear in early childhood can extend into
middle childhood as well. But ages seven through eleven
is a period when other symptoms of destructiveness may
also appear. In the main, these will be related to body size
and shape, experience with achievement, contact with
other people, and health.

Children aged seven through eleven are not usually
able to understand themselves in terms of personality
traits, such as cheerful, dedicated, etc. They usually think
about people (including themselves) in terms of what they
can see and feel. That is why children in the middle years
of childhood think about what is physically obvious. Those
boys who can run fast, throw far, hit balls hard, for example, will usually have higher status than those boys who
are physically less able. Girls may use other physical criteria
to evaluate themselves and others, such as prettiness or
thinness, but they, too, are focused on the shape, size,
and abilities of their bodies.

We recognize that not all children have the same abilities, and we might regret with tender sensitivity when it is our children who are less popular. There is wisdom in our recognizing two or three things about children's self-respect and their bodies. For one thing, relying just on physical abilities for self-respect is a mistake. Physical abilities can be changed by illness, injury, or just growth; their importance can be challenged by better competition. And as children mature, other things, such as social skills and talents, will play a greater role in their attractiveness to others and in their own feelings of worth.

We can be alert to our children's feelings about their bodies, and we can notice whether they have high or low status among their friends. All children are able to pay a certain amount of attention to caring for their appearance and to keeping clean. They can appreciate being able to walk, run, see, and hear. Children who dislike themselves because they are unable to succeed at being fashionably thin, handsome, or beautiful, could be asked to work for an hour or two with handicapped children. With their perspective restored, they will probably complain less after such an experience.

Childhood obesity is a physical condition that deserves our close attention. Overweight children are sometimes disadvantaged because they are not able to achieve positive status; they may be ridiculed and may struggle for self-respect. Obesity in children may result from hereditary tendency combined with low activity level, overeating, and rapid food intake. In this case, part of the solution is first to help our children increase their activity level and regulate their food intake and then to help them feel as comfortable with the body heredity has helped give them.

Obesity can also result from eating as a form of self-destructiveness. In this case, eating is an emotional crutch for depression and anxiety. Unfortunately, the "crutch" brings on a physical result that may lead to social isolation and further discouragement, depression, more eating, more weight gain, and more ostracism. A vicious cycle is begun that, if unchecked, can leave a permanent imprint.

Obesity from any cause makes it difficult for children to develop self-respect. Overweight children may miss or be hindered in many physical activities with other children (most children's games and activities involve them physically), and they are more likely to be extremely self-conscious and form negative attitudes about themselves because they know their size is obvious to others, whom they assume are disapproving.

In helping children lose weight for any reason, caution is necessary because the attention we give to our children's eating and weight can easily be interpreted by them as additional criticism, adding to their feelings of rejection. Some strategies can be helpful if we apply them with discretion. We can, for example, make certain that our children have skills other than physical skills to rely on as a basis for self-respect. We might help them develop skills in music or art; we might help them develop talents for writing or woodworking; we could encourage them with suggestions and praise to get involved in some social activities, such as Scouting. We should remember that school programs usually do not provide sufficient exercise and must be supplemented by such physical activities as jogging, playing physical games, karate, swimming, or weight lifting.

Instead of making a pointed issue of children's overeating, we can examine and adjust our family's eating habits. Just changing a few foods can help alter obesity without giving too much emphasis to dieting. Limiting the availability of foods with high fat and sugar content and reducing intake of such foods to small amounts help out more than we or our children may realize. In some cases, a more strict diet may seem warranted, but we should seek competent medical supervision before placing a child on a special diet.

If overeating cannot be brought under control by these

measures and if it seems to be a means to self-destruction, we may need to seek help from a child psychologist or psychiatrist. Obesity related to self-destructiveness is a psychological problem. Doing nothing about such obesity is a mistake because the problem will not go away by itself. We must begin by recognizing that the obesity is a symptom of an underlying emotional cause, stemming from things that have happened to the child that are being used to form the child's emotional conclusion that "no one cares," "it doesn't matter," so "why not eat?" Very often, change will take place if the underlying events are talked about. When children face their hurts and talk them out, a foundation is laid for changes to be made.

We can search for these experiences by telling our children that we know something has happened and then ask questions. If gentle questions do not yield good results, we can become firmer, though always loving, in our insistence that the children talk about what has happened that is related to their weight. There will be more than one experience, so we must listen without too much reaction until the children have talked through several experiences. We must avoid challenging what is said, but we must make certain that the children report the experiences in some detail and display the hurt, anger, and resentment toward others that have resulted. We should not be surprised if they are angry at us. Children are often irrationally angry at parents for "not preventing or understanding the hurt" they feel. Then, it is wise to help the children explain how those harmful experiences were channeled into the desire to hurt themselves by overeating. Once this point has been reached, some of the children's self-destructiveness will be reduced and some plan of action will make itself apparent.

I offer one note of caution here. From my experience I have determined that any attempt to solve the problem of obesity needs to be met with some immediate success. It is usually unwise to start by designing big programs with delayed reward. Rather, we need to start by doing something simple, even unrelated to eating, just to bolster the children's courage and confidence.

Obesity presents a moral crisis partly because it so often results in social isolation. But obesity, of course, is not the only cause of social isolation. In fact, social isolation in itself can be a form of self-destructiveness. It is fairly easy for us to see when children avoid others and spend long periods alone. If such isolation is temporary, we can assume that it is related to some specific event, and it might clear up if we talk with our children, understand what has happened, and encourage them to try again. Friendship problems, school failure, or sharp words with a parent are examples of specific things that result in temporary isolation. But, suppose children use isolation or withdraw without talking to anyone every time something disappointing happens. Or suppose children come home and spend most of their free time alone in the bedroom for several days or weeks. That is the kind of isolation that offers potential for self-destructiveness.

Children who use withdrawal as a response to such hurts as embarrassment, disappointment, or frustration use isolation to punish other people. They often become extremely defensive and blame others for their problems. Failing to learn conversation as a means of solving problems and testing reality, such children are unable to determine whether or not they think and believe what other people think and believe. If they are allowed to continue this pattern, there is a chance they will develop unreal, even strange, ideas about themselves and others. Prolonged isolation may at first represent a crushing, profound hurt, but can become something even worse—a mental or an emotional disturbance.

Sometimes professional help should be sought for this condition, especially if we think that the reasons for the isolation involve unusually strong or traumatic emotions associated with experiences or events. But we still must find ways to help children change the feelings that prompted the action of withdrawal. As usual, we first examine ourselves, this time to see how easy or difficult we are to talk with. If we have been critical or indifferent, we can apologize and ask for an opportunity to improve as a listener. We can make an agreement with children to talk about ourselves, in a personal way, and tell about our feelings and activities, hoping they will do the same.

If some traumatic event has precipitated the withdrawal, then it must be confronted and dealt with. Being able to talk with someone about the experience and its accompanying feelings is usually very helpful. In one extreme case I know of, the child had not spoken for several months. Her parents took her to a therapist who was as mystified about the child as they were. There did not seem to be any specific cause for the behavior. One day the counselor began to tell a story about a girl frog who used to sing and croak with other frogs. He made the story very detailed and noticed that the child had become engrossed in it. "One day," he said, "the girl frog stopped croaking, and no one knows why." As he paused for a breath, he heard the little girl say, "It was her birthday party." He went on with the story and stopped periodically to let her fill in the spaces between his words. He learned that something very unhappy had happened to the little girl at the party. Once she had talked about it with someone, she left her self-imposed isolation and began to speak again.

If we suspect some specific cause for a child's isolation, it is important to learn as much about it as we can before talking through it with the child. That may require talking with other people, visiting the place where the event occurred, and tracing all that led up to the experience until we have a good idea about what happened. When the withdrawn child notices that we are learning more about the traumatic event, he or she may become agitated and want us to leave it alone. But we cannot leave it; we must find out what happened and tell the child we know, or

the child may create of withdrawal a permanent, mala-
daptive way to live.

Failure and Illness

Some of us have children who, after trying, even trying
hard, will experience repeated failure. Under certain conditions, some of these children will give up entirely and
try no more. They may be so frightened of failing that they
will do only what is guaranteed to succeed and avoid trying
at all. One solution to this problem is to examine and
explore the "audience," the people who, the child believes,
witnessed the failure. The other solution is to learn how
the child interprets the meaning of the failures.

Sometimes children try things just to please someone.
The failures that result in no further efforts may be accompanied by the notion that so much disapproval, shame,
and embarrassment create risks too great for trying (and
failing) again. Helping children have the courage to try
again may depend on clarifying their thoughts about what
others think, changing the "audience" to a more supportive one for the next trial, or helping them feel more autonomy by setting personal goals and teaching them to be
less concerned about what others might think.

While I was watching one of my sons during a Little
League baseball game, I noticed that some parents made
rather intense comments about players and coaches. My
son came to bat in the last inning, the bases loaded, and
one run behind. "You can do it," some parents yelled. "A
hit's a run," someone else yelled. His coach called him
over to give some private but pressure-packed advice.
Some people were still yelling, "You can't do it." The
opposing players taunted him. As I sat there, I wondered
how anyone would be able to achieve anything in that kind
of situation. Attempting to relieve some of the pressure
for him, I waited until he stepped into the batter's box and
yelled, "It's all right with me if you don't get a hit!" People

in the stands quieted and looked around to see who had shouted such heretical words. My son recognized my voice, smiled just a little in my direction, and turned back to face the pitcher. As I recall, he got a hit.

Some children do not have a good understanding of mistakes and failures. They believe that success and failure clearly represent their complete value as human beings. As parents we need to help such children accurately interpret the meaning of their failures. Is the failure something important that should signal to the child a need for change? Or is it just a minor mistake of little consequence? Does the child feel responsible and crushed by the failure ("crummy, stupid, and will never be any good")? If we have loved our children well, they will be able to sense their worth even with the mistakes. If we have not, then we will have some recovering to do. We may need to "start over and do it right." We may have to apply the pressure of encouragement to try again. We may have to help them try in another area where success is more likely. We may need to tell stories of great people who failed but kept trying and succeeded at last. (Abraham Lincoln and Thomas Edison are notable examples.) And we may have to develop sayings that help carry our children along. My favorite is "Success is usually on the far side of failure."

The best solution, however, is to insulate children with real achievement and help them form "achievement motivation." That is accomplished when parents set reasonable expectations for their children's performance, involve children in choosing and deciding what they will accomplish, and give abundant positive reinforcement of children's successful effort. (McClelland, 1953.)

Another form of self-destructiveness common among children is using ill-health, actual or feigned, as a mechanism of avoidance. Many children use phony sickness as a means of avoiding responsibility. Most parents have experienced at least one or two attempts by children to miss school this way. Each time a child does this, however, self-respect suffers. Even children who have real, prolonged illnesses lose respect for themselves because they miss social reinforcement and opportunities for achievement. So complaints about illness create a dilemma for us: we want to provide good care if the illness is real; on the other hand, we don't want children to use the complaint as a means of avoidance.

Some psychosomatic complaints, with real pain and physical symptoms, but without a specific, identifiable physiological cause, are probably related to school and may represent such problems as missed assignments, social rejection, or stress. When children complain of headaches, sick stomachs, "flu," or other symptoms before school or some other event, the chances are good that they are anxious and wish to avoid the situation. Most of the time the feelings they complain about are actually felt. Thus it usually is unwise to argue with children, threaten to expose them, attempt to shame them, or just ignore the problem. The first time this happens it is usually all right to care for the children as long as the symptoms remain, as shown by their staying in bed, sleeping, or lethargy. If the illness or complaints are repeated, however, and we are certain that avoidance is involved, then the next step is to attempt talking children into facing what is being avoided. That may require us to find out about the situation and how children think about it. Then we may be able to intervene on their behalf to change the source of the fear.

If talking doesn't help, some other things might. We can use techniques similar to those we would use to discourage overdependence. We can, for instance, start caring for the children's "illness" in a way that causes discomfort. Spilling juice on the children is effective. Simply insisting that children stay in bed and lie still for long periods "to get well" also helps. If children are made uncomfortable enough, they are usually ready to face the feared event the next day.

In instances where the complaint about illness persists,

it is wise to get children a physical examination and consider seeing a professional therapist to help out. What starts out to be a technique to avoid some single event, such as an exam at school, can become a way of life. Our brains are so quick to respond that it is entirely possible for a child to act sick, complain about symptoms that originally have no physical basis, and eventually actually develop those problems. In these cases the illness will not go away, and the child will develop a pattern of using illness to manipulate and avoid. That is self-destructiveness. It may call for a radical change of environment, such as going to live with relatives, attending another school, and acquiring new friends. In some cases, a solution may come only from counseling.

A young teenager I treated had been in an automobile accident and sustained a few minor injuries that doctors expected would heal quickly. But after three years, she would still not go to school, play, or do much that was active. She could not, she said, because of her injuries. Her physicians referred her to me because she showed no physiological problems. Her parents had told me about the automobile accident in which she had received her injuries, but at first she could not remember much about the accident. As I reminded her with what I had learned from her mother, she began to talk more about it.

I learned that after the initial impact she was unconscious. She regained consciousness in time to see the other car catch fire and the occupant burn to death. She could not get out of the car to save him. As she talked, I could tell she felt responsible, and I could understand why she felt obligated to retain her "injuries" as a form of self-punishment. We talked until she disclosed her feelings about the accident. We discussed the extent of her responsibility for the death she witnessed. She could not shake the feelings of guilt, so I asked a geneticist who works with rare and unusual plants to give her some plants to care for. That required her to inform herself about the plants and set up a detailed routine of watering, cultivating, and providing light. As she succeeded in keeping the plants alive, the pain she felt from her injuries decreased.

Anorexia and Bulimia

It puzzles and frightens us that some teenaged children, who are for the most part beneficiaries of our hard work to make life good for them and who themselves have so much to give the world, seem to deny all this and give it all up in dramatic gestures of self-destruction. We have already discussed the widespread self-destruction in alcohol and drug abuse. Three other common ways modern adolescents demonstrate their hopelessness and emptiness are anorexia-bulimia, cultism, and suicide.

It is stark symbolism when children starve themselves. We can see in their behavior a wish for some part of them to end or a terrible drive to deprive themselves in some way. *Anorexia* means loss of appetite. It refers to a behavioral disorder in which food is avoided because of anxiety, and it is related to depression. It is treated much like an addiction to drugs, but that approach does not fully address the problem. It does not explain why children begin in the first place to starve themselves, and why, even in the face of evidence to the contrary, they think of their problem as a small thing, easy to stop if they wish.

Anxiety and depression related to food also takes another form, called *bulimia*. This disorder involves starving and then bingeing and purging. When children have starved themselves into extreme hunger, they will eat large quantities of food and then make themselves vomit until the stomach feels completely empty. I have known girls with this disorder who have vomited ten to fifteen times a day.

Children who develop these eating disorders (they are usually girls) are susceptible to anxiety, often from birth, and they may have family backgrounds that include harshness expressed several ways. They may have received criticism about eating habits and the possibility of weight gain. They may have been physically abused by parents. Perhaps they have been neglected or denied emotional support. In some cases the cause is simply raw anxiety about being overweight. Quite literally, eating makes such children ill.

One overly thin fourteen-year-old, with sallow skin and hollow eyes, told me how she hated her dad and mother. She was very likely hyperactive and undoubtedly difficult to rear, but she thought only of her parents' harsh treatment. After listening for a while, I said to her, "You are succeeding." "At what?" she asked, surprised. "You are certainly punishing them," I replied. Caught off guard, she could not prevent the corner of her mouth from turning upward in the small grim smile of the exposed.

Like others I have treated, she worries about being thin enough, she is anxious, and she has some deeper underlying emotional problems. Among those who have the problem of anorexia, about 34 percent will overcome the problem without help. Another 40 percent will benefit from counseling, and the rest, more than 25 percent, will die. (Berger, 1986.)

To help such children, parents must recognize the problem as soon as possible. Many children are embarrassed and will lie about it, so recognizing early warning signs and diligently investigating them is essential. These include exaggerated efforts to lose weight or stay thin, irregular eating habits, defensive responses when asked about food and eating, disappearing after eating (in order to vomit), mood shifts between anxiety and depression, and food that was planned for meals disappearing.

The next step is, once again, to learn as much as possible about the problem: How long has it been going on? Are friends involved? To what extent do children starve or binge? If children often refrain from eating or if they binge and vomit daily, the problem is serious enough to warrant immediate professional help. We will be better able to help if we try to understand the problem and learn how to respond constructively to it rather than assuming guilt for causing it. Special emphasis on love, warmth, and patience will help children know of our care and concern. It usually takes a long time and a great deal of love and support to help children overcome serious eating disorders and gradually regain the self-respect they have lost because of the disorder. In most cases, successful treatment will consist of enforced eating schedules, which may require hospitalization, and participation in a support group that exerts pressure and concern, in addition to steady parental love.

Cultism and Suicide

Another very disturbing form of self-destructive behavior among young people is their tendency to affiliate with bizarre and obviously harmful social groups. Many children are not anchored to religious values, family love, and strong friendships. These children are often susceptible to offers of membership extended by what appear to be small, tightly knit groups of people who feel disenfranchised by mainstream society. Sometimes these social groups are based on fashion and fads of the day—"punkers," for instance, whose group cohesiveness involves a certain kind of music and the life-style it promotes. The basis for membership in such groups is an "anti" feeling, an emotional opposition to whatever is established.

These groups vary in what they profess to be against—traditional dress, music, religious values. At a deeper level, however, which usually is denied by the participants, the groups are very much alike in that the leaders usually exert considerable control, bordering on possessiveness, and demand strict submission from their members. In some groups, children who are members are free to leave if they wish to, but may have difficulty doing so. In other cases, pressure is put on children to retain their membership and demonstrate their loyalty by espousing unusual beliefs or performing some acts of loyalty. These groups are called cults.

Membership in these kinds of social groups, or cults, harms children in two important ways. The first harm is the pervasive negativism, the "anti" feelings created and expressed by members, who are often unwilling to hope and work toward something better. Being against something one judges to be bad is not the same thing as being for something good. The result of this negativism is confusion, depression, and despair. The accompanying loss of self-respect is exploited by the group leaders. The second harm is the perverted form of morality the groups engender and maintain. Satanism, an all-too-prominent form of cultism, not only is negative but also actively promotes a morality of spiritual bondage instead of freedom, secrecy instead of openness, destruction and doom instead of uplift and support.

Children who become involved in cults most often have little autonomy and self-control to begin with. After becoming involved in these groups, they demonstrate even less. If they are to be helped, their involvement must be discovered. Indications are depressed moods, deception, extreme emotional intensity, withdrawal from other balanced activities, and intense reactions to pressure to participate in them. Once the involvement is discovered, children may have to be forcibly removed from contact with the group if they will not discuss their situation and cannot demonstrate the benefits of membership. A full solution requires that children learn a set of positive cohesive values that will replace the negative. These beliefs and values must be maintained by an organization that generates feelings of belonging—church or family, for example—and children must be surrounded by love and warmth as they rejoin their family and the larger society.

Participation in negative, twisted cults and other less extreme but still deviant social groups is self-destructive. Like other forms of self-destructive behavior, participation in such a group can increase a child's confusion about values. This confusion, combined with family discord, instability, and loneliness, can lead to the depression or impulsiveness that are the antecedents of the ultimate form of self-destruction. The increasing number of young people who are taking their own lives is shocking and saddening, and it should motivate us to learn how to help our children stay far away from whatever might lead to such tragedy.

Suicide victims are often depressed, but, surprisingly, some die when they are feeling better, not worse. They express their hopelessness in words and actions long before trying to take their lives. They may make unsuccessful attempts before they actually do it. They may withdraw from conversations with others and express a strong negativism similar to that displayed by cult members. We can be alert to these signs, and take them seriously.

Having told his thirteen-year-old son that he could not go to a high-school basketball game, a father settled down to read the newspaper. After a minute or two, he felt a strange silence. He ran to his son's room and found him hanging by the neck from the closet rod. The boy was unconscious but was saved by his father's quick action. I went to the hospital to see the boy. During our conversation, I asked what he had done the day he tried to hang himself.

He told me that he had spent the day listening to heavy metal music. I am not proposing that hard rock music is the cause of suicide; however, hard rock music is a factor in nearly every suicide of young people. As I talked with this boy I felt his loss of hope, nihilism, alienation. This loss may be demonstrated in depression, in angry rebellion, or in silent certitude, but however it is manifested, it will usually be acutely felt.

If we are to prevent suicide, we can renew our appreciation for the vitality we all gain when we belong, holding membership with groups of moral people and feeling that we contribute. If the family is in trouble or dissolves, if children fail in school, if they are not encompassed by a circle of friends, if they are not anchored by standards or values, then they are at risk, for they can find little to hope for and little to believe in.

Teaching children to reason, judge, and act morally is both the prevention and the cure for this condition. If children have moral standards, they will find that the principles of morality are also the key to membership in many beneficial and enjoyable social groups. They will have something to hope for and believe in outside themselves, and they will believe in themselves. At the very moment when children can choose to live or to die, it is their moral training that increases the probability they will choose life rather than death.

CHAPTER 13

DIFFICULT CHILDREN

Healthy children are born with fairly well developed sensory capabilities and more than one hundred reflexes to help them survive. Every child undergoes an identifiable pattern of mental and physical growth, but different children mature at different rates. Right from the beginning, some babies thrive, are healthy and intelligent, and are easy to care for. They seem to be calm and relaxed. Other babies do not grow up so easily. Some are handicapped by physical problems, and others have social and moral problems. We do not know exactly why that happens, but we do know that children differ in so many ways that just knowing about the course of child development does not explain why some children develop more readily into mature, moral individuals and some do not. So, in their attempts to better understand this phenomenon, scientists have begun to seek for explanations from sources other than children themselves. The family is an obvious source of information. By studying how individual children react to and interact with other family members, we have gathered a great deal of information that helps us better understand how moral thought and behavior develop. This information, added to what we know about child development, has enabled us to find better ways to help children grow into moral adults.

It has become very clear that children differ from birth in the way they approach life. These biological, inherited differences have many implications, but one very important implication for parents to think about is this: if all parents treated all children alike, with unfailing wisdom and great skill, some of the children would still turn out "better" than some of the others. That would happen because some children are born with characteristics that help them benefit from parental influence and some children have limitations that prevent them from learning.

Children who thrive seem to have a kind of inborn mental filter. They use this filter to limit the pressure and distractions around them, giving them a natural sense of autonomy. They are able to direct their thoughts in a way that enables them to concentrate on what they learn. They are able to work to apply what they learn and are relatively calm in their approach to life. Murphy (1987) describes such children as resilient. Generally speaking, these children —

Have trust and hope sufficient to withstand rebuffs and disappointments.

Use verbal and nonverbal communication, imitation, and identification. (They can be seen trying to be like someone.)

Have the capacity to communicate, cooperate, and love in their relationship with their mothers.

Display a range of emotion, including joy, curiosity, playfulness, and creativity.

Are able to keep on trying after failure.

Can forgive and forget.

Can delay gratification.

Can adapt to differing conditions in several environments.

Other children appear to have a weak filter and cannot mentally screen out enough of the world around them to concentrate on any one thing for any length of time. These children are likely to be impulsive, highly distractible, and very reactive to what they see, hear, and feel. They are less able than other children to work and learn effectively; they often fail in their attempts to achieve. Consequently, they receive less praise for success than other children do.

Since caring for them and teaching them requires a great deal of energy, they are less satisfying for parents and teachers to work with than are children with well-developed filters.

But even this information does not fully answer one particularly perplexing question: why do some children in strong families with competent parents grow up troubled and immoral? And why do some children with neglectful, unstable parents become highly competent, moral adults? These conditions contradict tidy theories of how family life generally influences children. We would like to be able to say that if parents are kind and warm and use effective and appropriate discipline, children will always turn out the way parents want them to. But though this very often happens, other influences make rearing successful, moral children more complex than that. It appears that promoting the positive development of children requires some knowledge of children as individuals, knowledge about the effects families have on children, and an understanding of how the environment influences the family.

Our children's environment is made up of friends, conditions in the immediate neighborhood and community, school, fashions and fads, and also of what is brought into their lives by movies, television, magazines, and books. Many of us learn firsthand about the role the environment plays when we are forced to struggle against people who entice our children into destructive activities and ideas that compete with our own values.

Because we are concerned with helping our children develop moral character, it is important for us to combine our knowledge of children and families with some ability to manage their environment. That will help us adapt to the unique traits of a particular child we are trying to teach and will greatly improve our influence. Some children will develop morally with what appears to be little help from us. Others will require more help but will succeed because of our efforts and love. Still others will be at greater risk because they have inborn characteristics that make it truly difficult for them to learn morality. They are vulnerable to all sorts of external influences and seem immune to our efforts to teach them what we want them to know to keep them from hurting themselves and others.

We call these children "difficult." We love them, and we ache for them, but they try our patience, often making us feel helpless and triggering anger that makes us feel ashamed and guilty. They may lead us to places we would rather not go, make us see what we would rather not see, and force us to face life and ourselves in ways we would rather not. They are our children, however, and even though they seem to require something more than our best, we feel responsible to do whatever we can do to teach them. And so we will.

What Children Inherit

Ideally we will identify difficult children early in their life. That way, we can apply our understanding of family and environmental influence to make sure that we do not make things worse for the child than they need to be. But whenever the identification is made, we can organize strategies for helping them, based on our knowledge of each child's particular personality.

The role of biological inheritance in the makeup of the human personality is shown in the work of Thomas Bouchard (1983). He conducted research with identical twins separated at birth and reared apart who did not know of each other's existence until they were adults. Bouchard's findings were astonishing. Those individuals, who have the same genetic makeup but who were raised in totally different environments, are amazingly alike in personality and preferences. Constance Golden (1985) described identical twin brothers who discovered each other at age thirty-nine. Both had law enforcement training and worked part-time as deputy sheriffs. Both vacationed in Florida; both drove Chevrolets. Both had dogs named Toy. One had a son named James Allan; the other a son named James Alan.

These findings suggest that parents are not the sole cause of what a child becomes; a great deal is determined by biological makeup. That does not mean that a particular child is genetically destined to be bad or good and that parents can do nothing about it. Neither does it mean that we can blame our children's problems on their genes and default on our parental responsibility to them. It does mean, though, that emotional, mental, and social characteristics may be inherited that make it easier or more difficult to learn moral behavior. And just as we should not feel totally responsible for all the good our children do, we should certainly not feel totally responsible and guilty for our children's mistakes. That kind of objectivity will help us be more effective parents.

I have often worked with parents who have difficult children to rear, but sometimes the parents are more difficult to deal with than their children are. These parents assume guilt for their children's problems. They feel exposed to public disapproval because of their children's actions, and they appear helpless to do anything constructive about it all. Sometimes the parents are so angry at their children's inability to learn quickly and easily that they shut these children out by withdrawing affection and attention. As a result children are hurt and confused. In one case, a mother grew so frustrated at her daughter, who was a difficult child, that she told the girl she would no longer be her mother and tried to shut this child out of her life. She learned, however, that her desire to be free from the hard work and frustration did not remove the child from her thoughts and her feelings. Even if the daughter had been sent to live elsewhere, this mother would not be able to escape memories, guilt, and a sense of failure.

It is better emotionally, and more effective practically, if we assume that children are biologically responsible for what they bring with them into the world as babies but that they cannot succeed without our help in becoming mentally and morally responsible adults. With that in mind, we can divide our responsibility from theirs. That separation will allow us to give them their share of responsibility and prevent us from assuming too little or too much responsibility ourselves.

Labels for Difficult Children

When parents have problems with children, it may be that little thought is given to whether children can or cannot learn morality. Therefore, children who have difficulty learning to be moral are given other kinds of labels, depending on who is working with them. At school or at home, these children may be said to have learning disabilities, such as an attention deficit disorder (ADD), formerly known as hyperactivity. This diagnosis may first be made when children have difficulty learning in school because they are distractible and unable to finish tasks. Further, boys may have problems with reading or math and boys or girls may have inappropriate moods and social behavior. These children may also demonstrate volatile emotions, which often take the form of anger toward others or tantrums. Such children often seem emotionally electric and impulsive, which adds pressure and tension at meals, during playtime, and at school.

Some children may be labeled as oppositional. Oppositional children may not have learning problems but are intense and insecure. When asked to do something, they oppose the request and resist with great intensity. Oppositional children are not very adaptive, and when asked to change (for example, to stop watching television in order to eat), they refuse to comply. Some observers have referred to oppositional children as engaging in power struggles. To prevent themselves from being controlled or swallowed up by others, these insecure children oppose instructions and directions, often doing exactly the opposite of what they are asked to do. This behavior may be accompanied by tantrums, anger, and disagreements in conversation. If a parent says, "It's going to be a beautiful day," an oppositional child will say, "No, it's going to be a bad day."

A less intense but still extremely insecure child may be labeled as withdrawn. These children show their insecurity by shyness, avoiding social contact, and extreme defensiveness. Such children complain excessively, are pessimistic, blame others for mistakes, and may periodically erupt in sudden anger. Withdrawn children feel ineffective and powerless. Their anger is usually unexpressed outwardly, but it can be expressed indirectly through self-destructive actions to punish those who they think caused their discomfort.

As they grow older, withdrawn children become increasingly dogmatic and show prejudice and limited concern for others. They insist that they are right about the ignorance or incorrect opinions of others. Usually these beliefs are narrow and extreme and may be manifested in fanaticism of many kinds. Their dogmatism allows them to shut out competing ideas so that they will not have to adjust their own views. They often are not aware of how their actions affect others but harshly judge and condemn the mistakes they see others make.

Withdrawn people may have negative, unhappy moods and be prone to sulking. These emotional states are accompanied by statements indicating that they believe they deserve things from others, and they may express frustrations and resentment when they don't get what they want. They may remove themselves from contact with people because they fear and suspect the intentions others have for them. Thus it is difficult for them to maintain close friendships, except with those who believe as they do. In extreme cases, such individuals isolate themselves in the name of self-protection or comfort. If their isolation continues, they will feel alienated from others, confident that they are not understood or appreciated. This extreme condition exists in many people who commit dramatic crimes to draw attention to themselves.

There are still more labels for difficult children. Autism is the name given to a broad category of communicational disorders characterized by difficulty in receiving and interpreting visual, auditory, and tactile sensation. The condition varies in severity, and extreme cases usually require institutionalization. But less severely affected children who are not able to deal competently with what they see, hear, and touch are not able fully to participate in emotional communication with others. They may learn language, may even be more intelligent than average, but they have gaps in what they hear and speak. Their inability to communicate with others makes them difficult to live with and to teach. They yell when frustrated and may eventually swear excessively or simply be indifferent to what they are asked to do. It is hard for them to learn how they affect others, and they usually demonstrate a lack of sensitivity and empathy. In some cases, they may be excited by someone else's pain or difficulty, smiling or laughing at displays of violence they see on television or elsewhere. This lack of regard for others may be manifested in excessive aggressiveness that leads to fighting and arguing. Children with communicational problems may not show a normal wariness and apprehension about risky or dangerous situations. They charge off into action with little or no thought of physical harm that might result.

Occasionally, this communication problem is related to thought disorders involving fear of others or strange, illusionary notions. Such a condition may be diagnosed as childhood schizophrenia. Most often this condition can only be modified somewhat by medicine and psychotherapy.

Sometimes it is difficult to assign a precise label to a child who has difficulty warming to others or being re-

sponsive to comfort and care. Some children have con-
genital physical or sensory handicaps; some have been
injured by a traumatic birth; some have been abused and
neglected by parents who themselves are troubled or
handicapped in some way. But regardless of how we label
them, we have judged them to be difficult because they
are vulnerable to many distractions, prone to impulsive
acts, and tend to be locked into emotional immaturity. They
may also be defensive, shifting blame to others; they may
be unwilling to openly disclose their feelings and ideas.
Their guardedness may appear as prejudice and negative
moods. They have difficulty complying with rules and
completing tasks. They may be disruptive to others and
have a difficult time making and keeping friends.

Although some parts of these descriptions can apply
to all children at some time or another, difficult children
consistently demonstrate many of these characteristics at
once. Even if parents do not know the exact nature of the
problem, or the label for it, any parent who has a difficult
child knows there is something wrong, because they and
the family are so affected and disturbed that they are unable
to ignore what this child does.

Difficult Children and Moral Behavior

Children who have emotional or cognitive limitations
have more difficulty than usual in learning moral behavior.
There are many reasons. For one, we can see that they
might have a difficult time learning about and understanding the parts of a moral circumstance. These difficult children do not easily complete tasks or develop task-oriented
skills. They are highly anxious individuals who are likely
to misperceive or misjudge other people because they do
not correctly interpret or understand such cues as facial
expressions, emotional reactions, or voice tones. Parents
may take for granted that these important cues are available

and clear to everyone. For these children they are available but not clear.

In some cases, children at risk know they are not understanding correctly and become afraid. They may, for example, make certain that a teacher does not like them; they may intentionally alienate friends. They may show intense reluctance to participate in activities where social skills are going to be required. Some avoidance of school, for example, can be related to children's inability to understand the interpersonal events of classroom and playground.

Difficult children tend to be controlled by whatever circumstance they are in because they do not conceptualize and recognize the situations that require rule-governed behavior. When knowledge of a moral standard is needed, they may be focused mentally on some other aspect of the situation and fail to evaluate correctly what is right and what is wrong. A ten-year-old child told me of throwing mud balls at the school building during recess. After he told of the details, I asked him what was right or wrong about throwing mudballs at the school building. His answer revealed his thought process. He said, "Anyone who hurts me [meaning his teacher] is going to get hurt." I asked again, "What is right or wrong about throwing mudballs at the school building?" He replied, "My friends and I were just having fun."

Every time I asked, he told of friends, being mad at a teacher he thought had hurt him, or trying to see who could throw the farthest. He never explained what was right or wrong because these ideas were not useful or relevant to him. He described virtually any situation the same way. He knew about people in some limited way, and he could describe what he had done, but he could not identify any standard of right or wrong.

Difficult children also are limited in their ability to carry out the moral tasks. They usually have difficulty in reasoning about ideas and integrating the information that comes from several sources (moral standard, other people, the tasks of a situation). They are often impulsive rather than deliberate in making decisions. Their emotions are so intense and variable that they often cannot manage or adapt them. And it is difficult for them to sustain a course of action to completion.

Although this long description may seem negative, even hopeless, there is much we can do. We can gather information and learn new skills. We can adapt our parenting styles to fit the special needs of these children. We will have to be patient instead of frustrated, understanding instead of judging. We can magnify and extend our ability to love them, for they will require all we can develop.

Parental Strategies for Difficult Children

The usual family group has parents (perhaps two parents, a single parent, or an older relative) who give some form of discipline, basic physical care, affection, and warmth, and who have other strong emotions. Difficult children stretch and pressure these normal family conditions. That is especially true if any child's behavior makes us organize or adapt our family life to deal with special needs.

As parents we can make some very specific adaptations that will help us teach such children. First, we can *reduce their anxiety* rather than just try to control their actions. Ordinarily, parents try to get children to do something or to stop doing something without worrying too much about their feelings. But when we set up a plan of discipline or attempt to teach children, especially difficult children, it is helpful to begin by communicating to them that we understand the need to help them be calm. That means we can talk in calm tones, use affection (if they will allow it), and ask them to calm themselves, before we correct them or teach them something.

Next, we need to *focus on one situation at a time*. When

children make many mistakes in many places, we tend to want them to correct everything at once. But we will be more effective in helping them if we temper our urgency and work on learning and succeeding in one situation at a time. We can, for example, work on friendship skills until a child is reasonably effective in friendships. Children can learn, for instance, what to do when a visitor comes to the home, how to answer the telephone, how to eat properly, what to do when leaving home to play, and how to come home on time. One mother, for example, purchased a digital watch for her son and had a training session with him every day until he could leave and come back in fifteen minutes, a half hour, and so on. We can teach children to follow through on one chore instead of several. We can help them handle one hour of school instead of an entire day, adding time until they have learned to do it all.

It will help if we can *concentrate on small successes*. Realistic expectations can prevent much frustration. Learning to say, "I'm fine, thank you," or doing one chore better, is not the same thing as becoming a model child, but any improvement deserves our attention.

And always it is very important that we *do not withdraw emotional support* from difficult children. Sometimes the frustration and embarrassment associated with their behavior is so great that we want to hide or at least disassociate ourselves. When that happens we may find that we feel less close to them or less loving. Moreover, difficult children may have difficulty loving us. We, however, are the teachers of love and support, and so we must give love and support in a sustained and consistent way. Children often do not understand why they do what they do, and they will only be hurt and confused, not motivated, if we withdraw our love in an attempt to discipline them.

In addition to these special adaptations, some specific strategies will help children to function better and to learn morality. They are based on recognizing children's emotional style. Some children are very intense; others are mellow. Some are insecure; some are confident. Combinations of the two types of intensity and the two types of security produce four emotional styles. Understanding all four emotional styles and how to respond to each of them can help us further adapt to our children.

When children's emotional style is *secure* and *high intensity*, children—
Are socially aggressive.
Show leadership among friends.
Make such social mistakes as talking too much or saying inappropriate things.
Are adventurous.
Challenge authority, often asking why or asking for reasons.
React quickly but calmly.
Can talk openly with parents.
Have fluctuating moods but are usually cheerful.
With children whose emotional style is secure and high intensity, parents can—
Show examples and require children to talk calmly about their reactions.
Require children to develop a strategy for what they want to accomplish.
Show high levels of affection, which quickly increases emotional control.
Require children to make choices about how they will act in a situation and then hold them to their choice.
Ask children to identify their emotions and talk about their feelings when they are talking about themselves.
Use strategies of positive reinforcement to improve children's responses.
Help children be aware of how to act in many different social situations.
Actively teach children ways to control their emotions by talking about ways to develop self-control: thinking about something else, using self-commands, realizing that

parents expect self-control as a disciplinary measure, or take time out to cool off away from the situation.

When children's emotional style is *secure* and *low intensity,* children—
Have mild fluctuations of mood.
Are generally cheerful and pleasant.
Are sometimes very passive and unresponsive.
Will play tricks or perform secret acts of deceit.
Occasionally say what people want to hear to remove pressure on themselves.
Avoid confrontations but will carry emotions for longer periods—for example, hold a grudge.
With children whose emotional style is secure and low intensity, parents can—
Expose them to social opportunities.
Actively teach children ways to control their emotions by talking about ways to develop self-control: thinking about something else, using self-commands, realizing that parents expect self-control as a disciplinary measure, or take time out to cool off away from the situation.
Use emotion words—happy, sad, angry, calm—and engage children in many conversations about feelings.
Ensure that children feel affection (it is easy to ignore these children if they do well).
Use routine discipline—systems of rules and consequences work well.

When children's emotional style is *insecure* and *high intensity,* children—
Are emotionally explosive (have tantrums).
Respond impulsively to external stimuli.
Talk excessively.
Lie to avoid responsibility.
Fail to follow through on tasks.
React oppositionally when they are told what to do.
Argue when told no.

Adopt excitement shown by others.

Express anger more readily when they are tired or hungry.

With children whose emotional style is insecure and high intensity, parents can—

Emphasize the children's need to control their emotions and to have strategies for how they will act in specific situations, to delay action while they think ("stop, look, and listen"), and to watch vigilantly for how people act and for the cues of social situations.

Use structured techniques for positive reinforcement to control behavior.

Remember to calm children before talking to them or correcting them.

Ignore their tantrums.

Rehearse with them how they should act in situations they may face in the grocery store, for example, or in church, at school, and so on.

When children's emotional style is *insecure* and *low intensity,* children—

Are socially inhibited (isolate themselves).

Show fear in many situations by shyness or blushing.

May have long periods of depression.

Avoid challenges and fear new situations.

Have difficulty talking to others.

With children whose emotional style is insecure and low intensity, parents can—

Involve them with groups of children and reinforce them when they get along well.

Work to create conversations (and it can be real work to do that).

Use pantomimes or charades to teach emotions.

Help them develop a talent that can be used socially (playing a musical instrument, for example, or reciting poems).

Use praise abundantly.

While we are learning to make adaptations, we can remember some additional things that will help us. One is that morality is learned over a long period of time, and though at any one time children may not seem consistently able to behave morally, the influence of our efforts to teach them may be seen later. Furthermore, they deserve to learn all they can in order to have the best chance for their own success. We can help them do that.

Successfully teaching difficult children is not easy. As parents we live in a world that requires more of us than rearing children. When children have needs beyond the ordinary, our lives are unavoidably affected and the decisions we face are often not easy or enjoyable to make. If we are not well prepared mentally, difficult children can provoke marital problems, raise the family tension level to maximum, and stimulate us to be our worst selves rather than our best. Our effectiveness in teaching children moral behavior will be diminished if we have difficulty exercising family leadership, if we fail to be unified as parents, or if we are poorly organized. We will be further hampered in our efforts if we face life with rigid, inflexible rules or expectations, if we suffer from excessive stress or pressure in our personal lives, or if we have low tolerance for the frustrations and exasperation children present to us.

Teaching morality to children requires us to learn and apply strong leadership and loving commitment. We can begin by being mature enough to adjust our expectations and recognize that children do not have to turn out a specific way and at a definite time for us to be successful parents. We need to appreciate that our children's actions often represent their own struggle with life more than they reflect on our parenting. Besides, it takes many years for children to mature. It is a bad idea to decide that any particular child has turned out badly at any point or age. Human development is unfinished as long as we live. Even if we are alone in trying to help a child when no one else can or will, we can better maintain the hope that fuels our efforts if we have a long-term perspective.

Robert and Ryan: More Parental Strategies

Cheryl and Max Simons adopted twin boys and later found that they both had attention deficit disorders (ADD). As infants they were intense, difficult to comfort, overactive boys. When they went to school, they could not follow rules or finish work, and they did not progress. Max and Cheryl decided to hold them back a year, and the boys repeated the first grade. Their pediatrician prescribed medicine, which helped the boys regulate their own behavior. Their classroom behavior and school work improved, but the boys were disruptive and aggressive in social situations. They broke family rules, swore vehemently when angry, and fought between themselves and with other children. Further, there was little evidence that they were developing any sense of right or wrong or concern for other people.

When they came to me for counseling, Max and Cheryl were often so exhausted and filled with stress that they wanted only to know how to maintain themselves. So our visits together were balanced between propping up the parents and developing plans to teach and control the children. We had to develop a rationale so that Max and Cheryl could feel good about leaving their sons in order to be alone and could avoid filling their entire lives with helping with homework and otherwise supervising them.

The boys seemed never to rest. They could not follow such simple routines as getting up, getting dressed, making their beds, and cleaning their room. They worked only with help and supervision. There were the problems in school to overcome and also in church. The boys were disruptive in Sunday School, jumping around, yelling, and refusing to obey their teacher. Most troubling to their parents, however, was that the boys stole things, lied, broke rules, and seldom showed remorse for what they did.

Together we worked out a plan that has seemed to help both parents and children. This plan was designed to achieve two goals: to help the boys develop self-control and improve their performance at school and home, and to help the boys develop morality.

The parents *adjusted what they expected from their children.* These boys were not going to develop in some areas at the same rate as other children did, so if the parents compared them with other children, they would feel discouraged and impatient. The school counselor arranged for Max and Cheryl to get in touch with parents of other children in a similar situation so that they would better know what to expect.

The parents *avoided yelling, scolding, spanking, and other common displays of frustration.* Children with ADD have elevated emotions and are tense and in turmoil. If parents yell and scold, the children will be hurt and confused rather than understand their parents' frustration. Both parents kept charts of the times when they "lost it" until they could go one full month without exploding. Sometimes they had to take turns dealing with the boys, each warning the other, "Your turn!" when the end of the rope had been reached.

The parents *structured a few chores and family rules.* They told the boys how to perform a few chores, showed them how to do those chores properly, and practiced doing the chores with them. Consequences were related to each task or rule so that if the boys failed, they lost a privilege such as playtime, going to a game with Dad, and so on. It was hard at first for Max and Cheryl to be as firm and definite as necessary. When they wanted to let the boys make it up or try again, I explained, "If you make a rule, enforce it, or get rid of it."

The parents *used incentives.* To begin with, each task was associated to a reward or incentive the boys could earn, such as a family activity, points that could be used toward buying a new toy, etc. After they had performed a task several times, the boys were rewarded if they did it without being asked. Then the rewards were no longer used every time.

The parents *met and communicated frequently with other adults who worked with the boys.* Max and Cheryl visited with schoolteachers, church leaders, Scout leaders, and neighbors. They found these people understanding and willing to help by sending notes, making phone calls, and keeping one another informed.

The parents *saw to it that misbehavior was followed by conversations and practice of the correct behavior.* When either boy misbehaved, he was first calmed down and then required to talk with his parents about what he had done. He was asked to discuss his feelings, and the parents talked about their own. The goal was to help the boys assume responsibility for their acts, identify what was wrong or right, and let them know they were cared for. Then the boys were required to practice the correct behavior until they got it right. For example, if one did not come home on time from playing, he had to put on a digital watch and practice going outside and returning in five minutes, then ten, and then fifteen minutes.

The parents *anticipated new situations and practiced in preparation for them.* Rather than wait for the boys to enter new situations and fail in handling them because they were excited and out of control, Max and Cheryl helped the boys practice what to do. In a weekly "family night," the parents used pantomimes and charades to teach correct or successful behavior for new situations the boys would face the following week. These practice sessions helped the boys realize greater success.

The parents *taught their children to use self-commands.* When either boy could not control himself in some situation, the parents had him practice what they wanted him to do. While he was practicing, he would whisper self-instructions. "Close the door," "Put my shoes in the closet," "Walk quietly into the school building," and "Do not talk until the teacher calls on me." The self-commands were especially useful to control impulsiveness. Each boy was taught to "stop, look, and listen" and to "go slow" to help him think before acting.

The parents *provided opportunities for their children to help other people.* To teach empathy and awareness, Max and Cheryl asked the boys to help each other and other children. On family night they reported what they had done to help. Sometimes the parents and the boys worked together to help someone. When one boy came home and told about a boy whose father had lost his job, the family planned a helping program that included giving food and money.

The parents *conscientiously taught that there is a right and a wrong.* Cheryl and Max asked each boy, usually at meals, what was right and wrong about many different acts, in many different situations. The boys developed clearer ideas about right and wrong. When they were asked, they could say what was right and and what was wrong about many actions. They accepted that doing right would be rewarded and doing wrong would result in teaching conversations and practice. These discussions, together with actions linked to consequences, helped them recognize the first level of morality: there is a right and a wrong. From that level they could progress to more complex reasoning, judgment, and conduct.

Melissa: Still More Parental Strategies

Bob and Heather Sunquist wanted a well-organized family that ran like clockwork. Bob expected Heather to have dinner at regular times, the children to do homework at specific times, and each child to do family chores at a prearranged time during the week. Bob's engineering background appeared to influence his concept of family leadership and organization. When their daughter Melissa had difficulties at birth, they were relieved when she seemed normal. But as she grew, she displayed signs that all was not well. The Sunquists were worried about her extreme emotional reactions, including yelling and screaming, tantrums, and oppositional reactions. When she grew older, she began to insult people and to swear.

Thinking their daughter was simply disobedient, they first attempted to find some way to control her. They tried to set rules and pressure her into following them. They told her what she should do and when to do it, reminded her often when she did not, became angry and sometimes used physical force to make her comply. They grounded her, scolded her, yelled at her, spanked her, and isolated her. Nothing seemed to work.

Melissa fought back. She resisted them in many ways. She did her chores, for example, only when forced or supervised; she sulked and pouted around the house and misbehaved at school and in the evening with friends. She tried different insults on her parents to see if she could get them to argue. When she did, even if she lost the argument and was punished, her parents reported that she smiled with satisfaction. As Melissa grew, the confrontations between her and her parents became more intense, so that by the time she was fourteen they had yelled, sworn at, and hit each other several times.

The parents were frustrated that she would not obey them and fit into their family plan. They began having difficulty with their other children because of Melissa's example in often not doing what the other children were required to do. Melissa was hurt and angry that she was treated "so badly." She was also extremely defensive, blaming others for her behavior and unable to express her own thoughts and feelings. She was certain that most people would hurt her if she grew emotionally close to them. As a result, she did not have close friends, and even though she spent time with girlfriends and boyfriends, she displayed suspicion toward them as she did everyone.

She often lied. Once when her parents had restricted her from school activities, she wanted to go to a school ballgame, so she arranged to visit a cousin who lived nearby and spend the night. Her boyfriend picked her up at the cousin's house and took her to the game. They stayed out most of the night. Melissa enlisted her cousin's help, and they both said they had stayed home and watched videos the whole evening. Lying was associated with several other forms of misbehavior, including shoplifting, skipping school, and drinking.

By age thirteen, she had developed an eating disorder. When her parents learned she was bulimic, they placed her in a hospital for a thirty-day program of regulation and therapy. While there, she performed well, adjusted her eating habits, and became calmer. When she returned home, her tension increased and her bulimic symptoms returned, as did the conflict with her parents.

Bob and Heather wanted to help Melissa and sought counseling for her. I explained that working with her alone would probably be necessary but not sufficient. They too would need to participate to reduce family conflict and teach Melissa a sense of morality.

Resolving defensiveness. Melissa was so angry, hurt, and afraid that it took several conversations before she would speak openly with me. I often sat in silence while she decided whether to speak to me at all. Gradually she began to voice her feelings, which at first were some anger at me and very intense anger toward her parents. These feelings were followed by frustration and despair with her situation, and then hurt and sadness. As I worked with her parents, they began to listen more than they explained, criticized, or regulated her. It was very hard for them to ask questions and listen attentively while she said things they thought to be untrue and that often hurt them. Over time all three formed an uneasy truce.

Reduce tension. It took a while before these parents were willing to understand that open conflict might be more

harmful than a child's disobedience, especially if the disobedience was minor. Then it took them a while to learn
to avoid conflict situations, whether they themselves pro-
voked them or Melissa attempted to. About the same time,
they agreed to do some enjoyable things with the whole
family. To their surprise, Melissa readily agreed to participate.

Adapting some family rules. I explained that the condition
they wanted in their family would be better achieved if
they used a method other than setting an explicit, rigid
rule and pressuring their children to comply. In Melissa's
case, this was an invitation to oppose and resist. We examined the rules, dropping some and making others
flexible, such as mealtimes. (*Flexible* meant that times and
expected conduct were not always rigid and fixed.) I suggested that we could help Melissa be less oppositional if
we helped her go through a process of making decisions
at every possible opportunity. When the parents asked
Melissa to do some task, if she opposed, they were to tell
her she was perfectly free to do her work and feel worthwhile about it, or she was perfectly free not to do her work
and receive the consequences. That was the first step in
helping her make decisions. When Melissa wanted to know
what the consequences would be if she did not do as she
was asked, her parents said, "If you cannot be trusted to
do some small task, when the time comes that you want
something from us, we will not be able to give it to you
because we haven't been able to see you be responsible
for yourself." Then they were to ask her again to decide.

*Making children earn what they want by participating in
relationship events.* Melissa was informed that allowance or
other privileges depended on whether or not she was able
to join in family activities, participate in conversations, and
manage herself respectfully and cooperatively with other
family members. This reinforcement system soon helped
her become more constructive in her relationships with
others and helped her feel more like she belonged.

Increasing the number of parental refusals in connection with children's extreme oppositional reactions. When Melissa became overly incensed at being refused something she wanted, her parents told her that her next request would automatically be refused also. If she could adjust to being told no, then they would try to give her permission as often as they felt they could do so.

Eliminating harsh words and physical punishment. To improve family relationships, everyone agreed to eliminate swearing, insults, and physical punishment such as hitting, hair-pulling, shoving, and kicking. We developed a penalty that each person would have to pay if any of this took place. For example, if the father did any of these actions, he agreed to take his wife, Melissa, and other family members out to dinner, or else to pay everyone some money.

Engaging in conversations about what helps and what hurts people. I asked the parents and Melissa to discuss how people are helped and hurt. These conversations gave them a chance to practice listening to each other and helped them focus on something other than arguing or blaming each other for past mistakes and hurts they had experienced. These conversations helped them become more aware of what helps and what hurts people.

Helping others. Melissa's parents began a program of helping others. Each family member drew the name of another. For one week each agreed to do helpful things for that person. The family also performed service for a neighbor and with their church. Curbing violent emotions, reducing tension, and starting positive and loving experiences helped these parents alter the course of life for their daughter. The great amount of effort required from them is not fully expressed in these paragraphs, nor is the frustration and emotional pain, but I believe they felt rewarded for their efforts when they watched their daughter begin to do more constructive things and gain some measure of control over her own life.

The two preceding examples illustrate techniques that work with some children. Because parents, children, and family circumstances vary considerably, these particular suggestions may not work in every case; however, they are based on the following principles, which can be adapted to suit many different families and many different difficult children.

Taking the offense. Difficult children are usually unstable and will cause people to react to them. Teaching moral behavior is usually most effective when parents have a plan and expect our children to participate in it as much as they want us to respond to them. We only need to balance our plan with healthy doses of what is reasonable to expect from them.

Taking our sails out of their wind. Children's verbal behavior is often mean and insulting. It provokes us because they are hurt, angry, and want to hurt someone. If we get entangled in it by arguing and blaming them, we will discover that the verbal arguments expand rather than solve problems. It is better to smile, ignore, walk away, or do virtually anything other than be drawn into a verbal tangle by an angry child.

Remembering that love is an end in itself. Many of us link the expression of our love to correct performance by our children. It is best to separate love and our expressions of it from anything else. We need to commit ourselves to express love often and regularly without regard to what children do. We love children who lie, who don't do their chores, and who insult us. This love may force us to be tough or gentle, firm or flexible, but never rejecting, withdrawn, or bitter.

Arranging for strategic separations. Family life can be strenuous under the best of conditions, but with difficult children the strain is magnified. If we recognize that, we can take time away from each other occasionally to give us a chance to rest and to give children a break from us. Many parents feel like prisoners in their own homes and fear leaving because of what their children might do. When parents can find adequate sitters, leaving will help them to get a different perspective. If there are two parents, they can also benefit from time alone together to renew their marriage partnership, but it is often even more important that single parents occasionally retreat to renew themselves. We just need to remember that bad things happen whether we are at home or away.

The World Outside the Home and Family

When difficult children are present in a home, it is generally wise to assume two things. First, the children will be susceptible to whatever influences they find outside the home, whether good or bad, because they are less able than most children to control themselves. Second, parents will usually have to interact with people outside the family to keep their children from getting involved in what might hurt them and to ensure that they will learn positive and useful things. The following practices have been developed by parents who have found them useful when dealing with children difficult to teach.

Organize groups of parents in the neighborhood, and establish some common ground rules for social activities. These groups can make rules governing how late children should be out, the number of activities they can join in each week, what activities are acceptable, and rotating parties or other constructive activities for them. Having such groups of parents will prevent children from using the leverage that "other kids have different and better," or more lenient, "rules." Knowing that other parents are following similar rules will strengthen us in our attempts to help our children.

Create participation in positive activities. Many parents help their children take piano, gymnastics, karate, dance, and other lessons. Difficult children also benefit from participating in Scouts, school plays, athletics, and any activity that brings adults and young people together for useful purposes. The trouble and inconvenience of helping them participate is usually less than the frustration of letting difficult children do nothing. We may have to become a leader or otherwise participate with our children for them to join in. Or, in some cases, we may need to stay home for them to feel free to participate.

Get acquainted with children's friends. We need to know the friends our children spend time with and ask to meet them. If we bring them into our home, unless they are truly deviant, they will be affected by our influence. When they are around, we can talk to them and listen to them. They will usually appreciate our attention to them.

Know high-risk situations. Difficult children are usually vulnerable to anything that provides them sensory stimulation. Pornography, drugs, alcohol, thrills (including shoplifting), and sex provide such sensory stimulation. Rather than assuming that we will be too restrictive if we prevent our children's going to places where these are available, it is best to explain proved alternatives and reduce their freedom. There is a point at which children get beyond our control, and then there may be less we can do in this regard. While they are young, however, it is usually best to be firm, even definite, about the issue.

Manufacture success. Difficult children have many struggles that contribute to feelings of failure and inadequacy. For one thing, they bring failure on themselves because of undeveloped social skills and inadequate performance skills. Whenever possible, we can encourage them to participate in activities we think they will succeed in. One set of parents enrolled their son (who was an ADD child) in a karate club and took him to his lessons. They all benefited from learning the philosophy of nonviolence, and the boy was able to succeed at something important to him. The secondary benefits of recognition he received from his friends also helped.

Arrange public displays of helping. In church, school, and civic programs, children can participate in public helping activities. These group activities make it legitimate for children to develop the desire and skills necessary to help others. One group of teens makes lap robes for aged women at a nursing home. They go to the home and deliver the robes and then visit and talk to the residents. Another group provides entertainment at a home for older people. Still another group cleans the litter from a two-mile stretch of nearby interstate highway. Other examples abound. Caring and concern for others is learned as a group and felt by individuals.

Identify social service agencies. Many organizations can help with the task of helping a difficult child learn to be moral. They can provide teaching materials, help impose consequences when children behave improperly, and they are usually concerned, too. To find these organizations, we can check with a church leader, school counselor, or government youth agency.

Communicate with anyone having regular contact with our children. When difficult children go out into the world, they may have difficulty with others. Often, our children are in a continuing cycle of frustration and failure because we have not communicated with others who are faced with teaching or training them. That means we need to visit schools, school counselors, teachers, church leaders, Scoutmasters, and so on. They are going to have the task of helping our child. In most cases, they are willing to help, but we make their burden lighter by letting them know we are interested and involved. By getting to know them and communicating regularly with them, what we and they do can be coordinated, making it less likely that our child will be treated carelessly or improperly.

The Best We Can Expect

Difficult children teach us as much as we teach them. If nothing else, we learn how precious childhood is, and we learn the power of love and devotion. Difficult children

may try us, but they make us enter into the drama of life.
No parent who cares can stand on the sidelines merely
observing. Difficult children require that we confront ourselves and grow in ways that we would not otherwise
grow. We may one day appreciate what we have shared
together.

The core of parenthood is not so much in developing
a child's talents or promoting academic pursuits as in preparing a child to live a mature, moral life. The formation
of character is the enduring part of our work, and in this
we find the dream and the power of being fathers and
mothers. In a world filled with enticements, pressures,
and opportunities, there are many who avoid rather than
seek the challenges of parenthood. We who have difficult
children may wish we had done so. But if we persevere
with children we know are at risk, and if we do our best
to teach morality to these difficult children, we will know
better than most parents that being good parents is the
best thing we have ever done.

CHAPTER 14

HYPOCRISY

Young children surprise and delight us because they show us humanity in its innocence, its beginning. We see their thoughts represented in very obvious actions. If children are looking at a cookie or a little red ball, we can, if we watch, see their intentions revealed in their actions. Childhood is a sincere and trusting time. Little children do not hide things from us because they cannot. What we see is what they are.

As they improve their language and other cognitive skills, children improve their ability to have inner experiences that are not shown in their outer behavior. They and we learn that they can show one thing but be feeling or thinking another. The age of innocence has been traded for the age of magic, where children's first attempts to live in a sometimes confusing world are both humorous and serious. They say words that do not fit the time or meaning. Their actions may not fit what is appropriate, but we do not care much; we enjoy what we see because it is evidence of life and growth.

As children grow up, they meet a greater variety of social situations, and more requirements are placed on them; they encounter more evaluations, more approval or disapproval. It doesn't take long for children to discover that appearing or seeming appropriate brings as much approval and avoids as much disapproval as actually *being* appropriate. Perhaps that is the birth of hypocrisy, when children find that protecting themselves from the disapproval of others is more important to them than saying honestly what they think, feel, believe, or have done. Thus it is important to protect our children from harsh judgment until they gain confidence in themselves and in those who evaluate them. If they are reared in love, acceptance, and warmth and have firmly set limits, most children will learn the peace of mind that results from integrity. If children are themselves anxious and fearful and if they are reared in harshness, they may learn that their safety depends of their ability to deceive and misrepresent.

We understand, of course, that keeping information from others is not always wrong. For example, we may rightfully and properly keep disappointing or embarrassing experiences private to protect ourselves or others from public criticism. As long as this hiding is not immoral — that is, as long as we do not hurt ourselves or others — we are not deceitful. The kind of hiding that leads to hypocrisy is the deceit of creating or maintaining a reputation or image before others that is not based on truth and accuracy and is designed to cover immoral or hurtful things that someone has done or intends to do.

When an insecure child fears the judgment of others and pretends or tells a white lie as a form of self-protection, that is not yet hypocrisy. When children have not acquired the ability or confidence to express themselves accurately and yet are confronted with people and situations that seem to demand certain beliefs and behavior, their "hypocrisy" is more incompetence than intentional deceit. They may not even know that they have done something other than what was called for. Adolescents may sometimes pretend in order to prevent their private thoughts and acts (which they are hiding to give themselves a sense of freedom) from being exposed. This pretense is an attempt to adjust the difference between what is expected and a child's less-than-acceptable behavior.

Hypocrisy is one moral issue that has received considerable attention. For parents, pretense and deception in children are moral issues because failure to grow out of them keeps children from learning morality. If we do not understand this well, we may unwittingly teach exactly what we do not want to teach. We may overreact when we see what appears to be hypocrisy in our children, even when their deviations from the truth may be a normal part of their development. By the same token, we may under-react and fail to appreciate how truly damaging many forms of deception can be. Further, if we don't understand the kinds of deception that are the roots of hypocrisy, we cannot teach integrity, the moral opposite of hypocrisy. We may fail to help our children learn how to succeed in life as moral people. Failing to teach them the significance of integrity may be thought of as permission for them to continue through life believing that something other than integrity is acceptable and good.

Values and beliefs are not stronger than actions. If children persistently behave contrary to their values, their values will change. They will not learn that hypocrisy is wrong or inappropriate. They will come to see it as an effective tool to use to get along in life. Many people assume that all criminals know what is right but that they choose to break the law. These people might be shocked to learn that many criminals believe that crime is the most effective way of living and believe in it just as strongly as law-abiding people believe otherwise. Similarly, many truly believe that hypocrisy is necessary, perhaps more important to life than integrity.

Some believe that they can get what they want from life only through deceit. These people use hypocrisy to acquire. Others are hypocritical to achieve recognition. The desire for reputation stems from the notion that being well known is synonymous with personal success and significance. All of us know of public personalities who pretended something to achieve their fame. Hypocrisy may be used as the means to acquire power over others when people think that position and authority stamp them with worth and importance.

To the degree that people are hypocritical they will lack a true sense of belonging with other people. Hypocrisy inhibits feelings of empathy and acceptance. It creates lives that are emotionally shallow rather than deep and rich, barren rather than fruitful. We want, then, to be aware of how pretense and deception rob children of their emotional membership in families and groups of friends, even if their friendships are based on deviance from the moral standard.

Pretense and deception serve numerous individual purposes. We may feel the need to pretend when a family problem is exposed to others. We may feel that someone's arrogance justifies our exaggeration of our own qualities. When we think our actions are being scrutinized by others, we may feel great apprehension and pretend in order to reduce our anxiety. All pretending may be dangerously close to the sinister deception of hypocrisy and therefore the enemy of moral character. If we wish to teach morality to our children, we must help them avoid the path to hypocrisy. We can do that if we have integrity ourselves and help our children learn that success, however defined, will always be more than just pleasing others or achieving reputation. When children work toward any goal, we can help them understand that their satisfaction will be incomplete unless their efforts have been honest and true.

Adult Examples

Most parents acknowledge the power of example in several ways. If we are aware that our own actions are not what we want our children to do, we tell them, "Do as I say, not as I do." We hope that making this statement will offset the times when our actions do not match what we say or preach to them. It is a weak rationalization for parents who cannot or who will not rearrange their example so that it matches what they say.

Children are vulnerable to the influence of adult example for at least two reasons. First, they are developing and changing. They are growing toward some goal that they think adults have achieved. If they think we are what they are striving to become, they assume our example is what they must learn in order to make progress. When they do as we do in many situations (in religion, for example, or in social settings, sports), they are highly reinforced when they see our pleased and happy response. Second, children are not able to tolerate much confusion. If they see two contradicting examples, they will shut one out of their minds to reduce tension or frustration. When they are confronted with actions that do not match what they are told, children usually shut out the words they hear and respond to the actions they see.

James Bryan and his colleagues (1969) supported the idea that children follow what they see people do. They organized a bowling game for third- and fourth-grade children. If the children scored high enough, they received certificates that could be redeemed for money. The children were then shown a box where they could contribute donations to poor children. Adult supervisors talked to some of the children about the importance of giving to others (generosity). Other children listened to adults who talked about the importance of keeping money and using it for personal needs (greed). The results of the study showed that if the adults gave money, the children were more likely to give also, regardless of what the adult said.

Interestingly, in some conditions children were not affected by hypocrisy. Even when adult models told children to give but did not give themselves or preached avarice but gave donations, the children continued to be self-sacrificing. Children exposed to models who preached goodness, but practiced avarice were not less likely to sacrifice their winnings than children exposed to a consistently generous model. In this case, the children had learned that giving was important whether the adults told them to give or not to give.

Another important result of Bryan's research is that the

children liked the adult models who consistently talked about generosity and acted generously. They disliked the adults who talked about generosity but acted greedily. These children, eight or nine years of age, showed that they were willing to trust in those whose actions matched their words. In summary, then, children in this study were not put off by adult inconsistency but tended to do what they saw adults do; however, they would not enter into affectionate relationships with adults who were inconsistent.

Thinking about this finding as it applies to our relationship with our own children should give us pause. We understand that children are more influenced by those with whom they have emotional ties. One act of giving or not giving may be an isolated event, but moral character forms over a long period in relationships with trusted people. If our examples fail to match the words or exhortations we give children, they will find us less attractive. Once we lose their confidence, we will lose our ability to teach and influence them. They will have removed themselves from us.

Arnie Rochik learned this lesson the hard way. His son, Arnie Junior, was caught shoplifting at age fourteen. The boy had already gone through the juvenile court system and had made restitution for a previous crime. This time, Arnie Junior received a harsher sentence from the juvenile judge, but he continued to steal. Later he was caught breaking into a store. He and his parents were required to seek counseling.

During one of their family sessions, Arnie pleaded with his son to stop. "Why do you keep doing this?" he asked. "You're ruining your life." Turning to me, the father said, "He has everything he wants or needs. I don't see why he does this."

The boy sat stonefaced, looking at the floor. With mixed frustration and fear, Arnie Senior continued. "Why won't you listen to me and your mother?" The boy had shown no response to the first question, but now his head came up. He looked hard at his dad, but he still said nothing.

I realized something was on his mind and spoke to him. "If you can tell us, Arnie, I would like you to say why you won't listen to your parents."

His answer was a classic. "Dad tells us to go to church and to be good, but he's a crook." Startled, Arnie Senior protested. I quieted him and asked the boy to continue. "Yes, you are!" he defended. "You don't get the cars inspected, and you make your own sticker every year. You tell us how you weaseled money out of some guy at work or how you got some guy to buy more than he wanted." I could tell from the stricken look on Arnie Senior's face that his son was telling the truth. His wife sat in silent condemnation.

This conversation revealed that the family had two problems. One was that the boy was breaking the law and refused to stop. The other was that he was beyond his father's reach because the father's hypocrisy had disqualified him as a source of influence. The second problem is by far the worse. Arnie Junior might have made an unwise choice to steal, but if he had trusted his dad, he might have been willing to stop stealing when his father begged him to. But his father's pleading washed off, not felt. The boy was truly out of control.

Although it may be true that children tend to do what they see others do, example being more powerful than preaching or telling, it is consistency as part of integrity that determines whether or not we retain influence with our children. Over time, as we know, this emotional leverage may be the only thing that permits us to give direction or teach an important idea. Our consistent, or congruent, acts and words are like investments in a savings plan. They accrue with interest until the time comes when we need them to reach, teach, or influence our children. Over time, a child's moral future may depend on whether we have invested enough congruent acts and words.

What to Do When Children Are Deceitful

Children can learn hypocrisy as readily as they learn integrity, and they are influenced by the consistency or inconsistency of parents' words and acts. Now we need to identify the signs of hypocritical behavior in children, understand some reasons for it, and think about how to correct it.

To begin with, it is important to distinguish between the normal inconsistency of behavior that marks childhood and harmful, hypocritical behavior. Young children lie. They may impulsively say what they think will win them approval without regard for what they actually do, intend to do, or do not do. And, of course, they pretend in many ways. We accept much of this for a while because we assume it is a part of growing up.

If there is not a gradual change so that children get better at telling the truth, if the correspondence between what they say they do and what they actually do does not increase, then we suspect a problem. Most children, especially those who are young and inexperienced, have difficulty disguising their real feelings. We may see that their facial expressions do not match what their words mean, and even though we may not know what is true, we can at least tell that there is a discrepancy or conflict. It is this incongruence that cues us to trouble. Usually we are curious enough to suspect and to get more information than we are first given.

I learned about some difficulty one of my sons had had with a friend. I was not overly concerned, but I happened to watch him quite closely as we talked, and I noticed his nonverbal reaction to my question. He quickly tried to erase all emotion from his face, and a little too quickly he said, "Everything's all right now." His attempt to show no feelings meant to me that he still had some rather strong feelings. Rather than put pressure on him to tell me more about the problem, I decided to wait a while and talk to

him about the importance of telling his true feelings. He
never did say more about what had really happened with
his friend, but he did admit that sometimes he had a hard
time letting people know what he really felt. We decided
that sometimes it is hard even to know our own feelings,
but, if we are to feel good about ourselves, it is important
to make our words match what we feel and think.

Living in the privacy of our homes and families, we
get a pretty good idea about how our children ordinarily
act and feel. There will be times in the company of other
people when children's behavior is different from the
usual. Children may want to impress others and put their
best foot forward, so to speak. But if the change in children
is dramatically different in the company of others from
what it usually is at home, children have begun to learn
hypocritical behavior. In this case, hypocrisy may reflect
low self-esteem, an impulsive response to the situation,
or fear of others. But any of these reasons indicate that we
need to give increased attention to helping the child be
more comfortable in expressing himself authentically.

Around home and with her family, Heather was somewhat pessimistic, quiet and somber. During a birthday
party at their home, her mother overheard Heather make
exaggerated statements to several of the guests about her
family, her clothes, and her summer plans. As she listened,
it seemed clear that her daughter felt it was necessary to
pretend that things were more exciting than they really
were. At first the mother thought the child might be a little
embarrassed about her family, because earlier she had
made some apologetic comments about the living room
furniture being too old. Then it seemed more that Heather
was exaggerating to compensate for her own sense of inadequacy and was trying to find reassurance through the
acceptance and approval of her friends.

When the girls left, Heather went to her room. Her
mother went after her to talk. She first asked Heather if
she had had a good time. Then she complimented her

about the way she had dressed and the gracious way she had entertained her friends. Then she told Heather what she had overheard. Heather was about to disagree or tell her mother to go away, but seeing that her mother felt concern instead of criticism, she did neither. Instead, she nodded and said quietly, "Yeah, I guess I did."

"Do you know," her mother asked, "why you thought or felt it necessary to do that?" This question led to an exploration of the feelings of inadequacy Heather had around her friends. After talking this over, they came up with some more honest ways for Heather to win acceptance. Heather said later that the most impressive thing about the talk was her mother telling her, "If you gain acceptance from your friends by telling a lie, they might think you are neat, but it won't help because what they think is you is not really you."

Not all situations turn out as well as this one, and even this mother and daughter had more to do to solve the problem. The important thing to note, however, is that the mother in this case did not ignore this situation but attempted to help her daughter correct it before it led to something much worse.

A more harmful form of pretense is accompanied by lies. There are several reasons why children lie. Young children exaggerate. Older children lie because they fear exposure; they intentionally mislead to cover up something. Adolescents lie to overcome self-consciousness or to intentionally deceive. Although we may not be able to discern the truth immediately or the first time this happens, living with children allows us to detect when something recurs. When a child repeatedly lies, something is seriously wrong.

It is important first to analyze whether we ourselves are so aggressive and critical that our children lie because we have made them fearful. Loud, angry voices spewing accusations and criticism can make most children so afraid that lying seems a good alternative. If we are like that, we must make our conversation calmer and less critical before our children will feel free enough to speak what is true.

The next step is to identify the situations in which the lying takes place. Are they usually related to children's activities with friends? Do children lie about chores or schoolwork? Are the lies about family relationships? Knowing when lying takes place or what the lies are usually about moves us closer to understanding the real problem. If friends are involved, for example, it is reasonable to assume that they are up to something our children think will not be acceptable to us. And they are usually right.

Greg and Barbara Peterson went away for a weekend. They told their daughter Ann that she was not to have any friends over while they were gone, and they asked her to care for her younger brothers and sister. When they returned, one of the younger boys commented about a party Ann had had with her friends on Saturday night.

When confronted, Ann hotly denied that her friends had come over at all. Then, faced with a few facts, she acknowledged that they had come just for a visit, but had left early in the evening. After being told that her parents would call her friends in order to get the truth, Ann admitted that her friends had come over, brought some food, and stayed until early morning hours.

At this point, many of us would have reacted angrily and punished our children to show our displeasure. Ann's parents did a very wise thing. Greg and Barbara told her they wanted to talk with her again.

As the parents talked together about the problem, it occurred to them that Ann had lied other times about her friends. These lies involved how late they had been out for the evening, what friends she was with, and where she and her friends went. They also remembered that Ann had restyled her hair and insisted on getting some clothes that were extreme compared to her usual style but that were like clothes her friends wore. The parents had allowed these changes, thinking it important for Ann to be a part of the group.

During the talks they had with Ann, Greg and Barbara learned that Ann had not asked her friends over. But because her friends knew that Ann's parents would be gone, they arrived, uninvited, around nine o'clock Saturday night. They went into the house, began playing music, and eating and drinking. One couple found a bedroom and went in alone. Ann knocked on the door and told them that she didn't want them to be in the bedroom alone. "We're only talking," was the reply. Ann told her folks that she didn't know what to do after that, but the boy and girl soon left the house.

Then the parents learned that a water fight had been started and Ann was unable to stop it. Finally, around one o'clock, the kids began to leave, telling each other they would meet Monday at school. After hearing these details, the Petersons recognized that Ann was unable to maintain her standards around her friends. When caught up in the pressure to do something with them, Ann gave in, even when she knew it was not the best thing.

Then Greg and Barbara took a creative step. They called the parents of the other children who were involved and asked them to come over one evening. During their short meeting, the parents all expressed concern about what their children were doing. Together they decided to set some rules that all could and would follow. One was to decide how often they would allow the friends to get together. Another was to decide what activities they would give permission for the children to participate in. Because all the young people were thirteen and fourteen, they also decided on a curfew time.

Life returned to normal for the Petersons. In a few days, Ann told her parents that her friends were going to a dance at a place the group of parents had decided was off limits. Greg and Barbara told her she could not go. Ann got angry and asked, "Why not? Everyone else is going." "No, they aren't," she was told. "Just call them and see." Ann took the challenge and began to call her friends. To her surprise, she found that none of her friends could go because their parents wouldn't let them. Ann didn't protest anymore.

Similar things happened in the next few weeks. One day Ann fixed her hair almost the same way she had worn it before. She also seemed to lose interest in some of her friends and began to meet new ones. These changes were viewed as positive by her parents. These results were achieved by wise parents who recognized that often when children are together, no one person is in control but each child thinks the others are.

The Public and Private Lives of Teenagers

For some parents, their children's teenage years are some of the best times of family life. Other parents have different experiences, and their horror stories about adolescents make us nervous as our own children enter into this complex stage of life. If we view our teenaged children with sensitivity and compassion, we can notice that they are faced with particular and striking challenges. There is pressure to perform, to belong, but not to make waves. Many adults do not take teenagers seriously but expect them to understand very serious things. Teenagers are part of several groups or relationships that compete for time and effort. They are often pulled between friends, who accept them and offer little judgment, and adult authorities, who do judge and evaluate them.

Furthermore, adolescents are passing through puberty. Most develop physically at about the same time and experience the usual self-consciousness, social frustrations, and mixed happy-sad, excited-worried states. Some children, though, develop earlier than others. Boys seem to benefit from early development, from being better at throwing, running, jumping, and being more emotionally mature than their age mates. In our culture, girls who develop early are not so fortunate. Their more mature bodies often increase their self-consciousness and increase their sense of inadequacy. Boys who develop later than others are often emotionally immature, and they often have problems with self-esteem and difficulty with authority. Late-developing girls have more pleasant social experiences, and they tend to find satisfaction in achievement, but they may be quite insecure about themselves.

Children find various ways to adapt to the complexities brought on by physical development and other aspects of adolescence. One way is to develop a private and public life. Being private—doing things alone or with same-age friends—allows children to feel separate from the scrutiny of those who regulate. Being private—not communicating with others—also helps children test and evaluate parental rules against, or according to, their own experiences. That may help adolescent children achieve a sense of independence. Being private also allows children to experiment with new ways of acting, allowing them a sense of security that what they do will not be judged by others.

Having a public life means meeting and interacting with people outside the private realm. That requires children to avoid disapproval of those in authority in order to protect their private life. Usually a public life includes those activities that impress others (courtesy and conversation), as well as joining with others in socially approved events (going to church, getting decent grades, doing volunteer work). These are important to children because they build a positive reputation.

Some teenagers live a public and private life successfully and in this way find a modest sense of freedom and growth toward increased maturity. Others have a wide discrepancy between what they do privately and what they do publicly. They discover that public life seems to satisfy those who judge as well as to disguise what they do privately. That gives rise to the idea that they can experiment widely with many things, including things that are forbidden, and still avoid the attention of anyone who might regulate or disapprove. That is the beginning of lifetime hypocrisy.

John Mitchell (1980) writes that adolescents display four types of hypocritical behavior that are associated with their dual public and private lives: (1) to pretend to be what one is not; (2) to pretend not to be what one is; (3) to say negative things about someone in private but say positive things in public; and (4) to act or say what is expedient or what others want to see or hear.

We can see how these behaviors prevent positive moral development. Pretending to be something they are not enables children to impress someone in a public sense and achieve a good reputation even when private acts do not really earn them the reputation. Then, even though their private acts are immature or devious, it is possible to maintain their reputation and thereby satisfy parents and others by continuing the pretense. As a part of such pretense, speaking positively in public to or about someone perpetuates the reputation but permits private opinions to exist even if they are negative and critical. Finally, saying or doing something purely to satisfy others can protect children from having private acts exposed. Mitchell writes that the adolescent who says only what the school principal wants to hear, who behaves only in the way the gang leader expects, who feigns sincerity to win the confidence of a sweetheart, can be likened to an imposter, a con man, or a charlatan. These labels apply because saying or doing what is expedient manipulates others to achieve selfish results.

While some parts of the private-public life duality may be healthy and advantageous to our children, it is also apparent that this duality is dangerous. Therefore, one important task we have as parents is to distinguish for ourselves what part of this duality is healthy and what part is not. Then we can adapt what our children do.

That is not as easy as it may at first appear. Most of

us support our children, have strong feelings for them, hope for them, and wish them well. We are not looking for signs of deceit or deviance. Even when the signs are obvious, so obvious that everyone else can see them, many of us refuse to accept the meaning of what we see, preferring instead to hope blindly that our children are not doing wrong or immoral things. Yet, if we fail to act, we will make a mistake worse than those our children make. We will have failed to confront the issue, allowing it to continue and probably get worse.

Many parents, for example, finding pornography under children's mattresses, do not speak of it when, instead, we should take it immediately to our children and ask directly about it. We might pass it off as a minor thing when we hear children speak harmfully about others behind their back. We might see skipping school or minor scuffles with the law as insignificant, instead of recognizing that these acts may be part of a larger problem. We might think of insincerity and manipulation as a necessary part of adolescence and consequently fail to bring our children to an awareness of the harm they do to themselves and to others by such action.

Many of us can look back with the sad realization that had we acted when we first saw the "early warning" behavior in our children, we might have prevented the much more serious problems that appeared later.

That was the case with Hal Michaels. He was a single parent who loved his kids. His teenaged daughter Robin was upset at the divorce, the move away from the family home, and the reduced financial circumstances that resulted. She fought with her mother, and so she lived with her dad. Hal was attentive to her and her brother, but he worked full-time and as a result was often tired. Robin started to date, and she spent excessive time with her boyfriend. When Hal talked with her, she agreed to stay home more often, but things didn't change much. Her grades at school were still pretty good and she worked at her part-time job, so he thought she was doing okay. She was often silent around him and walked away when he tried to talk. He decided that trying to talk would only cause problems, so he didn't push it. He once overheard Robin say on the phone to a friend, "No one really knows me." At other times she talked about girls or women at their church who thought she was "neat" when she felt she really wasn't. She also said such critical things about her friends that he thought she would never be friends with these girls again. Later these same friends would show up, and Robin would act as though she liked them very much.

One evening when Hal was out, Robin had a few friends over for pizza and videos. She had asked in advance, and Hal had agreed. During that evening, Robin and her boyfriend had sexual intercourse for the first time. Robin had a strong religious background, and she felt much guilt and shame. The next day she found some pills and took an overdose in a genuine attempt to kill herself. She failed, however, which gave the father and daughter another chance. This time, Hal would recognize the danger signals and do something about them.

All of us face times when it is difficult to tell the truth. These moments are the touchstones of integrity. Our children deserve our help in learning to meet such moments with courage. If our children have grown to adolescence without having changed their immature tendencies to protect themselves by some form of hypocritical behavior, they will need our intervention so that they can develop more integrity. If we see our children handling the public-private duality of adolescence with all four types of hypocritical behavior noted by Mitchell, if we see that our children usually lie for the sake of convenience or self-protection or self-aggrandizement, if our children attempt to cover up or lie about immoral or improper acts, then our children are at risk, and we need to act immediately.

Using Children's Misbehavior to Teach Them

Not one of us wants our children to misbehave. We find, however, that they do it without coaching or instruction. Sometimes we become angry because we think our children's misbehavior reflects negatively on us. Sometimes we are disappointed, having expected more from our children. Sometimes we are indifferent, knowing that others do not know about the misbehavior and hoping that it will not happen again. Catching children in misbehavior is an emotionally charged experience for them and for us. We can be sure that they will notice and remember what we do at such a time.

The important part of correcting misbehavior is to do it in a way that helps children understand the consequences of their actions for themselves and for other people. Other guidelines for correcting misbehavior include matching punishment to the wrongdoing, keeping calm so that children will not be tempted to blame us instead of recognizing that they are responsible for their own actions, and, finally, getting children to practice doing right what they have done wrong.

When children are old enough and mature enough to know that they have done something wrong, their misbehavior not only violates some rule but also alienates them from family and friends. This sense of alienation, of not belonging, increases the risk of further immorality. Children are more likely to do wrong things when they believe that no one cares or that they do not matter than when they feel that they belong with people who love and support them.

The times when children misbehave and are found out are the times to help them learn the benefits of integrity and openness and the harm of deceit and secrecy. If children have misbehaved and been found out, we should remember that they will have thoughts and feelings about what was done and will be alert to what we do and say when the wrongdoing is discovered.

Before we act, we need to consider the actual wrongdoing and children's motives or reasons for the behavior. And if we are to teach morality and prevent the development of destructive hypocrisy, we need to consider the issue of deceitful secrecy itself. That means that we examine what children do to perpetuate the secrecy or deceit associated with their actions. We consider whether or not our children are willing to admit their responsibility and honestly tell what they did. When our children willingly confess their misbehavior, we must recognize the action of confessing as more responsible than if we learn about their actions another way and then have to pry facts out of them. An honest confession resolves the discrepancy between private and public acts and rids children of deceit.

When children are accused of wrongdoing, or when we learn of their misbehavior from someone else, we need certain skills to correct the misbehavior and teach children the pitfalls of secrecy and deceit. If we react too quickly or too harshly, they may bury their acts deeper in excuses and further deceit. We also prevent them from having the emotional time necessary for them to bring their private acts willingly into public knowledge. They may instead learn that hypocrisy is safer than making themselves responsible and honest.

Children do not need to review and retell every detail about their actions in order to move away from secrecy. But wrongdoing creates alienation, one aspect of hypocrisy, and we need to help our children correct their misbehavior in a way that also helps them regain their sense of belonging. Otherwise we may respond to a specific misbehavior but fail to address secrecy and alienation, which are even more damaging.

We need to be sensitive to the importance of helping our children return to us and feel a part of our family. Then we need to develop a method of helping them correct their behavior that accomplishes this important goal. It is not a simple, step-by-step process but one that must be adapted to the level of children's confidence, or lack of it, and we must continue to adapt it as we proceed to bring correction about. The method can be described as a series of stages.

Gathering information. During the initial confrontation, we talk with our children about what we know of their actions and ask them to tell us what they did. We begin by setting an emotional climate that is warm but factual and honest. We cannot discover deceit all of the time, but there are some things to look for to help us recognize it. One is the amount of information children tell spontaneously in contrast to what they withhold. If we ask a question and get either a terse answer or an elaborate explanation, we may suspect they have a motive to hide facts. If children talk on their own and include descriptions of their own actions, they are being more honest. Another clue to honesty, of course, is whether the description children give matches what we know. A third is the mannerisms displayed by children while they are talking. Honesty is usually indicated when children talk with some eye contact, and their voice tones fluctuate within ordinary limits, neither too loud nor too soft. Additional cues of honesty may be that they show emotions that fit the situation they are in, and their attempts to control themselves are not excessive. Dishonesty is usually indicated when children obviously force facial expressions, tell facts contrary to what we already know, and show extreme or confusing mannerisms when they are talking.

The phase of information gathering continues until we are confident that we have accurate information and have helped our children be more honest than dishonest. This process may require more than one conversation. If we see that our children are unprepared to talk freely, or if we believe they are dishonest, it is generally better to suspend the conversation by saying something like "I can see that you are not quite ready to talk about this." We can encourage our children to be honest and tell them the importance of it, but accusing them of dishonesty is usually not helpful except as a last resort.

The admission. Entry into any group requires some price of admission. In our case, reentry into the emotional bond of our family requires that children come close to admitting honestly what they have done wrong and indicate in some way that they want to belong.

The purpose of setting the emotional climate and gathering information is to encourage that admission. Our saying, "Can you tell me . . . ?" or "I want to know about . . . " can give children the feeling of freedom to be honest. In cases where children have a history of lying, we may need to be more aggressive in our approach by asking, "Who did . . . ?" "When did this happen?" "Who else was involved?" or "What did you actually do?" We can even say we cannot believe them but we want to, and then plead for them to tell the truth.

In the admission phase we ask our children to tell us honestly what part they had, or believe they had, in the wrongdoing so that we can find out whether they will accept and admit responsibility for their choices and their actions or shift this responsibility by blaming others. If they blame or deny, then we must continue questioning, because they are demonstrating that they are not ready to be fully honest. Usually, by exercising patience and showing an understanding attitude, we can help them get to the point where they will state what they did and that they were responsible for it, blaming no one else.

Consequences. What happens after children admit what they did and accept responsibility for it? For us, an important result has been achieved. They are no longer hypocritical, and we need to direct their attention to that point. Now we can help them examine their feelings as we share our feelings, and we can invite them to talk about the difference between having the truth known and carrying the burden of maintaining a lie.

Then we need to help them understand the effects of their actions on themselves and others. We can ask them, "What do you think this has done to you?" and we can share our own thoughts. We can follow that by talking over other consequences that fit the situation. We can decide if there was faulty reasoning about who could be helped or hurt. We can go over the moment of choice and ask them about each decision they made and why. Then, for every wrong or immoral thing they have done, they can do something moral, something that helps themselves and others. Feeling the freedom and happiness that comes from behavior that bears up under scrutiny, they will find that morality is more inviting after all than hypocrisy.

CHAPTER 15

LOVE AND MORALITY

In hidden picture games children are challenged to find figures or diagrams embedded in other pictures. At first glance the pictures seem to contain only the obvious objects—a house, a tree, a car, some children. The instructions, however, say that it is also possible to find, by looking more closely, a lion, a bicycle, an ice cream cone, a bird, a trumpet. The children look again and may still not see what is hidden, but careful scrutiny reveals first one embedded shape and then another. Soon most are found. If children have difficulty finding all of the hidden pictures, they may come to us for help. We read the instructions and begin to look for the hidden pictures. Sometimes we are better at discerning detail, and we find the pictures our children have missed. Sometimes our children will discover them on their own while we are helping. After all the hidden pictures have been found, it is no longer possible for us or the children to look at the obvious house, tree, and car without also seeing the lion, ice cream cone, and trumpet. What was once hidden has become an integral part of the overall picture.

This example represents a truth about life. As children grow, their innate tendencies combine with instruction and experience to increase the realm of the obvious as more and more of the world becomes familiar. Children continually discover that there is more to life than they used to think there was, and each new discovery becomes a lasting part of the picture thereafter.

Children start out in life motivated to learn or to become

more competent. Babies urgently and insistently attempt to become better at moving, sitting, crawling, standing, walking, and talking. Healthy children are curious about their world—touching, tasting, looking at, and listening to things in it. Inborn curiosity and motivation to achieve competency move children to increase their effectiveness in knowing about the world and living in it. Their senses are supremely adapted to life; children seem to want to know when and where to look, what and how to listen, and how and why to touch. Newborns seem to have an inborn understanding that the more they discover, the better off they will be.

Interestingly, children are more motivated to learn about some things than they are about others, and they show at an early age that they prefer to learn about people. Brazelton, Koslowski, and Main (1974), for instance, demonstrate that given a choice, infants prefer to look at the human face. Children do find stimulation and happiness from their discoveries about people. In his book *The Brain* (1984), Richard Restak cites a report by Alexander Luria, a Russian psychologist. Dr. Luria had worked with a patient named "S" who could remember remarkable details from his infancy. From the writings of Dr. Luria we can see the development of an infant's ability to perceive what at first were "hidden pictures." Dr. Luria wrote that "S" once gave the following description.

"This is the sense I had of my mother: Up to the time I began to recognize her, it was simply a feeling—'this is good.' No form, no face, just something bending over me from which good would come . . . pleasant. . . . Seeing my mother was like looking at something through the lens of a camera. At first you can't make anything out, just a round cloudy spot . . . then a face appears, then its features become sharper." (P. 221.)

Later the newborn's natural interest in other people takes new forms. Researchers find that infants learn to initiate more than 80 percent of the contact between themselves and their caretakers. (Berger, 1986.) By learning different styles of crying, smiling, and noise making, infants stimulate watchful adults to give attention to them. As children grow, they learn many other things. Where once we thought children's Why? questions indicated their curiosity and interest, we now understand that these questions perpetuate contact between them and people around them.

Another indication of children's considerable interest in people is shown in parent-child relationships. The mutual bond between parents and children is enduring. If children become too dependent at an early age, they tend to remain that way throughout life. Rather than independence being the natural condition, easily attained by children, it must be developed in children. In its best forms, independence is seldom complete separation and indifference. Children and parents retain good feelings for each other throughout life, despite the anger or frustration they once may have felt toward each other.

Several important implications of these ideas relate to the moral development of our children. Children's contact with their parents often determines what children come to see and understand about themselves and others. That in turn determines the quality of life for them. Children who experience happy things seem to expect happiness and believe that life is made up of happy experiences. Children who experience emotional pain and unhappiness often seem to see pain all around them and believe the world is an unhappy place.

Parents must recognize another truth, a less obvious one but even more important. Children may look for but not find many things about life unless they are actively helped to discover them. We all know people who have lived for years, perhaps their entire lives, having failed to understand something, even something others take for granted that everyone knows. I can think of men and women who have found so little warmth in life that they believe they will never receive it from anyone, and so they give little of it themselves. I have asked parents whose children are not doing well in school if they can recall happy memories of their own school days. Often, there is no response to my question. One woman, after I coaxed her a bit, told of a time she had slipped on the ice and bumped her head, and the school nurse was nice to her. If these parents never "found" excitement in school, how could they teach their children to find it? The low performance marks of their children, who were just as intelligent as the high performers, seemed to show that the parents who did not find excitement in learning were teaching their children to see the world in the same way they saw it.

If, as parents, we accept our primary role in teaching morality, if we have decided that we will teach our children moral standards and moral skills by precept and example, what else do we need to know and do that will make children more receptive to our teachings?

First, we can understand that all children have an inborn or inherited sense of right and wrong. Arnold (1960) and Osgood and others (1974) report research findings suggesting that in every culture, primitive or advanced, children's first judgment is the judgment of good and bad. Children are not empty or blank pages waiting for life's experiences to fill them. Rather, children have a mental structure that exists at birth, or is developed shortly afterward, that functions for survival and is the foundation for morality. That innate tendency is refined and enlarged simply as part of maturing. But the fundamental sense of right and wrong does not reach its fullest bloom in mature morality without another element, which will be unseen and unlearned by children unless we teach it to them. That essential element is love.

Love has a unique role in teaching and learning morality. It unifies the separate conversations, lessons, consequences, lectures, and examples that children are exposed to. When love does not exist in their lives, children have more difficulty comprehending that morality is of great value. Love motivates children to integrate moral values into their actions. The presence of love in children's lives helps them weave single or isolated moral thoughts or acts into the wholeness of a moral person. This integration is found in the ideal of a moral character. Without love, children may at times help one another, and they may at times avoid hurting themselves or others. They do that because it is expected or a situation might determine it. But they will not form the abiding sense of concern for one another that can be found in virtually every significant act of the mature and complete moral individual.

If children do not learn love, will they learn that humans are base, weak, animalistic, and prone to destructiveness? Will they learn to manipulate and despoil, thinking that humans are gullible and that there is a sucker behind every tree ready to be taken by anyone crafty or shrewd enough to do it?

People who are highly moral believe that they are linked to others in a way that is necessary for a happy life. Therefore, they must be concerned about their associates and be prepared to help. When such individuals act, they consider whether their actions will hurt others or help them. On their own initiative they act to help, to give, to nurture. Why? These people have learned about themselves and others, but what they have learned has been accompanied by love. Therefore, they know that people are worth sacrificing for, that people are more noble than base, more filled with potential than stunted. They know that people can always grow and improve if they are helped and loved.

Children will not see and learn about love without someone's help. Love is embedded in the flow of life like a hidden picture and will stand out sharply to be seen, understood, and felt only if it is pointed out in a variety of ways and at numerous times. If we fail to help our children know love, we will also fail in teaching them to be moral. This lesson is often learned by tyrant parents who teach moral standards enforced by fear. Their children need only to know the rules and follow them to avoid displeasure and disapproval. But since their motivation to be moral is fear of authority, when strong authority is absent, so is morality.

Love can be expressed in many forms. It may be displayed in affection, in compliments, in companionship, and in the desire for romance. In its truest sense, love is expressed in caring and sacrificing for the welfare, especially the spiritual welfare, of someone else. Though this definition of love is easy to write, it implies many things not obvious at first glance. To contribute to the welfare of others, a loving person must recognize a commitment of time, because human life is expressed in time. Contributing to someone's welfare requires some idea about human growth. Someone who has no knowledge about human potential cannot direct or encourage anyone else to a better place. We have a tendency to become more loving as we grow older. Is it simply age that makes that happen? Or is it our growing awareness about where we humans are going and the perspective that allows us to see children at one point and ourselves at another point, but all on the same path?

The love that makes morality possible is more than a few specific things we do. This love is a general intention, an overall attitude integrated in the character of a loving person who can almost always be relied upon to express it. This reliable love shown by parents over many years helps children see love in the world and believe in it. This love enables our children to make sense out of our attempts to teach morality. Learning to see love this way, children cannot thereafter consider life without looking to find love.

People Are More Important Than Things

If more years mean more experience and wisdom, then adults should know that things are not as simple as they seemed when we were children. Younger people may think that affluence and possessions are highly desirable. Older people may have had experiences that taught them that other things may be more valuable than affluence and possessions. Money is useful only if we treat it carefully and make it a tool to accomplish worthwhile things for people. It can bring food to starving people and medical care for the disadvantaged. It can bring opportunities for education and cultural enrichment that would not be possible otherwise.

Unfortunately, children do not naturally know that money is good only if it is used morally. Children see many demonstrations of wealth that appear to suggest that the wealthiest people are also the happiest. With so much affluence visible in our culture, it is understandable that many of our young people formulate materialistic attitudes. Their goals are to make money and possess attractive things, and their time and efforts are directed to these ends without consideration of the responsibilities related to money. When they develop such materialistic attitudes, possessions become more important to them than people.

Morality is a system of standards that encourage us to act toward one another in ways that sustain us individually and perpetuate the common good. Materialism is inherently selfish. It is a philosophy that fails to take into consideration the relationships we have with other people, because in the pursuit of money, people are less important than achieving the material goal.

A high-school counselor in Seattle gave this moral problem to the forty members of the student council: A large boat loaded with cocaine lies at anchor off the coast of Florida. Someone offers them one million dollars to bring the boat to shore. That is all they would have to do for the money. A person would meet them at the dock and pay them then. Would anyone do it? Only one of the forty said no. This solitary student said he wouldn't do it because he knew the drugs would harm the people who purchased them. The other thirty-nine said that was not their responsibility. What happened to the drugs after they were brought to shore was up to someone else. For them, morality in this situation meant doing what they were paid to do.

That kind of thinking is not uncommon. Researchers at the University of Utah surveyed high-school seniors in the western United States about what made members of the opposite sex attractive. More than half the girls indicated that the amount of money boys had determined whether the girls found the boys attractive or not.

Remember that children start life finding other humans more fascinating than anything else. When we think about teaching children to love themselves and others, our first task is to encourage their fascination with people. That will help them grow in the understanding of the relative value of people and things. It will help them see, for instance, that it is a mistake to think of themselves or other people in the same way they think about a toy or a pet. What makes a person happy or sad? What hurts people or helps them? What motivates people? What are the highest and best qualities in people? What are the worst? Why does a person act a certain way in one situation and act a different way at another time? What helps someone grow intellectually? emotionally? physically? We can help our children learn to love by helping them learn to ask and then to answer these important questions.

The love that blends with moral values relies on other people and on an understanding of how our own behavior helps or hurts others. One of my colleagues requires students to secure a fresh, unboiled egg with a string, tie the string to their wrist, and carry the egg wherever they go for one full week. That includes sleeping and showering or bathing. Some wrap the egg in a protective cover. Most hold the egg in their hand and carry it everywhere. These students report that they learn a greater sensitivity to the requirements of protecting something fragile and how much attention can be required to care for something important.

This example can remind us to show attentiveness and sensitivity to our children. When we do that, we show them we regard them as unique and interesting. We can listen to our children, acknowledge their desires and needs, and accept what they do as part of their stage in life. A couple I know placed a crib for a new child at the foot of their bed. The father noticed many things about this child that he had missed with his older children. Certainly the proximity of the new baby made a difference, but essentially he noticed more because he was more practiced—he had sharpened his observation skills with his older children.

We ourselves need to be reminded to understand people as more important than material things. One study of what schoolteachers thought about their students asked two thousand teachers across the country to rank fifty items according to their own perception of their importance to education. Twenty-five items were related to students' characteristics, such as self-esteem and integrity. The other twenty-five items were related to material things, such as textbooks, salaries, and school boards.

No teacher placed any of the twenty-five "human" or student items higher than the mid point. (Frymer, 1972.) All apparently thought that the material or physical trappings of education were more important than the students themselves, the people who were being educated. These teachers were demonstrating the all-too-human tendency to think that the things that influenced their comfort, security, and status were more important than the people they themselves influenced.

This condition need not exist in our families. We can help our children develop the perspective about people and things that makes morality possible. That perspective is love, and it is a challenge to teach children to believe in it. But we can do it. The experience one twelve-year-old boy had with his parents will illustrate one way to try.

Derrick Hansen was ordinarily a pleasant and cooperative boy. One morning he failed to get up in time for breakfast. He did not get up at the first call, and his father, Don, had to go to his room and shake him awake. When he arrived at the breakfast table, Derrick was at first quiet and then made cutting and sarcastic statements to his brother and sister. An argument followed, and Don's attempts to stop it led to his telling Derrick to leave the table. Derrick did, yelling back, "You're all alike. No one cares." After things settled down, Don asked his wife, Mary, if she knew anything about Derrick that would explain his behavior. She didn't. Don asked the other children if they knew anything. His brother said that Derrick had gotten into a fight at school, and his sister told of catching Derrick up late at night watching television.

The next night, Don got up around 1:30 A.M. and found Derrick watching a movie. Derrick's explanation was that he couldn't sleep. When Don asked why not, Derrick said, "Get off my back!" and ran to his bedroom. Don told Mary what had happened. Both parents were confused. When Derrick did not appear for breakfast again, the family had another discussion about him. Derrick's brother told how Derrick's favorite pigeon had recently been killed by a cat. Because this event coincided with the change in Derrick's behavior, the parents guessed that this might have been the reason for Derrick's actions.

When Derrick came to breakfast, Don told him he knew what had happened. His voice hushed in sadness, Derrick whispered in reply, "She was sitting on some eggs, and a cat broke into the cage and killed her." This revelation let Don and Mary respond to the real problem with affection and understanding instead of punishing Derrick for his unruly behavior.

Don and Mary did something about teaching love. They taught by their example that human beings are worth understanding before being judged and that they deserve to be understood with love. Their continued efforts will help their children learn the same sensitivity.

In great contrast to their example is the father who was referred to counseling because he had severely beaten his two sons. This man asked me, "Do you ever hit your children?" I told him that I might on rare occasions spank them, but I never hit them in the way he was talking about. "Why not?" he asked. "First," I replied, "it doesn't help anyone to do it. Second, my father loved me and never hit me."

Certain as he was that his way of thinking about children and disciplining them was at least as good as mine, he saw no need to change. In his mind, he, as a father, was within his rights to reinforce his parental authority by abusive beatings. To protect her sons, his wife had to divorce him and use the courts to keep him away from them.

How different from the message this man gave his sons is the message of a sign in a Catholic Youth Center: "God don't make no junk." If the young people who go there believe in God and believe that God created them, then there is only one possible conclusion. They are of great value themselves, because their Maker made them. Sometimes it is hard to keep that in mind in the face of racial prejudice, insensitivity, insults, and other demeaning behavior. But if children regularly find the tender caress, the warm attention given in companionship, the gentle embrace, and the sensitive inquiry to understand, then the idea that people are more important than things, that *they* are more important than some *thing*, is easier to believe. The gestures of love that teach our children their importance to us help them understand that promoting human happiness and well-being is more important than other things they might do.

Overcoming Fear and Jealousy

Fear and jealousy prevent children from learning to

love. Most children feel fear or jealousy at one time or another, and we can learn to help them overcome these feelings and learn to love instead. Many theorists believe that fear is inherited by all children. Some have studied fear as a cross-cultural phenomenon. They write that fear first appears around six months of age and is a part of life that must be managed thereafter. Because children differ in their levels of emotional intensity, some learn to love quite easily and others have more difficulty. In their exhaustive research about infant temperament, Thomas and Chess (1977) found that some children respond easily to parental affection, are warmed by it, and are easy to care for. Other children have more difficulty participating in loving experiences. Still others exhibit qualities of temperament that make them even more difficult to love and to learn love. These children stiffen at affection and return little of what they receive. Although some of these conditions change as children grow older, children reflect individual differences about love throughout life.

Knowing that some children require more effort than others helps us adapt to the differences we find between our own children. Excessive fear, for example, can prevent children from learning to love. Frightened children see the need to protect themselves as greater than the motivation to care. Fear leads to caution and a defensive inability to give of themselves, and such children mistrust what others give. Jealousy, an extension of fear and mistrust, is often expressed in the desire to diminish someone else who is feared and thought of as a threat.

Childhood is an opportune time for fear to grow. Children see, hear, and participate in new things. They imagine and dream about frightening things. They may feel fear when separated from their parents. When school begins, many children feel pressure to perform and feel afraid of teachers who judge and of other children who may also judge. They may also express fears without any identifiable cause. These feelings are simply a part of life, especially a life that is changing from month to month.

One morning before going to school, fifteen-year-old Jimmy Swenson complained of headaches. The pain seemed to be intense, so his mother kept him home from school. The next day Jimmy went to school but called at noon to tell his mother the headache had returned. When his mother picked him up, he looked pale and in pain. Their family doctor examined Jimmy and diagnosed his headaches as migraine headaches. The doctor prescribed some medication that helped him. During that year Jimmy missed so much school that he was far behind in his homework. Ordinarily he did well, though, so the teacher assumed he would do all right in the next grade and passed him. The last day of school, however, was the last day Jimmy had a headache—at least for three months. Just as school was starting in the fall, the headaches returned. The school counselor advised Jimmy's mother to consult a psychologist.

In my interviews with Jimmy and his parents, I learned that Jimmy had an older brother who excelled in school. His parents were excessively performance oriented and exerted great pressure on their children. They extolled the virtues of the older achieving son. They nagged all their children about getting work done. They talked more often about high grades, awards, and scholarships than about anything else. Jimmy had no friends at school, and when he was alone with me he told about unhappy and embarrassing experiences with his teachers. His mother added that he spent much time alone daydreaming and reading science fiction. While she was talking to me, Jimmy picked up a book and began to read, tuning us out of his thoughts so that she had to say his name three or four times before he raised his head and paid attention to the conversation.

Jimmy was very bright. He talked often about the books he was reading. In addition, he was a computer whiz and had inventive, imaginative ideas about electronic devices he hoped to create. None of his interests, however, involved other people. He appeared to be comfortable only when he was alone or with some mechanical device.

We did several things to help him overcome his fear. First, we developed a plan to help him make friends. Getting him to invite an acquaintance to a movie was a major task, but once he was over that hurdle, other things came more easily. Soon he had someone in each class whom he considered a friend. Then we started on friendships with girls and dating. Though he was scared of girls, they were fascinating to him. He first went on a group date with some of his friends, and he eventually went out alone with a girl for an evening without any friends. The success of these social occasions could be seen in his improved mood. He was animated when he told about the girl and what they did on their date.

The family went out together more often. They went on short trips so that Jimmy could be exposed to more social and cultural things. His parents were asked to anticipate what he would find to be new and prepare him for newness by talking over what would happen. Later they practiced meeting the new people and seeing the new sights. They held family meetings in which the children gave simple performances by telling stories, giving small speeches, reading aloud, or singing. His parents used many compliments and much praise.

Jimmy's headaches stopped. He was learning that he could go out into a wider world and be successful. He was less afraid and felt more insulated from the pressure he had once felt from his parents.

Schulman and Mekler (1985) give other helpful suggestions for overcoming childhood fears. Children should seldom be forced to participate in anything they are frightened of, and parents should prepare them before they participate. They also remind us to avoid ridiculing children about their fears. Instead, we can model what children are afraid of while giving them specific reassurances. We can talk over a frightening situation and talk about the frightening parts of it. When each part is discussed, parents can then reassure their children. When children are afraid of something, simply saying, "There is nothing to be afraid of," will rarely produce calm. Modeling children's fears also means to put into words what the parents think the children might be feeling. For instance, if children are afraid of being left out of a game by friends at school, a parent would voice that fear: "Oh boy, I'll bet no one chooses me." Then parents can give specific suggestions for what children might do, such as saying, "I want to play, too." Using the information we gather about our children's specific and routine activities, we can be specific and concrete about what we model and what reassurances we give.

Many fears can be resolved by close contact and warmth. Children benefit from our affection, attention, and time we take to understand them. When we see their fear, if we respond first with contact and warmth, we will usually be able to comfort them. If we see them afraid of other people—usually shown by an exaggerated motivation to avoid new people—we can tell children that most people are "nice and will not hurt them," "Most new situations are fun because they are exciting," "New friends can be made and kept by learning to ask questions and listen," and "Fear need not prevent happiness and love."

Fear about oneself in relation to others often takes the form of jealousy. Helping children overcome jealousy requires different skills from those that help them overcome other kinds of fear. Most jealousy, for example, manifests itself in competitiveness and intense concern about whether another person has or does something better. Usually, jealousy is diminished by increasing the sense of confidence children have in themselves combined with the ability to avoid judging others. Jealousy in childhood can be resolved by individualizing and customizing children's clothes, chores, and bedtime routines to preserve each child's sense of uniqueness. Giving each child an individ-

ual plan will help each one focus on his or her own schedule
and set of tasks rather than worrying about someone else.
When children display jealousy, it is useful to remind them
to think about what they are doing rather than what someone else is doing as well as on how their own actions might
make someone else feel.

Ingrid and Tom Stauffer had difficulty with their children, who claimed that they as parents were not fair. These
complaints came when they treated any child differently
from the others by buying clothing or a toy for one and
not for the others. The parents said they felt guilty and
sometimes tried to make it up to the other children.

This method didn't seem to be working because the
children continued to complain about their parents' un-
fairness. I suggested that the parents admit that they were
not fair and had no intention to be fair, at least as far as
fair meant treating each child the same. Then they could
show how they treated each child differently in some re-
spects, as their age and needs required. That was a new
idea to the Stauffers, but they found it effective in reducing
jealousy.

Another way to combat jealousy is actively to build
confidence. Children benefit from confidence-building experiences. We can help them develop talents, praise them
for successes, communicate with them about traits or characteristics we admire, and help them overcome obstacles.
One father took his son on several camping trips and taught
him how to succeed at that. Later, when his son went on
trips with the Scouts, this boy was recognized as a good
camper. Other parents have taught cooking, carpentry,
reading, writing, music, and sports for the same reasons.

Finally, children's jealousy can be reduced by loving
explanations of what they are feeling and pointing out
times when they display it. This procedure often takes time
and a willingness to be patient, but it will help us help our
children know what to do instead of acting jealously. A
man I know has two daughters who are about the same

age. They are quite different in looks and personality, and they are often jealous of each other. Their mother is working with one in an attempt to help her share, give, and do things for the other. Their father is working with the other to help her do similar things. It is fun and satisfying for each parent when "his" or "her" child explains what she did instead of feeling jealous of her sister. Each has, for instance, let her sister go first at the bus line. Each has learned to express delight in her sister's successes. Each has also been excited when her sister received recognition during such times as birthdays and Christmas. Someday the parents will tell their daughters what they have done to help them along in life, but right now, they are keeping secret that each girl is being helped to love instead of being jealous of the other.

Giving and Receiving Love

When we teach children to love, it is useful to think of love as a circle. Love can be stopped either by the failure to give it or by the failure to receive it. Usually, however, we are so concerned about teaching children to give love or show it that we do not help them learn to receive it. During one of our family gatherings we talked about this as a family. I went over to one son, told him I loved him, and kissed him on the cheek. He returned this gesture by squeezing me back. Then I turned to the rest and asked, "What would happen if Jeremy had not received my demonstration of love for him?" Even the younger ones understood that I might be unhappy and that maybe I would stop giving demonstrations of love to him.

If the circle of love is to be big enough to gather every member of a family into it, then every family member needs to learn to receive it as well as give it. We can read stories to our children about the kind things people have done. We tell them about gratitude and appreciation, and we demonstrate in our actions the importance of showing both. As parents, we want our children to receive much more love than hatred or neglect. Because gratitude and appreciation reinforce the person who gives, we can teach thank you's and other expressions of gratitude to our children, both by our words and by our actions.

Tough Love

We ordinarily think of love as soft and kind, warm and gentle, honest and giving, patient and pleasant. But sometimes love requires us to be hard and unpleasant, withholding and abrupt. When we are trying hard to express the love that is pleasant and warm and worrying about whether or not our children actually feel loved, it is easy to forget that love sometimes means we must be very tough if we are to contribute to the welfare of our children.

All children make mistakes, but some of those mistakes are not isolated events. Breaking a vase is a mistake; a drug habit supported by theft is something else. Children who are out of control for one reason or another may hurt others repeatedly unless they are stopped. There are times when our children try to manipulate us to get what they want. They may devise ways to get for themselves some of the money we bring home. They may want us to feel guilty so that we will give them more than they ask for. They may present us with difficult situations between themselves and others, hoping we will choose their side. These situations require a toughness that many of us find foreign because we have always thought of love as being warm and gentle.

I know parents who learned that their son forged checks to pay for his excesses. After they told me what the money was used for and the many months they had been struggling with him to no avail, I suggested that they call the police and turn him in. Silence followed. Finding the words that matched his feelings, the father said, "What will he think of us, if we do that?" My answer was, "What

will he continue to do if you don't bring him under control?" After some additional discussion, they called the
police. He was picked up and placed in youth detention.
He was convicted and placed on supervised probation. He
was embarrassed; so were they. He stopped his drinking
binges.

Many drug-dependent children have parents who
could be called co-dependent because they seem to give
or do anything to make their children "happy." In one
case, a father and son occasionally argued about what the
son was doing. Their verbal battles were very heated. At
the end of each one, a truce of sorts would begin with the
father giving the son some money to go out and have a
good time. Getting the son into a drug treatment center
was not as difficult as getting the father to correct his own
habit.

In some ways, this part of parenthood is the most
uncomfortable part, but our being able to be tough at the
right time teaches children about love in ways the other
forms cannot. One father allowed his son to drive the car
to and from school with the provision that he never use
the car to do anything to hurt himself or anyone else. If
he did, the keys would be taken without a second thought.
The boy handled the car and disciplined himself very well.
One day the parents received a notice from the school that
the boy missed a class five times. When asked about it,
the boy claimed that he had been there but was late and
the teacher had failed to give him credit. Since he was
usually honest about things, his parents had no reason to
disbelieve him.

When the second notice came from the school, there
was a direct and forthright discussion between father and
son. When confronted with the evidence, the boy admitted
he had skipped the class. "Why this class?" the father
asked. "It is boring, and besides, I don't know what is
going on." His father asked, "What did you do when you
skipped?" "We went into town and got something to eat,"

the son replied. "How did you get there?" came the question. "I drove the car," was the answer. After a long look of joint realization, the father said, "Get me all of the keys."

They did not speak for several days. Then, after another discussion, they arranged a way for the son to earn the use of the car again. A few years later, I heard the son tell about this incident. He said that moment was when he knew his father loved him.

If we keep in mind that love is sometimes tough, then we can keep from being manipulated and make ourselves do what is necessary to help our children avoid pitfalls and correct their mistakes. It may hurt us to be tough, but that pain is less than the pain we would feel when our children hurt themselves or others further because we failed to prevent it.

Our Decision

Maturity includes the wisdom that we do not have to do anything in particular to have problems or challenges. We can do nothing special, and still they confront us and our children as a normal part of their growing up. We must, however, do *something* to help our children avoid problems and survive their mistakes. Part of that active role is to teach them the principles of morality, which make greater sense to them when we do it in the climate of love.

Most books about child discipline that I know of place parental behavior after the child's behavior. That is, while explaining disciplinary techniques, the writers suggest several possible parental responses to several types of actions by children. This discovery made me uncomfortable, because just responding to what children do does not give parents a creative, inventive perspective on parenthood. We are older than our children. We hope we are wiser. We have learned things children do not know. Without being tyrants or even overcontrolling, we have the privilege, perhaps obligation, to help our children learn what we believe will enhance their success. We need not impose our beliefs very much to help them discover and consider what we believe to be right and wrong for them. It is not intrusive for us to help them understand what will help them or hurt them and others. It is not too demanding for us to help them make wise choices and learn to apply a set of standards that contribute to self-respect and self-esteem. None of that is excessive if we do all of it out of genuine love.

Sharp differences and confrontations are part of relationships between parents and children. We do not look for confrontations, but we ought not to fear them either, if we love our children enough to declare that they should stop something they are doing or start something they are not doing. These times may be painful, but the pain of these moments is usually less than the long-term pain we and our children have when they are not able to make their way in the world, when they have wasted their lives, or when we have failed to teach active morality in the name of love. The emptiness and sadness of these conditions are the real sources of pain, because they mean that we are all living with something less than what might have been.

Teaching morality and love is the way we increase our chances and our children's chances of avoiding that pain. Love and morality are also the means by which we may restore happiness when we or our children make mistakes. Love and morality are active, not passive, parts of family life. They are things we can do rather than be on the sidelines confused and wondering.

Guiding children, teaching them, and helping them grow involve many different choices. Whether we are aware or unaware, we decide how much freedom we give them, the opportunities we expose them to, how to help them in school, how much to control their activities, and we influence countless other aspects of their lives. In the midst of all the tumult, happiness, fun, and struggle that is childhood, we are granted the power to choose whether children will know or not know about love from us. If we want our children to be moral and know about the significance of life, we will choose to love them so that they will choose to be moral.

LIST OF REFERENCES

Arnold, M. B. 1960. *Emotion and personality*. New York: Columbia University Press.

Bandura, A., and MacDonald, F. J. 1963. Influence of social reinforcement and the behavior of models in shaping children's moral judgments. *Journal of Abnormal and Social Psychology, 67*, 274–81.

Becker, W. C. 1964. Consequences of different kinds of parental discipline. In *Review of child development*. M. L. Hoffman and L. Hoffman, eds. Chicago: University of Chicago Press.

Berger, K. S. 1986. *The developing person through childhood and adolescence*. New York: Worth Publishers.

Birdwhistle, R. 1970. *Kinesics and context*. Philadelphia: University of Pennsylvania Press.

Blasi, A. 1980. Bridging moral cognition and moral action: A critical review of the literature. *Psychology Bulletin, 88*, 1–45.

Blatt, M., and Kohlberg, L. 1975. Effects of classroom moral discussion upon children's level of moral judgment. *Journal of Moral Education, 4*, 129–62.

Blum, L. A. 1980. *Friendship, altruism and morality*. London: Routledge & Kegan Paul.

Bouchard, T. J. 1983. Do environmental similarities explain the similarity in intelligence of identical twins raised apart? *Intelligence, 7*, 175–84.

Boyd, D. R. 1984. The principle of principles. In *Morality, moral behavior, and moral development*. W. Kurtines and J. L. Gewirtz, eds. New York: John Wiley & Sons.

Brazelton, T. B., Koslowski, R., and Main, M. 1974. The origins of reciprocity: The early mother-infant interactions. In *The origins of behavior*. M. Lewis and J. Rosenblum, eds. New York: John Wiley & Sons.

Brody, L., Rozek, M., and Muten, E. O. 1985. Age, sex, and individual differences in children's defensive styles. *Journal of Clinical Child Psychology, 14*, (2), 132–38.

Bryan, J. 1969. How adults teach hypocrisy. *Psychology Today,* Dec., 3.

Burton, R. V. 1984. A paradox in theories and research in moral development. In *Morality, moral behavior, and moral development.* W. Kurtines and J. L. Gewirtz, eds. New York: John Wiley & Sons.

Cameron, M. I., and Robinson, V. M. J. 1980. Effects of cognitive training on academic and on-task behavior of hyperactive children. *Journal of Abnormal Child Psychology,* 8, (3), 405–19.

Damon, W. 1984. Self-understanding and moral development from childhood to adolescence. In *Morality, moral behavior, and moral development.* W. Kurtines and J. L. Gewirtz, eds. New York: John Wiley & Sons.

Douglas, V. I. 1972. "Stop, look and listen": The problem of sustained attention and impulse control in hyperactive and normal children. *Canadian Journal Behavior Science Review,* 4.

Fromm, E. 1976. *To have or to be.* New York: Harper & Row.

Frymer, J. R. 1972. Teaching the young to love. Address to NEA convention, Las Vegas, Nevada.

Golden, C. 1985. "Twins reunited." *Science magazine.*

Grando, R., and Ginsberg, B. 1976. Communication in the father-son relationship: The parent-adolescent relationship development program. *The Family Coordination,* Oct., 465–71.

Hand, H. H. 1981. The development of concepts of social interaction: Children's understanding of nice and mean. Unpublished doctoral dissertation, University of Denver.

Hartshonne, H., and May, R. 1928. *Studies in service and self-control.* New York: Macmillan.

Henry, R. 1983. The cognitive versus psychoanalytic debate about morality. *Human Development,* 26, 173–79.

Hoffman, M. 1988. Development of prosocial motivation: Empathy and guilt. In *The development of prosocial behavior.* N. Eisenberg, ed. New York: Academic Press.

Johns, G. 1987. The great escape: Why so many skip out on work. *Psychology Today,* Oct., 31–33.

Johnston, L. D., O'Malley, P. M., and Backman, J. G. 1985. Use of licit and illicit drugs by American high school students, 1975–1984. National Institute of Drug Abuse. U. S. Department of Health and Human Services, Washington, D. C.

Keller, M. 1984. Resolving conflicts in friendship: The development of moral understanding in everyday life. In *morality, moral behavior, and moral development.* W. Kurtines and J. L. Gewirtz, eds. New York: John Wiley & Sons.

Keniston, K. 1965. *The uncommitted: Alienated youth in American society.* New York: Harcourt, Brace, & World.

Kohlberg, L. 1969. Stage and sequence: The cognitive developmental approach to socialization. In *Handbook of socialization theory*. D. A. Goslin, ed. Chicago: Rand McNally, 1969.

Kohlberg, L. 1983. Essays in moral development. In *The psychology of moral development*. New York: Harper and Row.

Kohn, A. 1987. It's hard to get left out of a pair. *Psychology Today*, Oct.

Kurtines, W. M. 1984. Moral behavior as rule governed-behavior: A psychosocial role theoretical approval to moral behavior and development. In *Morality, moral behavior, and moral development*. W. Kurtines and J. L. Gewirtz, eds. New York: John Wiley & Sons.

London, P. 1980. The rescuers: Motivational hypothesis about Christians who saved Jews from Nazis. In *Altruism and helping behavior*. J. Maculey and L. Berkowitz, eds. New York: Academic Press.

McClelland, D. C. 1953. *The achievement motive*. New York: Appleton-Century-Crofts.

Meichenbaum, D., and Goodman, J. 1971. Training impulsive children to talk to themselves: A means of developing self-control. *Journal of Abnormal Psychology*, 77, 115–26.

Milgram, S. 1963. Behavioral study of obedience. *Journal of Abnormal and Social Psychology*, 67, 371–78.

Mitchell, J. 1980. Adolescent hypocrisy. *Psychology Today*, Fall, 19, 59.

Morrison, D., Siegal, M., and Francis, R. 1983. Control, autonomy, and the development of moral behavior: A social cognitive perspective. *Imagination, Cognition, and Personality*, 3, (4).

Murphy, L. B. 1987. Further reflections on resilience. In *The invulnerable child*. J. Anthony & B. Cohler, eds. New York: Guilford Press.

Nisan, M. 1984. Content and structure in moral judgment: An integrative view. In *Morality, moral behavior, and moral development*. W. Kurtines and J. L. Gewirtz, eds. New York: John Wiley & Sons.

Nucci, L. 1981. The development of personal concepts: A domain distinct from moral or societal concepts. *Child Development*, 52, 114–21.

Osgood, C. E., May, W. H., and Miron, M. S. 1975. *Cross-cultural universal of affective meaning*. Urbana: University of Illinois Press.

Patterson, C., and Mischel, W. 1976. Effects of temptation-inhibiting and task-facilitating plans on self-control. *Journal of Personality and Social Psychology*, 33 2, 209–17.

Piaget, J. 1965. *The moral judgment of the child*. New York: Free Press.

Rest, J. R. 1983. Morality. In *Handbook of child psychology*. P. H. Mussen, ed. New York: John Wiley & Sons.

Rest, J. 1984. The major components of morality. In *Morality, moral behavior, and moral development*. W. Kurtines and J. L. Gewirtz, eds. New York: John Wiley & Sons.

Restak, R. 1984. *The Brain*. New York: Bantam Books.

Robinson, I. E., and Jedlicka, D. 1981. Change in sexual behavior of college students from 1965 to 1980. A research note. *Journal of Marriage and the Family*, 44, 237–40.

Sabini, J., and Silver, M. 1982. *Moralities of everyday life*. New York: Oxford University Press.

Sanford, N. 1966. *Self and society*. New York: Atherton Press.

Schulman, M., and Mekler, E. 1985. *Bringing up a moral child*. Reading, Mass: Addison-Wesley.

Scoresby, A. L. 1988. Successful teenagers: Who they are and how they achieved. Unpublished paper, Brigham Young University.

Selman, A. P., and Selman, R. L. 1980. Children's ideas about friendships: A new theory. *Psychology Today*, 13, (4), 13–14, 71–80, 114.

Shannon, K., and Kafer, N. 1984. Reciprocity, trust, and vulnerability in neglected and rejected children. *The Journal of Psychology*, 117, 65–70.

Staub, E. 1984. Steps toward a comprehensive theory of moral conduct: goal orientation, social behavior, kindness, and cruelty. *In Morality, moral behavior, and moral development*. W. Kurtines & J. L. Gewirtz, eds. New York: John Wiley & Sons.

Strickland, B., Hale, D., and Anderson, L. 1975. Effect of induced mood states on activity and self-reported affect. *Journal of Consulting and Clinical Psychology*, 43, (4), 587.

Thomas, A., and Chess, S. 1977. *Temperament and development*. New York: Brunner/Mazel.

Turiel, E. 1979. Social convention and morality: Two distinct conceptual and developmental systems. In *Nebraska Symposium on Motivation*, 25. C. B. Keasey, ed. Lincoln: University of Nebraska Press, 1979.

Turiel, E., and Smetana, J. G. 1984. Social knowledge and action: The coordination of domains. In *Morality, moral behavior, and moral development*. W. Kurtines and J. L. Gewirtz, eds. New York: John Wiley and Sons.

Varni, J. W., and Henker, B. 1979. A self-regulation approach to the treatment of three hyperactive boys. *Child Behavior Therapy*.

INDEX